Beds and Chambers in Late Medieval England

YORK MEDIEVAL PRESS

Beds and Chambers
in Late Medieval England

Readings, Representations and Realities

Hollie L. S. Morgan

THE UNIVERSITY *of York*

YORK MEDIEVAL PRESS

First published 2017

A York Medieval Press publication
in association with The Boydell Press
an imprint of Boydell & Brewer Ltd
PO Box 9, Woodbridge, Suffolk IP12 3DF, UK
and of Boydell & Brewer Inc.
668 Mt Hope Avenue, Rochester, NY 14620–2731, USA
website: www.boydellandbrewer.com
and with the
Centre for Medieval Studies, University of York

ISBN 978 1 903153 71 0

A CIP catalogue record for this book is available
from the British Library

The publisher has no responsibility for the continued existence or accuracy of URLs
for external or third-party internet websites referred to in this book, and does not
guarantee that any content on such websites is, or will remain, accurate or appropriate

This publication is printed on acid-free paper

Typeset by
Frances Hackeson Freelance Publishing Services, Brinscall, Lancs

*This book is dedicated to the homeless and vulnerably housed people of York,
past and present, who do not have a bed or chamber to call their own.*

CONTENTS

LIST OF ILLUSTRATIONS

The author and publishers are grateful to all the institutions and individuals listed for permission to reproduce the materials in which they hold copyright. Every effort has been made to trace the copyright holders; apologies are offered for any omission, and the publishers will be pleased to add any necessary acknowledgement in subsequent editions.

PREFACE AND ACKNOWLEDGEMENTS

The premise of this book is that everyday objects and spaces matter. We, as individuals and as a society, are shaped by our everyday surroundings. In late medieval England, a society in which chambers and even beds were still a rarity, such objects and spaces left imprints in its literary, artistic and pragmatic productions. They affected the ways in which people understood less tangible subjects such as marriage, trust, communication, politics and God, which in turn affected how they used and thought about their own beds and chambers. For this reason, this book presents these higher concepts within a framework of the everyday. I have not covered every function or meaning of the bed and chamber (if such a feat were even possible). For instance, I have not touched on the bed's perceived role in death and dying, though it is a subject in need of more research. This book is about late medieval life; death will just have to wait.

I am grateful to the editorial board of York Medieval Press and Boydell & Brewer, for this opportunity and for their support and patience. I am also indebted to Mark Ormrod and Nick Perkins, for their careful reading and invaluable comments. Thanks are due to the Arts and Humanities Research Council for providing the funding to support the early stages of this project. Thanks also to the British Library, the Bibliothèque Nationale de France, the Bibliothèque Mazarine and Ian Coulson for allowing me to use their images. I am also indebted to Ian Coulson for allowing me to examine the 'Paradise Bed' and to Jonathan Foyle for sharing his unpublished research with me.

As our surroundings shape ourselves and our productions, this book is a product of my environment. In particular, its sources and interdisciplinary methodology reveal my York doctoral upbringing. Without the support, guidance and patience of Nicola McDonald and Jeremy Goldberg this book would never have been written and

I remain eternally grateful. Others have indirectly shaped this book's production: Orietta Da Rold taught me to question everything and the voice in my head asking 'What are the implications?' will always be hers; Monica Manolescu encouraged the pursuit of 'surprising connections' when I was an undergraduate and Natasha Hill, my GCSE English teacher, first showed me the value of studying (rather than just reading) books. While this was my monster to slay, the victory is down to a willing and steadfast band of supporters. For this, thanks are due to the University of York's Centre for Medieval Studies community, especially to Kate Giles, Justin Sturgeon, Kats Handel, Jane-Héloïse Nancarrow, Jenn Bartlett, Heidi Stoner, Gillian Galloway and Brittany Scowcroft. I am also grateful for the support of Takako Kato, Johanna Green, Rachel Thwaites, Isabelle, Paul and Aelwen Hamley and my York Vineyard family. Love and thanks to Andrew Kidd, without whom this would have been completed much sooner. Finally, I owe so much to my family, who have supported me and encouraged me from the start, and especially to my parents, Sharon and David Morgan for, among other things, *Little Bear Grows a Flower*. This book is for them, with love.

ABBREVIATIONS

BL	London, British Library
CCR	*Calendar of the Close Rolls Preserved in the Public Record Office, Edward I–Edward IV*, 37 vols. (London, 1892–1963)
CPR	*Calendar of the Patent Rolls Preserved in the Public Record Office, Edward I- Henry VI*, 49 vols. (London, 1891–1907)
DIMEV	*The Digital Index of Middle English Verse*, ed. L. R. Mooney, D. W. Mosser and E. Solopova (2012) <www.dimev.net>
MED	*The Middle English Dictionary*, ed. F. McSparren, in *The Middle English Compendium* (Ann Arbor, 2006) <http://quod.lib.umich.edu/m/med/>
NIMEV	J. Boffey and A. S. G. Edwards, *A New Index of Middle English Verse* (London, 2005)
OED	*Oxford English Dictionary Online*, 2nd edn (Oxford, 2012) <www.oed.com>
TNA	Kew, The National Archives

Introduction

It is a bitterly cold, grey January morning. The snow is pelting down cruelly, the wind is howling across the hills, driving deep snow drifts into every dale, and Gawain is getting ready to face what he considers to be his biggest challenge yet. This time last year an imposing stranger, a giant green man swathed in green and gold, had interrupted the New Year's feast at Camelot and challenged the court to a beheading game. Gawain had valiantly beheaded the man with one swing of a great axe and the party had recoiled in horror when the Green Knight picked up his head, held it aloft and announced that Gawain must seek him out for a returning blow in one year's time. Gawain has travelled far in search of the Green Knight, enduring harsh conditions and battling fierce monsters. He has enjoyed brief respite in a castle called Hautdesert, where he has been allowed to lie in bed until late in the day and be entertained in the warmth of the castle by his host's wife, who met him every morning in his chamber while his host Bertilak went out hunting. His break is now over, and he must confront his destiny. He dresses in the finest clothes, dons the brightest armour and adds as a final touch the green and gold silk girdle given to him by his host's wife on their last morning together in his chamber. Despite the terrified warnings of his guide, Gawain seeks out the Green Knight to receive his beheading. Though he stands to receive the blow, he flinches away from the axe and the knight misses. Duly admonished, he stands stock-still, awaiting death as the gleaming great axe swings down for a second time towards his bare neck.

To the surprise of both Gawain and the modern reader encountering *Sir Gawain and the Green Knight* for the first time, the Green Knight does not kill Gawain, but instead gives him a small nick on his neck before releasing him.[1] While Gawain is satisfied with the explanation given to him by the Green Knight, that his real trial took place in his bed in Hautdesert and not before the axe, modern critics are more akin to members of Arthur's court upon Gawain's return, widely celebrating Gawain's adventures but not really understanding what they mean. A great deal has been written about *Sir Gawain and the Green Knight* – so much so that a comprehensive bibliography of criticism of this text exceeds the word count of this book – and yet the text is still not fully understood. It is clear that the three chamber episodes, described by critics for decades as 'temptation scenes', are at the centre of Gawain's ordeal and trial.[2] However, there is more depth and meaning to these chamber episodes than mere temptation. A modern reader might see Gawain's chamber at Hautdesert as simply the place where the young knight talks to his hostess in bed, does not succumb to her sexual advances but accepts a gift of a piece of lace, which earns him the small wound on his neck. However, the cultural context of the romance must not be overlooked: the chamber must be considered as part of a larger scheme of romance architecture, which is built upon and feeds into the late medieval understanding of space. Piecing together each section of *Sir Gawain and the Green Knight*, one is left with the impression that the whole is greater than the sum of its parts and that something obvious is missing from our current understanding of the romance. Why are those three chamber episodes so important that the outcome of the entire narrative swings upon them? A greater understanding of the cultural resonances of that crucial space, the chamber and the bed within it, would shed new light on this celebrated but often misunderstood text. The key to understanding what is really going on in this romance fits, as it were, the chamber door.

---

[1] *Sir Gawain and the Green Knight*, ed. J. R. R. Tolkien and E. V. Gordon (Oxford, 1925), ll. 2239–2342.

[2] See, for example, D. Mills, 'An Analysis of the Temptation Scenes in "Sir Gawain and the Green Knight"', *The Journal of English and Germanic Philology* 67.4 (1968), 612–30; C. Dean, 'The Temptation Scenes in "Sir Gawain and the Green Knight"', *Leeds Studies in English* n.s. 5 (1971), 1–12; E. Brewer, *Sir Gawain and the Green Knight: Sources and Analogues*, 2nd edn (Cambridge, 1992), p. 7; A. Putter, *Sir Gawain and the Green Knight and French Arthurian Romance* (Oxford, 1995), pp. 100–48; J. Cooke, 'The Lady's "Blushing" Ring in *Sir Gawain and the Green Knight*', *The Review of English Studies* n.s. 49 (1998), 1–8; C. S. Cox, 'Genesis and Gender in "Sir Gawain and the Green Knight"', *The Chaucer Review* 35.4 (2001), 378–90 (p. 378).

This book takes a firmly interdisciplinary approach to the wider cultural meanings of beds and chambers in late medieval England. Its central focus is not on the physical bed and chamber, nor is it on imagined beds and chambers in literature, though it does encompass both areas. Instead, the focus of this book is on the idea of the bed and chamber in the late medieval imagination: the semiotics and cultural associations of object and space. It explores how the presence and use of the bed and chamber affected and were affected by late medieval society's collective ideas and social practices, from prayer to politics, gender roles to marriage vows, socialising to sex. It is based on the assumption that both space and objects are meaningful, and that their meanings both impact and are impacted by people who encounter them. As such, my research is situated at the intersection between two paradigms: the spatial and material turns.

An increasing theoretical interest in both space and objects within humanities scholarship has helped shape my approach towards cultural meanings. Henri Lefebvre's sociological theorisation of space has been influential in spatial discourse, particularly after its translation into English in 1991, and has opened up the discussion on how spaces are 'produced' and 'used' by the society inhabiting them.[3] Michel Foucault's argument that space can only be understood if one considers simultaneously 'the effective practice of freedom by people, the practice of social relations, and the spatial distributions in which they find themselves' is influential in this discourse.[4] Representational modes of spatial thinking, in works such as Gaston Bachelard's *The Poetics of Space*, influenced scholarship on landscapes and architecture within literary texts.[5] Crucially, spaces represented in literature are under-

---

[3] H. Lefebvre, *La production de l'espace* (Paris, 1974); H. Lefebvre, *The Production of Space*, trans. D. Nicholson-Smith (Oxford, 1991). Lefebvre's conceptual triad defines space in three dimensions: the social ('spatial practice', or the active uses of a space by society); the physical ('representations of space', or the production of conceptualised space), and the mental ('representational spaces', which include imagined spaces, symbolic meanings within spaces and artistic representations of spaces) (p. 35); Lefebvre's influence on spatial theory is charted in E. Soja, *Thirdspace: Journeys to Los Angeles and Other Real-and-Imagined Places* (Oxford,1996), pp. 6–12, 26–82.

[4] M. Foucault, *Space, Knowledge and Power*, in *The Foucault Reader*, ed. P. Rabinow (New York, 1984), pp. 239–56 (p. 246).

[5] G. Bachelard, *La poétique de l'espace* (Paris, 1958), trans. M. Jolas as *The Poetics of Space: The Classic Look at How We Experience Intimate Places* (New York, 1964); For a survey of literary analysis using spatial theory see E. Jones, 'Literature and

stood by scholars to be products of a combination of lived experience and individual or collective ideals and desires. Bachelard's focus on the significance of objects also opened up the opportunity for historians to see the study of everyday objects as a serious pursuit.[6] Discourse on the meaning of historical objects is often anthropological and takes the viewpoint that the study of objects facilitates the resurrection of past systems of meaning.[7] Dan Hicks notes that material culture studies can be approached from various disciplines, but argues that materiality is best looked at through one disciplinary lens.[8] I disagree. In order to study cultural meanings of objects and spaces, it is necessary to explore their physical and symbolic function in society. This book draws heavily from sources which are traditionally understood to belong to two separate fields of study: Literature and History, as well as making use of evidence usually associated with History of Art and Archaeology. I also hope that scholars belonging to those disciplines will find something in here which informs their own thinking. I strongly encourage anyone researching cultural ideas to think outside the box and, in some cases, to rip the box to pieces.

There is a paucity of scholarship on beds and chambers and their cultural meanings in late medieval England. Although there is some French ethnographical scholarship on beds and the social production of the modern bedroom, its focus is pan-European and not limited to

---

the New Cultural Geography', *Anglia* 126.2 (2008), 221–40. For a survey of the use of space in the analysis of medieval literature, see J. Ganim, 'Landscape and Late-medieval Literature: A Critical Geography', in *Place, Space and Landscape in Medieval Narrative*, ed. L. Howes (Knoxville, 2007), pp. xv–xxix.

[6] Before scholars such as Bachelard, attempts to study everyday objects were often confused as participation in the Arts and Crafts movement, and so were rarely taken seriously as historical cultural scholarship. For a survey of material culture studies, see D. Miller, 'Materiality: An Introduction', in *Materiality*, ed. D. Miller (Durham, 2005), pp. 1–50, and H. Green, 'Cultural History and the Material(s) Turn', *Cultural History* 1 (2012), 61–82; D. Hicks, 'The Material-Cultural Turn: Event and Effect', in *The Oxford Handbook of Material Culture Studies*, ed. M. C. Beaudry and D. Hicks (Oxford, 2010), pp. 25–98.

[7] See, for example, the essays in *Materiality*, ed. Hicks; K. Ames, *Death in the Dining Room and Other Tales of Victorian Culture* (Philadelphia, 1992); the essays in *The Social Life of Things: Commodities in Cultural Perspective*, ed. A. Appadurai (Cambridge, 1986); the essays in *The Oxford Handbook of Material Culture Studies*, ed. Beaudry and Hicks; the essays in L. Daston, *Things That Talk: Object Lessons from Art and Science* (New York, 2008).

[8] Hicks, 'The Material-Cultural Turn'.

the Middle Ages.⁹ The few Anglophone scholars concerned with the cultural history of the bed do not consider the bed as a meaningful object and are so general that they add very little to our knowledge of late medieval English beds and chambers.¹⁰ This book seeks to address that gap while building on a larger tradition of research on late medieval domesticity which has, to date, gone some way towards approaching the bed and chamber.¹¹

We know from scholarship on medieval domesticity that rooms considered to be chambers could vary greatly in terms of space and content. Access analysis and social/anthropological theories applied to large medieval buildings such as palaces and monasteries have indicated that the chamber occupied the 'deepest space' within the building, noting that female-only chambers were often deeper still.¹²

⁹ P. Dibie, *Ethnologie de la chambre à coucher* (Paris, 2000); M. Perrot, *Histoire de chambres* (Paris, 2009).

¹⁰ M. Eden and R. Carrington, *The Philosophy of the Bed* (London, 1961); L. Wright, *Warm and Snug: The History of the Bed* (London, 1962); L. Worsley, 'The History of the Bed', in L. Worsley, *If Walls Could Talk: An Intimate History of the Home* (London, 2012), 3–17.

¹¹ See, for instance, C. M. Woolgar, *The Great Household in Late-medieval England* (New Haven, 1999); P. J. P. Goldberg, 'Space and Gender in the Later Medieval House', *Viator* 42.2 (2011), 205–32; *Medieval Domesticity: Home, Housing and Household in Medieval England*, ed. M. Kowaleski and P. J. P. Goldberg (Cambridge, 2008); *The Medieval Household in Christian Europe, c. 850– c. 1550*, ed. C. Beattie, A. Maslakovic and S. Rees Jones (Turnhout, 2003); B. A. Hanawalt, 'Medieval English Women in Rural and Urban Space', *Dumbarton Oaks Papers* 52 (1998), 19-26; D. Vance Smith, *Arts of Possession: The Middle English Household Imaginary* (Minneapolis, 2003); see also R. Sarti, *Europe at Home: Family and Material Culture, 1500-1800*, trans. A. Cameron (New Haven, 2002), pp. 199–23.

¹² R. Gilchrist, 'The Contested Garden: Gender, Space and Metaphor in the Medieval English Castle', in her *Gender and Archaeology: Contesting the Past* (London, 1999), pp. 109–45 (p. 122). See also R. Gilchrist, *Gender and Material Culture: The Archaeology of Religious Women* (London, 1994), esp. 125–49; R. Gilchrist, 'Medieval Bodies in the Material World: Gender, Stigma and the Body', in *Framing Medieval Bodies*, ed. S. Kay and M. Rubin (Manchester, 1994), pp. 43–61; P. A. Faulkner, 'Domestic Planning from the Twelfth to the Fourteenth Century', *The Archaeological Journal* 115 (1958), 150–84; P. A. Faulkner, 'Castle Planning in the Fourteenth Century', *The Archaeological Journal* 127 (1963), 150–83; G. Fairclough, 'Meaningful Constructions: Spatial and Functional Analysis of Medieval Buildings', *Antiquity* 66 (1992), 348–66; A. Richardson, 'Corridors of Power: A Case Study of Access Analysis from Medieval Salisbury, England', *Antiquity* 77.296 (2003), 373–84; A. Richardson, 'Gender and Space in English Royal Palaces, *c.* 1160–*c.* 1547: A Study in Access Analysis and Imagery', *Medieval Archaeology* 47 (2003), 131–65; J. Grenville, 'Urban and Rural Houses and Households in the Late Middle Ages: A Case

Meanwhile, scholars such as Felicity Riddy have noted that inventories of bourgeois houses each include a room called a 'camera' or chamber, in which at least one bed was kept, though often more, along with other stored items.[13] This varying information suggests that a secluded room containing one bed in a palace and an upper room in a merchant's house containing two or three beds could both be understood to be 'chambers'. Additionally, several scholars have noted that medieval domestic space is often gendered female.[14] Furthermore, it is suggested by Jeremy Goldberg and others that, in bourgeois and aristocratic houses, the specifically 'female' space was the chamber.[15] Diane Wolfthal goes as far as to argue that in late medieval and early modern Europe, the chamber was understood by some to be an extension of the female body.[16]

The small amount of scholarship on late medieval beds tends to focus on the bed as a symbol of power. Penelope Eames argues that the canopied bed was 'inseparably associated with prestige, honour, power, wealth and privilege'.[17] Glenn Burger discusses the chamber as a space which marks the social status of its inhabitants and the bed

Study from Yorkshire', in *Medieval Domesticity: Home, Housing and Household in Medieval England*, ed. Kowaleski and Goldberg, pp. 92–123.

[13] F. Riddy, '"Burgeis" Domesticity in Late Medieval England', in *Medieval Domesticity: Home, Housing and Household in Medieval England*, ed. Kowaleski and Goldberg, pp. 14-36 (p. 23); M. Gardiner, 'Buttery and Pantry and their Antecedents: Idea and Architecture in the English Medieval House', in *Medieval Domesticity: Home, Housing and Household in Medieval England*, ed. Kowaleski and Goldberg, pp. 37-65; Faulkner, 'Domestic Planning'.

[14] S. McSheffrey, 'Place, Space, and Situation: Public and Private in the Making of Marriage in Late Medieval London', *Speculum* 79 (2004), 960–90 (p. 960); Riddy, '"Burgeis" Domesticity', p. 15; S. Salih, 'At Home; Out of the House', in *The Cambridge Companion to Medieval Women's Writing*, ed. C. Dinshaw and D. Wallace (Cambridge, 2003), pp. 124–40 (especially p. 125); D. S. Ellis, 'Domesticating the Spanish Inquisition', in *Violence Against Women in Medieval Texts*, ed. A. Roberts (Gainesville, 1998), pp. 195–209 (p. 196).

[15] P. J. P. Goldberg, 'The Fashioning of Bourgeois Domesticity in Later Medieval England: A Material Culture Perspective', in *Medieval Domesticity: Home, Housing and Household in Medieval England*, ed. Kowaleski and Goldberg, pp. 124–44 (p. 138); R. Lee, 'A Company of Women and Men: Men's Recollections of Childbirth in Medieval England', *Journal of Family History* 27.2 (2002), 92-100; Salih, 'At Home', p. 130.

[16] D. Wolfthal, *In and Out of the Marital Bed: Seeing Sex in Renaissance Europe* (New Haven, 2010), p. 79.

[17] P. Eames, 'Furniture in England, France and the Netherlands from the Twelfth to the Fifteenth Century', *Furniture History* 13 (1977), 1–303 (p. 86).

as an 'at once privileged and anxious location for self-identification' within bourgeois households.[18] The bed's role as a symbol of power is explored by Mark Ormrod, who discusses the ways in which Jean Froissart and Thomas Walsingham use royal beds in their accounts of the attack on the Tower of London during the Peasants' Revolt.[19] He demonstrates that late medieval beds – particularly royal beds – had meaning, both for the peasants supposedly attacking the beds and for the chronicles' authors and audience. More recently, the discovery of a Tudor bed has opened up the discussion on the significance of royal beds. Jonathan Foyle's current research on the provenance of the so-called Paradise Bed and its iconography has linked it to Henry VII and suggests that it is the marriage bed that was presented to Henry VII and Elizabeth of York in 1486.[20] His research shows that a great deal of thought and work by a large number of people went into the production of the bed, and indicates that its creators were aware that the bed, in itself, was an object that conveyed significant meaning. Foyle treats the bed as a public expression of Henry VII's motives and aspirations, and conjectures that Henry had some agency in the bed's design. While Foyle's research seeks to place the bed within the context of its production and reception as the bed of Henry VII, nobody has yet sought to place the Paradise Bed in its context as a product of the wider cultural understanding of beds.

While existing scholarship has brought up some issues surrounding the late medieval bed and chamber, including ideas of status and power and the suggestion that the chamber is gendered female, it is clear that there is still much left to understand about how beds and chambers were understood in late medieval England. Taking into account spatial theory, which argues that the meaning of a space is only apparent when viewed in the context of its social production and use, and the Saussurian idea of the *signifié* – bearing in mind that the ideas signified by the words 'bed' or 'chamber' (or their late medieval vernacular equivalents) had nuances that extended beyond a mental

[18] G. Burger, 'In the Merchant's Bedchamber', in *Thresholds of Medieval Visual Culture: Liminal Spaces*, ed. E. Gertsman and J. Stevenson (Woodbridge, 2012), pp. 239–59 (p. 239).

[19] W. M. Ormrod, 'In Bed with Joan of Kent: The King's Mother and the Peasants' Revolt', in *Medieval Women: Texts and Contexts in Late Medieval Britain. Essays for Felicity Riddy*, ed. J. Wogan-Browne, R. Voaden, A. Diamond, A. Hutchinson, C. Meale and L. Johnson (Turnhout, 2000), pp. 277–92.

[20] My thanks to J. Foyle for sharing his unpublished research with me.

picture of their physicality – this book takes a holistic, interdisciplinary approach, seeking to explore evidence of actual beds and chambers and their use alongside beds and chambers found in literary or artistic sources. [21] The aim of this book is to explore the cultural meanings of beds and chambers in late medieval England. It draws on historical, literary, archaeological and visual evidence in order to discover the semiotics and socially constructed associations of the late medieval bed and chamber: what the idea of the bed and chamber was in the late medieval public imagination, and how it related to everyday practice and experience.

Before we move on, it is important to clarify the terminology used in this book. I use 'bed' to describe the object signified by the Middle English term 'bedde' (in its various spellings), which, as I discuss in the first chapter, can mean the bed frame, some of the soft furnishings or the whole ensemble. I have chosen the term 'chamber' over 'bedchamber' deliberately, usually to refer to a room purposefully set aside to contain a bed, but with the understanding that 'chamber' means more than merely a room with a bed in it and that a room could have been understood to be a chamber even if a bed is not physically present.

All material culture is meaningfully constituted, being produced by someone for a specific reason, as an inherently conscious and often meaningful act.[22] As such, evidence to suggest that an object or space has meaning does not exist solely within any one discipline, and it is for this reason that this project crosses traditional discipline boundaries. As very little was written or disseminated in late medieval England with a primary focus on the bed and chamber, wider concepts surrounding the bed and chamber only become apparent as patterns emerge from a broad range of sources, considered simultaneously. An important source for this book is Middle English romance, which, although it was the most popular secular genre in medieval England, has until fairly recently been held widely in disregard or disdain by scholars of medieval literature, rejected as 'more amusing than useful' on the basis that romances are formulaic and designed to entertain the masses.[23] It is precisely these qualities which make Middle English

[21] F. de Saussure, *Cours de linguistique générale*, ed. C. Bally, A. Sechehaye and A. Riedlinger (Paris, 1916).

[22] I. Hodder, *Reading the Past: Current Approaches to Interpretation in Archaeology*, 3rd edn (Cambridge, 2003), pp. 6–10.

[23] 'Introduction' to *Reliques of Ancient English Poetry: Consisting of Old Heroic Ballads, Songs, and Other Pieces of Our Earlier Poets*, ed. T. Percy (London, 1857),

romances invaluable for my research. The romance genre, abounding with tropes and patterns, draws from and adds to our understanding of everyday spaces such as the chamber. It is also a genre rarely considered alongside many other genres or disciplines. In this book, romance texts are explored alongside wills, probate inventories, court documents and laws, letters and literature including devotional texts, dream visions, conduct texts and lyric poetry, as well as manuscript illuminations, archaeological evidence of space and the material bed.[24] However, while existing scholarship on the late medieval bed and chamber often draws on evidence from continental Europe alongside sources from the British Isles, without questioning whether the same associations exist across different cultures, this book focuses specifically on England, while understanding that communication and migration meant that ideas and objects continued to cross boundaries. As such, the majority of the sources used in this book were produced or widely disseminated in England. As the focus of this book is on ideas in late medieval England, rather than medieval history or medieval literature, I do not seek to produce a history of the medieval English bed, nor do I offer a revisionary reading of each literary text mentioned. Each source is instead considered in light of what it can tell us of how late medieval society viewed the bed and chamber.

This book is structured around 'Arise Early', a set of 'precepts in –ly' surrounding aspects of everyday life – variants of which were popular and well known in late medieval England – which begin and end with their male addressee in bed.[25] I have chosen to use the version which is

p. xix; for a survey of early critics' treatment of Middle English romance, see N. McDonald, 'A Polemical Introduction', in *Pulp Fictions of Medieval England: Essays in Popular Romance*, ed. N. McDonald (Manchester, 2004), pp. 1–21. A recent exception is *Sexual Culture in the Literature of Medieval Britain*, ed. A. Hopkins, R. A. Rouse and C. J. Rushton (Cambridge, 2014).

24 Whenever appropriate, I give the date of each source the first time it is used and place each reference within its textual context, though I only give a synopsis of the text where it is needed. A synopsis of each literary text mentioned in this book would not add to its overall argument and can be found elsewhere. Summaries of Middle English romances can be found in *The Database of Middle English Romance*, ed. N. McDonald (York, 2012). <www.middleenglishromance.org.uk> [accessed 17 June 2014].

25 At last count, there are thirteen extant manuscript copies, three early printed copies and one inscription on a wall of a second-floor chamber in 3 Cornmarket Street, Oxford. See *A New Index of Middle English Verse*, J. Boffey and A. S. G.

extant in New Haven, Yale University, Beinecke Library MS 365 (otherwise known as the Book of Brome) because it is the most complete and because it intrigues me that, unlike all other versions, it does not instruct its addressee to sleep at the end of the day, but instead makes sex with his wife the ultimate goal. I quote it here in full:

Fyrst arysse erly
Serve thy god deuly
And the warld besylly
Do thy warke wyssely
ʒyffe thy almesse sekyrly
Goo be the wey sadly
And awnswer the pepll curtesly
Goo to thy met happely
Syt therat dyscretly
Off thy tong be not to lybraly
Arysse fro thy met tempraly
Goo to thy sopper sadly
Arysse fro sopper soburly
Goo to thy bed myrely
And lye therin jocundly
And plesse and loffe thy wyffe dewly
And basse hyr onys or tewyis myrely.[26]

The addressee of these precepts, having risen, goes about his day until it is time to return to bed, at which point he is instructed to have sex with his wife, whom we as an audience encounter for the first time. The bed bookends the addressee's day and gives him structure. The precepts suggest that there is an appropriate time for all things, including when the addressee is allowed to be in bed. They give as much value to the expression of the addressee's sexuality as they do to piety and industry, but insist that each must be done at the most appropriate time and place.

Edwards (London, 2005) [Hereafter known as *NIMEV*], no. 324; *The Digital Index of Middle English Verse*, ed. L. R. Mooney, D. W. Mosser and E. Solopova (2012),<www.dimev.net> [Hereafter known as *DIMEV*], no. 560; N. McDonald, 'Fragments of (*Have Your*) *Desire*: Brome Women at Play', in *Medieval Domesticity: Home, Housing and Household in Medieval England*, ed. Kowaleski and Goldberg, pp. 232–58.

[26] New Haven, Yale University, Beinecke Library MS 365, f. 1v, my transcription; for another edition, see McDonald, 'Fragments of (*Have Your*) *Desire*', p. 255.

The first five chapters take their titles from the Brome precepts. In my first chapter, 'Fyrst Arysse Erly', I tackle the problem of what the terms 'chamber' and 'bed' meant to people living in late medieval England, a task necessary before any further nuances associated with the terms can be discovered. It also explores what it might have been like to wake up in a late medieval chamber and discusses the significance of arising early. Having determined what the terms 'bed' and 'chamber' meant in late medieval society, I move on to their wider cultural meanings in the late medieval imagination and how they affect everyday life. The relationship between the bed and chamber and religion is addressed in Chapter 2, 'Serve Thy God Deuly', in which I argue that the bed was at the heart of late medieval society's understanding of a personal relationship with God. Following the idea of the bed as an intimate space in which to communicate with God, my third chapter explores communication between people in the bed and chamber. As well as looking at the larger political stage, this chapter uses evidence from the Paston letters and papers to show how the bed and chamber's roles as a place of trust and good judgement were used in family legal disputes. I continue to explore how the bed's physical or implied presence in the chamber gives it meaning as a place of intimacy and trust in Chapter 4, 'Go to Thy Bed Myrely/ And Lye Therin Jocundly'. In the fifth chapter, I turn to the relationship between the bed and chamber and sex. I explore the ways in which the bed was understood in relation to both licit and illicit sex. Finally, I explore the relationship between the bed and chamber and the bodies which occupy them.

The 'Arise Early' precepts tell us nothing of the addressee's wife, or what she was expected to do. In terms of narrative, she does nothing until the appointed time for sex. Are we to presume, then, that she lies in bed all day? Nicola McDonald argues:

> From the moment when she too awakes, no doubt just as early, her shadowy presence attends her husband's throughout the day, at home and abroad, at table and in devotion, in the management of the household and in promoting, and regulating, its sociability.[27]

While, in reality, it is unlikely that a bourgeois or aristocratic wife of a householder would have spent all day in the chamber, within the realms of the narrative she does just that, a pattern which is reflected

---

[27] McDonald, 'Fragments of (*Have Your*) *Desire*', p. 257.

in many Middle English literary texts.[28] The final chapter of this book, 'The Invisible Woman', seeks to redress the gender balance of the precepts, giving form to the wife's 'shadowy presence'. It returns to the suggestion by medieval household scholars that the chamber is the 'female space' within the house, exploring the real and perceived relationships between women and the chamber and focusing on the idea of the chamber as an empowering space for women.[29]

This thematic approach highlights the complex and deeply ingrained nature of the structures of meaning behind the late medieval cultural phenomenon which was the chamber and the bed within it. It explores how values attributed to the bed and chamber informed day-to-day life in late medieval England, as well as affecting broader aspects of society such as religion, politics, sex and social structures. Beds and chambers mattered to everyone, and their cultural meanings extended far beyond the chamber walls.

---

[28] See ch. 6 below.
[29] Goldberg, 'The Fashioning of Bourgeois Domesticity', p. 138.

1

'Fyrst Arysse Erly'

What might it have been like to wake up in a late medieval English chamber? The eleven-year-old narrator of a lament on the loss of childhood pleasures in the anonymous collection of fifteenth-century *vulgaria* in London, British Library, Arundel MS 249 provides an evocative glimpse of a chamber:

> when I was a childe, from iij yere olde to x (for now I go upon the xij yere), while I was undre my father and mothers kepyng […] than I was wont to lye styll abedde tylll it was forth dais, delitynge myselfe in slepe and ease. The sone sent in his beamys at the wyndowes that gave me lyght instede of a Candle. O, what a sporte it was every mornynge when the son was upe to take my lusty pleasur betwixte the shetes, to beholde the rofe, the beamys, and the rafters of my chambre, and loke on the clothes that the chambre was hangede with![1]

The nature of the purpose of the text, as an exercise in translation from English to Latin for the scholars of Magdalen School, Oxford, means that this description is almost certainly not a representation of an actual chamber.[2] Instead, we can take it as a literary imagining of the late medieval idea of what a chamber should be. As such, we could take from the text that the ideal chamber, in the late medieval cultural imagination, is richly hung, light and airy, with more than one window and a ceiling open to the roof. The ideal bed would have

---

[1] *A Fifteenth Century School Book, From a Manuscript in the British Museum (MS Arundel 249)*, ed. W. Nelson (Oxford, 1956), pp. 1–2.
[2] Ibid., pp. i–xxix; N. Orme, 'Schoolmasters, 1307–1509', in *Profession, Vocation and Culture in Later Medieval England: Essays Dedicated to the Memory of A. R. Myers*, ed. C. H. Clough (Liverpool, 1982), pp. 218–37 (p. 237).

been comfortable, so that one would wish to stay there late into the day, would not be completely enclosed and, if the pre-pubescent narrator were to have his own way, would have been entirely to himself. Could such a chamber have existed in late medieval England, and if so, would it have been at the disposal of a small child? Is this what a late medieval person imagined when thinking of a bed? The aim of this chapter is to explore the composition of both real and imaginary beds and chambers, to discern what real chambers would have contained and how real beds were constructed, as well as what 'bed' and 'chamber' meant in the late medieval English consciousness.

There is little archaeological evidence of late medieval beds. At the same time, archaeological evidence of chambers is problematic, as it is often impossible to discern which room or rooms within a house would have been used as or considered to be chambers, even in buildings where well-meaning modern owners or curators have produced signs and maps indicating otherwise. Visual sources such as manuscript illustrations are useful, but must be considered within their production contexts. Similarly, documentary and literary sources have their own limitations, as we do not know the extent to which nuances of meaning of certain words have been lost over time. The *Middle English Dictionary* is helpful in terms of tracking etymologies and orthographical differences, but it is less useful as a tool for determining the exact meanings of words.[3] For example, the first definition given by the *MED* for 'bed (n.1)' is 'bed (for sleeping, resting, etc.)', which means that, for instance, when we hear Mary tell the baby Jesus in the York Nativity play that 'here is no bedde to laye thee inne', we can understand that she has given birth in a space without a bed.[4] We cannot discern from the definition given to us by the *MED* what Mary or her medieval audience imagine such a bed to be like, should there have been one present. As such, it is necessary to look beyond the given definitions of chamber-related vocabulary in the *MED*, to reconstruct an understanding of the semantics of chamber-related vocabulary, using a range of different sources in conjunction with each other. While the definition of 'chaumbre (n.)' in the *MED* focuses on ideas of privacy and containment, thus theoretically including any enclosed space, for the purpose of this book, unless stated otherwise,

---

[3] *MED.*

[4] 'bed (n. 1)', *MED*; 'Play 14: The Nativity', in *The York Corpus Christi Plays*, ed. C. Davidson (Kalamazoo, 2011), l. 115.

I will focus on the chamber as a room which usually contains at least one bed.[5] This is primarily because my interest is not in beds or chambers alone, but how the two concepts interacted, were interacted with and thought about by their owners and occupants.

The chamber

The intended purpose of rooms in post-conquest domestic buildings has been the subject of much debate. Back in 1958, Patrick Faulkner suggested that post-conquest houses contained 'lower and upper halls', with the upper halls comprising the sleeping, eating and living quarters for the owner and his family.[6] John Blair later put forward the idea that in manorial houses, these 'upper halls' were 'in fact chamber blocks which were once accompanied by ground-floor halls of the normal kind', suggesting that chambers were more intimate spaces than previously thought.[7] Anthony Quiney argues that the distinction between chamber and hall is fluid, as its definition depends on both the function and what the occupier thinks about the space:

> it might be more appropriate to ask what the surviving buildings represented in the minds of their builders, regardless of whether they called them halls or chambers […] perhaps an upper hall on one day could become a chamber on another with a simple change of furniture but, in its occupant's mind, remain as a symbol of his assumed nobility even were it only purchased by the depth of his purse.[8]

I agree with Quiney that the early chamber was more likely to be distinguished by its furnishings and use than by its architectural features. Towards the later Middle Ages, as chambers became more popular and were built with their specific function in mind, the level of access to the chamber was a vital consideration for builders and owners.

What is clear from written sources is that, regardless of architectural styles and sizes of domestic buildings, the idea of the chamber

---

[5] 'chaumbre (n.)', *MED*.

[6] P. A. Faulkner, 'Domestic Planning from the 12th to 14th Centuries', *Archaeological Journal* 115 (1958), 150–83.

[7] W. J. Blair, 'Hall and Chamber: English Domestic Planning 1000–1250', in *Manorial Domestic Planning in England and France*, ed. G. Merion-Jones and M. Jones (London, 1993), pp. 1–21 (p. 2).

[8] A. Quiney, 'Hall or Chamber? That is the Question. The Use of Rooms in Post-Conquest Houses', *Architectural History* 42 (1999), 24–46 (p. 42).

was firmly implanted in the English cultural imagination by the later Middle Ages. It is also clear that the chamber was a status symbol in late medieval England. The relative privacy afforded by a chamber physically separated those who could afford a chamber from those who could not. As shall be demonstrated throughout this book, the idea of the chamber was present in the minds of those in the community who did not have chambers, as well as those who did. If the distinction between the hall and chamber was fluid with the meaning resting on the contents of the room, in order to piece together what 'chamber' meant, we must begin with what it was likely to contain. In probate inventories, which list contents under headings for each room, the bed is the principal feature of most rooms defined as chambers by their occupants or surveyors. The relative importance of the bed in the chamber is immediately obvious when several inventories of chambers are considered alongside one another, as illustrated in Fig. 1 on the following page.

The word cloud is created from all the inventories which explicitly refer to a chamber in Philip Stell's edition of *Probate Inventories of the York Diocese, 1350–1500*.[9] The words included in the cloud are words that occur most frequently in the inventories. The larger the word, the more frequently it occurs. This visual representation of a large corpus of inventories clearly illustrates that beds and bedding were the most likely articles to be found in the chamber. It indicates that upon waking, the colours one would most likely have seen would have been combinations of red, blue, white and green; that as well as the bed and bedding, there would probably have been curtains, a tapestry, a chest, a table, cupboard or board, some clothes and towels and miscellaneous household items such as bowls, trestles, candles and presses; that the decorative motifs might have been roses or other flowers, arms, animals such as lions and griffins, wheels or stripes. We know from the Paston records that it was sometimes difficult to accommodate all of the things one might want within the chamber. Around 1454, Margaret

---

[9] *Probate Inventories of the York Diocese, 1350–1500*, ed. and trans. P. M. Stell (York, 2006). While this volume is by no means exhaustive and its existence in modern English translation only hinders its use for complex analysis, the modernised spellings work in its favour for this exercise, as variant spellings do not affect the results. Similarly, the small area in which these inventories are written avoids discrepancies resulting from dialectal variation. All word clouds in this book are created using software from Tagxedo <www.tagxedo.com>.

Figure 1: Word cloud representing inventories of chambers in the York Diocese, 1350–1500.

Paston, recounting to her husband her plans to house him and his belongings at Norwich, reports:

> I haue take the mesure in the draute chamer þer as ye wold your coforys and your cowntewery shuld be sette for the whyle, and þer is no space besyde the bedd, thow the bed were remevyd to the dore, for to sette bothe your bord and your koforys there and to haue space to go and sitte be syde.[10]

Such accounts as this illustrate that chambers were used to house goods considered valuable, as well as goods one might use in the chamber. It also suggests that there was not as much room in a chamber as the idyllic description in the Magdalene schoolbook implies.

As inventories usually only list moveable goods, we cannot know from the inventories alone whether the walls would normally have been painted, but we can deduce from such documents that some chambers had hangings. The 1485 inventory of the chamber of Margaret Pigott

---

[10] *Paston Letters and Papers of the Fifteenth Century*, ed. N. Davis, 2 vols. (Oxford, 2004), I, 253; BL Additional MS 34888. 'Cowntewery' refers to the board used for counting money.

in Ripon refers to 'eight separate pieces of green say hanging round the edges of the room'.[11] The youthful narrator of the Magdalen schoolbook similarly recollects 'the clothes that the chambre was hangede with', which suggests that the items found in Yorkshire chambers portrayed in the word cloud are indicative of a wider experience of the chamber.[12] In addition, the objects included in Fig. 1 fit well with contemporary illustrations of chambers, which indicates that it is a fair representation of what a chamber was like. For instance, the illustration below of the birth of St Edmund in Henry VI's copy of Lydgate's *Lives of St Edmund and St Fremund*, contemporaneous with the inventories, includes many objects and colours in the word cloud.

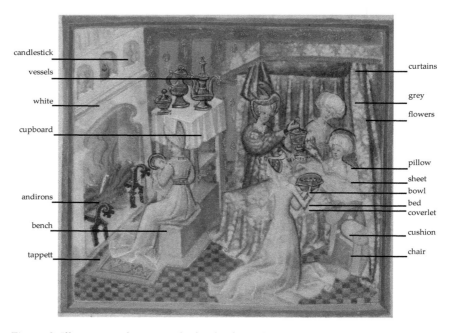

Figure 2: Illustration depicting the birth of St Edmund, *c.* 1434–9, annotated with terminology from Fig. 1. © The British Library Board. BL Harley 2278, f. 13v.

---

[11] *Probate Inventories,* ed. and trans. Stell 653; Leeds, Brotherton Library, Archives of the Dean and Chapter of Ripon MS 432.1.
[12] *A Fifteenth Century School Book,* ed. Nelson, p. 2.

London, British Library, Harley MS 2278 was produced between 1434 and 1439, whereas the birth of St Edmund represented by the miniature was in the ninth century. The illustration in Fig. 2 is clearly designed with a fifteenth-century chamber in mind, rather than as an accurate portrayal of St Edmund's birth. Because it is a representation of an historical birth, however, the illustration is unlikely to be a painting of a specific, existing chamber, but is instead the artist's idea of what a birthing chamber might look like. As the colours and objects correlate with documentary sources, we can assume that other details of the miniature can be taken into account as being part of a typical, if high-status, chamber. For instance, this image, like many illustrations of chambers, depicts painted walls. As a non-moveable feature of the chamber, wall painting does not appear in probate inventories. There is evidence of extensive wall painting in the now-lost painted chamber at Westminster, as analysed in detail by Paul Binski.[13] Chamber wall paintings are occasionally described in Middle English romance. For instance, the 'chaumbur of love' in the early fifteenth-century romance *Sir Degrevant* is painted with Biblical images, while the narrator of Chaucer's late fourteenth-century dream vision *The Book of the Duchess* finds himself in a chamber 'ful wel depeynted'.[14] It seems probable, therefore, that chamber walls, especially when they were not hung with cloth, would have been painted.

The miniaturist's depiction of the fireplace where the baby is being warmed is reflected in literary descriptions of chambers. As I will discuss later on, in Langland's *Piers Plowman*, written *c.* 1360–87, Dame Studie laments that lords and ladies are increasingly dining 'in a chambre with a chymenee', so that they are not socialising with people of lower status.[15] In Chaucer's *Troilus and Criseyde* from the early 1380s, Pandarus 'drow hym to the feere' in his chamber.[16] John Russell's *Boke*

---

[13] P. Binski, *The Painted Chamber at Westminster* (London, 1986); see also P. Tudor-Craig, 'The Painted Chamber at Westminster', *The Archaeological Journal* 114 (1957), 92–105; A plan of the painted chamber, drawn in 1800, is in BL, Maps Crace Port. 11.47.

[14] *Sir Degrevant*, in *Sentimental and Humorous Romances*, ed. E. Kooper (Kalamazoo, 2005), l. 1439; G. Chaucer, *The Book of the Duchess*, in *The Riverside Chaucer*, ed. L. D. Benson. 3rd edn (Oxford, 1987), l. 322; for more on the wall paintings in *The Book of the Duchess*, see ch. 4 below, pp. 127–30.

[15] William Langland, *The Vision of William Concerning Piers Plowman*, B-text, ed. A. V. C. Schmidt (London, 1995), x, l. 100.

[16] G. Chaucer, 'Troilus and Criseyde' iii, in *Riverside Chaucer*, ed. Benson, l. 975.

of Nurture, written about 1460–80, instructs the king's chamberlain to 'se þer be a good fyre in þe chambur conveyed,/ with wood & fuelle redy þe fyre to bete & aide'.[17] We can take from this that certain chambers had fireplaces. In 1577, the Elizabethan rector William Harrison notes that the old men dwelling in his village agree that one of the three things that has 'marvellously altered in England [...] is the multitude of chimneys lately erected whereas in their young days there were not above two or three, if so many, in most uplandish towns of the realm (the religious houses and manor places of their lords always excepted, and peradventure some great personages)'.[18] The addition of chimneys would, for the most part, be due to the growing number of chambers built in late medieval England, as in many houses, the fire was in an open hearth in the centre of the room until around the end of the fifteenth century.[19] Harrison's comment suggests that chimneys are signifiers of status. As such, 'a chambre with a chymenee' must be especially high-status.[20]

The bed

It is clear that the bed features prominently in the chamber, but it must be observed that the late medieval understanding of 'bed' is difficult to define. A definition by primary function would allow almost any surface upon which someone could possibly sleep to be considered a bed, but in wills and inventories the term is used to denote something specific. The *MED* defines a bed as 'a pallet, a small mattress', and the

---

[17] J. Russell, *The Boke of Nurture*, in *The Babees Book, Aristotle's A B C, Urbanitatis, Stans Puer ad Mensam, The Lvtille Childrenes Lvtil Boke, The Bokes of Nurture of Hugh Rhodes and John Russell, Wynkyn de Worde's Boke of Keruynge, The Booke of Demeanor, The Boke of Curtasye, Seager's Schoole of Vertue, &c. &c. with Some French and Latin Poems on Like Subjects, and Some Forewords on Education in Early England*, ed. F. J. Furnivall (London, 1868), pp. 929–30.

[18] W. Harrison, 'A Description of England', in *Holinshed's Chronicles of England, Scotland and Ireland*, ed. L. Withington (London, 1876), pp. 118–19.

[19] A. Emery, *Greater Medieval Houses of England and Wales, 1300–1500*, vol. III: *Southern England* (Cambridge, 2006), p. 32; J. Grenville, *Medieval Housing* (Leicester, 1997), p. 86; G. Sheeran, *Medieval Yorkshire Towns: People, Buildings and Spaces* (Edinburgh, 1998), p. 149; C. M. Woolgar, *The Senses in Late Medieval England* (London, 2006), p. 248; A. Emery, *Discovering Medieval Houses* (Princes Risborough, 2007), pp. 48–54; J. E. Crowley, *The Invention of Comfort: Sensibilities and Design in Early Modern Britain and Early America* (Baltimore, 2003), pp. 7–9, 13–14.

[20] Langland, *Piers Plowman* x, p. 100.

Oxford English Dictionary suggests that the bed's 'essential part' consists of 'a stuffed sack or mattress', 'as in "feather-bed"'.[21] Both define the bed as somewhere or some object upon which to sleep, rather than as a meaningful ensemble of materials connoted by the word 'bed'. While the *OED* acknowledges that 'bed' can also be used to describe 'the whole structure in its most elaborate form', its definition assumes a certain degree of knowledge on the part of the reader, as it does not list every article that may be included in the term 'bed'.[22] It is obvious that the modern meaning of 'bed' is not exactly the same as the late medieval meaning, although it is clear that neither meaning is clear-cut, and could well include both the 'essential part' and the complete ensemble. For example, in 1426, John Credy bequeathed Alison Burdon 'a blewe bedde of Tapacery', which indicates that Credy understood the 'bedde' to refer to soft furnishings.[23] On the other hand, in the stanzaic *Guy of Warwick*, Guy is thrown into the sea along with his bed while he is sleeping, and a fisherman 'seth that bed floter him by'.[24] In this case, the bed is buoyant, and so we must assume that 'bed' refers to either the wooden bedstead or a mattress stuffed with supernatant material. In 1424, Roger Flore bequeathed 'a bed' to each of his children, 'þat is to say, couerlide, tapite, blankettis, too peyre schetes, matras, and canvas'.[25] This suggests not only that Flore thought the bed to be a construct made up of the soft furnishing, but that he was aware that the term 'bed' was one requiring elucidation.

It must also be taken into account that beds varied according to status, even within the upper bourgeois and aristocratic circles on which this book is focused, so that what comprised a complete bed set for one person may have been different to a bed set considered complete by another, in terms of the number, type or quality of articles. However, it should not be presumed that only the upper aristocracy had expensively furnished beds. While the status of bed items varies, it is evident from inventories that even among the lower bourgeoisie,

---

[21] 'bed, *n.*', *OED*.

[22] Ibid.

[23] TNA PROB 11/3/108, ff. 27r–28v (f. 28r); *Fifty Earliest English Wills in the Court of Probate, London: A. D. 1387–1439; with a Priest's of 1454*, ed. F. J. Furnivall (London, 1882), p. 76.

[24] *Stanzaic Guy of Warwick*, ed. A. Wiggins (Kalamazoo, 2004), l. 2371.

[25] TNA PROB 11/3/174, ff. 70r–73v (f. 71r); *Fifty Earliest English Wills*, ed. Furnivall, p. 57.

care and money would be spent on furnishing a bed to a high stand-ard.[26] For example, the 1426 inventory of John Cotom, a York mason, itemises very few belongings, but includes 'a bed cover impaled with birds and bosses in rings', which, at '1s. 4d', was the most expensive thing he owned, suggesting that the bed was of some importance to him.[27]

The most useful evidence of the physical makeup of a late medieval bed is found in the mnemonic allegory of conscience, 'Bonum lectum', which survives in seven extant fifteenth- and sixteenth-century man-uscripts but probably existed in some form from an earlier date.[28] It instructs the male or female addressee (both genders are mentioned in the text) to 'take here hede and lerne howeʒ þou schalt make an honest bede and a good plesinge vnto god profitabel and worschipful/ vnto þi soule' (ll. 2–4). What follows is a step-by-step account of the construc-tion of the bed, with each component of the bed assigned an attribute, virtue or devotional activity required to make one's 'chambour of þi soule' (l. 5) a suitable resting place for Christ.[29] As it is allegorical and has a wide readership in mind, having been transmitted to both re-ligious and secular owners, the material bed it describes is probably not exceptional, except in the fact that it is imaginary. It is both wholly a bed and wholly not a bed at the same time, but the aspect which we could consider to be wholly a bed is likely to be representative of the typical bed for its readership. Considering this text alongside royal household ordinances and Russell's *Boke of Nurture* as well as documentary evidence of late medieval beds makes it possible for us to have a very clear idea of how a bed would have been assembled.[30]

Before moving on to a reconstruction of the physical bed, it is first necessary to discuss vocabulary. The late medieval English bed as a whole comprises several different material components, some of

---

[26] Goldberg, 'The Fashioning of Bourgeois Domesticity', pp. 124–44.

[27] *Probate Inventories*, ed. and trans. Stell, p. 549.

[28] A. I. Doyle, ed., '"Lectulus Noster Floridus": An Allegory of the Penitent Soul', in *Literature and Religion in the Later Middle Ages: Philological Studies in Honour of Siegfried Wenzel*, ed. R. Newhauser and J. A Alford (Binghamton, 1995), pp. 179–90. Doyle suggests that the variations between the texts of four of the extant manuscripts is indicative of a wider and longer circulation than is now apparent (p. 183).

[29] See ch. 2 below for a discussion on Christ in the chamber.

[30] *A Collection of Ordinances and Regulations for the Government of the Royal Household, Made in Divers Reigns, from King Edward III. to King William and Queen Mary* (London, 1790).

which are not present in every bed set, and some of which are necessary in order for the collective materials to be considered a bed. A good indication of the vocabulary that tends to be associated with actual beds can be found in Fig. 3.

Figure 3: Word cloud representing Middle English bed terminology.

This word cloud represents the words used most frequently in sentences referring to 'bedde' in its various forms.[31] As the source material is in Middle English, the variations in spelling results in some repetition of terms, so the size of the word is less of an indication of which article would have been the most frequently used as part of a bed set. However, this word cloud gives an indication of the many components that went into a late medieval bed, as well as the ways in which their owners distinguished between them, using terms such as 'good' and 'best'. It suggests that the most common colours for bedding are red, green, white and blue, and that curtains are popular but not as

[31] *Fifty Earliest English Wills*, ed. Furnivall; *Paston Letters and Papers*, ed. Davis; *Lincoln Diocese Documents, 1450–1554*, ed. A. Clark (Michigan, 1914); *Kingsford's Stonor Letters and Papers 1290–1483*, ed. C. Carpenter (Cambridge, 1996); *The Medieval Records of a London City Church (St Mary at Hill) A. D. 1420–1559*, ed. H. Littlehales (London, 1904–5); *Wills and Inventories from the Registers of the Commissary of Bury St Edmund's and the Archdeacon of Sudbury* (London, 1850), ed. S. Tymms; *Somerset Medieval Wills. 1501–1530. With Some Somerset Wills Preserved at Lambeth*, ed. F. W. Weaver (London, 1903).

common as sheets and blankets. The rest of this section will comprise an analysis of each layer of the bed, using terms directly from the word cloud as well as those in various written sources, including 'Bonum lectum', in order to work out exactly what is meant by these terms, how the components worked together, and what 'bed' meant in late medieval England.

A litter of straw

According to 'Bonum lectum', one must begin making one's bed with 'a liter of strey'.[32] The instructions for making the king's bed in the Household Ordinances of Henry VII also refers to 'the litter'.[33] In 'The Merchant's Tale', Chaucer describes lust as 'perilous fyr, that in the bedstraw bredeth'.[34] It seems likely that straw was often used in late medieval beds, although it is never mentioned in inventories of the chamber (given that it is not valuable once used). Straw was brought in for bedding at Hanley Castle in December 1409 and March 1410, while the duke of York was visiting.[35] Chris Woolgar argues that this could be indicative of a three-month use and replacement cycle, though it is possible that it was stored in enough quantity that it was changed monthly.[36] If we are to take 'Bonum lectum' as reflective of actual practice, the straw is shaken to remove the dust and then, once the bed is made, it 'must be borded lest þe streye wille falle ouȝt'.[37] Such a practice seems to have been widely known, as in Caxton's 1489 *The Four Sons of Aymon*, Mawgys is able to pitch a torch 'bytwyne the strawe and the bedsted soo that it helde faste', without it setting fire to the bed or its occupant.[38]

---

[32] 'Bonum lectum', ed. Doyle, p. 186.

[33] *A Collection of Ordinances*, p. 121.

[34] G. Chaucer, 'The Merchant's Tale', in *Riverside Chaucer*, ed. Benson, l. 1783.

[35] Northampton, Northamptonshire Record Office Westmorland (Apethorpe) 4. xx. 4, ff. 13v, 32r; c.f. 'A Household Account of Edward, Duke of York at Hanley Castle, 1409–10', ed. J. P. Toomey in *Noble Household Management and Spiritual Discipline in Fifteenth-Century Worcestershire*, ed. R. N. Swanson and D. Guyatt. Worcestershire Historical Society 24 (Bristol, 2011).

[36] Woolgar, *The Great Household in Late Medieval England*, p. 170.

[37] 'Bonum lectum', ed. Doyle, p. 189.

[38] *The Right Pleasaunt and Goodly Historie of the Foure Sonnes of Aymon. Englisht from the French by William Caxton, and Printed by Him about 1489*, ed. O. Richardson (London, 1884–5), p. 399.

Canvas

'Caneuas' is a prominent term in Fig. 3, and is the next component of the bed in 'Bonum lectum', following the straw. Roger Flore's explanation of 'a bed' starts at the top layer, with the 'couerlide', and works downwards to 'canvas', so one could assume that he considers the 'canvas' to be the lowest layer of re-useable bedding, below the mattress.[39] Similarly, in the Household ordinances of Henry VII, the yeoman is instructed to 'lay downe the canevas to the bedd's feete, and shake the litter, and laye on the canevas againe', which suggests that the canvas was meant to cover the straw.[40] While the *MED* suggests that it is a bed covering, it is much more likely that canvas was usually used towards the bottom of the bed. In addition to written evidence which implies that it covered the straw, its relative robustness, which made canvas useful for tents, bags and kitchen strainers, meant it was ideally suited to be the layer that would rub against straw-covered pallets and floors and protect other layers of the bed.[41]

Mattresses and featherbeds

In a reconstruction of the layers that would have comprised a bed, the first hurdle to overcome is not the unfamiliar terms presented in Fig. 3, but rather the assumption that the familiar terms meant the same in late medieval England as they do now. Despite the *OED* and *MED* definitions of 'bed' including references to mattresses and the *OED*'s implication that a 'feather-bed' is a 'stuffed sack or mattress', the Middle English 'fetherbed' is not necessarily synonymous with the modern-day 'mattress' or 'feather-bed', and a late medieval 'materas' almost certainly does not resemble a modern-day mattress.[42] This is evident from the way in which they are itemised in wills. In 1450, Joan Buckland left several bed sets to beneficiaries, often using the terms 'fetherbed' and 'matrasse' within the same bed set: 'the best

---

[39] *Fifty Earliest English Wills*, ed. Furnivall, p. 57.
[40] *A Collection of Ordinances*, pp. 121–2.
[41] 'pro canvays pro le Tent.', *Extracts from the Account Rolls of the Abbey of Durham, from the Original MSS*, ed. C. Fowler, 3 vols. (Durham, 1901) III, 603; 'on of the canvas baggis jn the gret coffer', *Paston Letters and Papers* I, ed. Davis, I, 98; 'take þan a clene canvas, & caste þe mylke vppe-on, & with a platere stryke it of þe cloþe', *Two Fifteenth-century Cookery-books: Harleian MS 279 (ab 1430), & Harl. MS 4016 (ab. 1450), with extracts from Ashmole MS 1439, Laud MS 553, & Douce MS 55*, ed. T. Austin (Oxford, 1962), p. 27.
[42] 'bed, n.', *OED*; 'bed, n.1', *MED*.

ffetherbed, & the best Matrasse with the best bolster'; 'j. good ffetherbed with j. large matrasse'; 'j. good featherbed, j. good matrasse', and 'the federbed, & a matrasse'.[43] Similarly, in 1533, shopkeeper John Lee bequeathed 'to Agnes Cokkes, one fetherbed, a mattresse, and all that longith to A bed'.[44] The use of these terms in wills suggests not only that mattresses and featherbeds differed from each other, but that they were often considered to go together as a pair. Towards the end of Joan Buckland's will she bequeaths some bed sets that contain a mattress but do not include a featherbed. As these bequests were to servants and people of a lower social standing than herself, then it can be deduced that the mattress was often the staple and constant component of a bed, while the featherbed was more of a luxury additional item.

Literary evidence shows that the featherbed was certainly a component of the bed upon which one would sleep, rather than as a stuffed covering. Gower uses the phrase 'upon a fethrebed alofte/ He lith' in his *Confessio Amantis*, written in the late fourteenth century, and the prose *Brut* refers to the Duke of Gloucester 'aslepe on a Fetherbed', which his killers took from where it 'lay vnder him' and placed 'apon hym', in order to smother him, inverting the norm for nefarious purposes.[45] Where 'bed' is used in wills and inventories to signify a specific soft component of the bed, such as 'a bed of red and grene' in Thomas Tvoky's will of 1418, it is likely that the item in question was a featherbed.[46]

Late medieval mattresses were not always, as they are today, the main stuffed layer of the bedding upon which one would sleep. The *MED* does not have a precise definition of 'materas', suggesting 'a mattress or pad for a bed', a 'bedcover, quilt' or a 'support'.[47] It also lists 'standard-materas' as possibly meaning 'a mattress on permanent frame', though I am inclined to think it is more likely a mattress

[43] Lincoln, Lincolnshire Archives, REG/20, ff. 55r–56r; *Lincoln Diocese Documents*, ed. Clark, pp. 39–41.

[44] Ibid., p. 164.

[45] J. Gower, *Confessio Amantis*, ed. R. A. Peck (Kalamazoo, 2003), Book 4, ll. 3020–1; *The Brut, or The Chronicles of England. Edited from MS Raw. B171, Bodleian Library*, ed. F. W. D. Brie, 2 vols. (London 1906–8), II, 351–2; for information on the date of the prose *Brut*, see L. Matheson, *The Prose 'Brut': The Development of a Middle English Chronicle* (Tempe, 1998).

[46] *Fifty Earliest English Wills*, ed. Furnivall, p. 36.

[47] 'materas, n.', *MED*.

perceived to be of a standard size.[48] In any case, the multiple meanings imply that the use and form of the 'materas' changed over time or varied depending on region or estate. For instance, in an early fifteenth-century English translation of *An Alphabet of Tales*, a man is described as 'slepand vndyrnethe a matres', which correlates with the *MED*'s suggestion of 'bedcover' as a possible meaning.[49] Conversely, the *Promptorium Parvulorum* of 1440 defines 'matteras' as 'vndyr clothe of a bed'. [50] In addition to the varied positions within the bed set implied by the term 'materas', there is a discrepancy in physical composition. The use of the word 'clothe' in *Promptorium Parvulorum* is suggestive of a piece of woven or felted fabric, which implies that the mattress was a length of unstuffed material.[51] In contrast, the Mystery of Upholders, who made mattresses and featherbeds, understood both items to be stuffed. In 1474, they complained to the Mayor and Aldermen of the City of London that some untrustworthy merchants were selling 'Federbeddes pylowes matrasses Quysshens Quyltes and suche othere which the Bier seeth withoute and knoweth not the stuf within', which included 'Fetherbeddes and bolsters stuffed with thistill downe and Cattes Tailles Materas stuffed with here and Flokkes and sold for Flokkes Materasse of netis here and hors here'.[52] In 1552, the 'Acte for the true stuffynge of Featherbedds Mattresses and Quyssheons' was passed, which ordered that featherbeds be stuffed with only 'drie pulled feathers or cleane Downe onely, without mynglinge of scalded Feathers fendowne thistledowne sande lyme gravell heare or any other unlaufulle or corrupte stuffe', while mattresses could only be stuffed with 'Fethers Wool or Flock'.[53] The complaint and subsequent

---

[48] Ibid.

[49] *Alphabet of Tales: An English 15th Century Translation of the Alphabetum Narrationum of Etienne de Besançon, from additional MS Add. 25719 of the British Museum*, ed. M. Macleod Banks (London, 1904), p. 145.

[50] G. Grammaticus, *Promptorium Parvulorum Sive Clericorum, Lexicon Anglo-Latinum Princeps*, 3 vols., ed. A. Way (London, 1853), II, 329; 'cloth, n.', *MED*.

[51] Grammaticus, *Promptorium Parvulorum*, p. 329.

[52] Letterbook L, in *Calendar of Letter-Books Preserved among the Archives of the Corporation of the City of London at the Guildhall*, ed. R. R. Sharpe, 11 vols. (London, 1912), XI. My expansions.

[53] *The Statutes of the Realm, Printed by Command of his Majesty King George the Third in Pursuance of an Address of the House of Commons of Great Britain, from Original Records and Authentic Manuscripts*, ed. T. E. Tomlins (London, 1819), p. 156; J. F. Houston, *Fetherbedds and Flock Bedds: A History of the Worshipful Company of Upholders of the City of London* (Sandy, 1999), p. 34.

act imply that it was widely understood that mattresses were stuffed, albeit with some occasionally unsavoury items. It also suggests that, at least by the later Middle Ages, the main difference between mattresses and featherbeds was that featherbeds were stuffed with soft materials, whereas mattresses were essentially firm.

From the available evidence, it can be deduced that as time went on, mattresses were more likely to be stuffed and were intended for lying upon, rather than used as unstuffed coverings. Featherbeds were used in a similar way to mattresses, as a bed component on which to lie, but were usually treated as an addition to, rather than as an alternative to, the mattress.

Sheets, fustians and blankets

Terms that occur very frequently in wills and inventories in relation to beds are 'shetis', 'fustyans' and 'blankettis'.[54] Like 'canvas', 'fustian' can refer to a certain type of fabric, which, according to Kathryn Berenson, was 'woven with linen warp and cotton weft', as in 'fustyan pillow' or 'dobelet of blak fusteyn'; or an article in itself, as in 'a payer of fustyans'.[55] Due to the use and frequency of the terms 'sheet' and 'fustian' in documentary sources, it is clear that each term has a specific meaning. For instance, Joan Buckland's will of 1450 includes 'blankettes', 'Shetes' and 'Fustyance'.[56] However, they do not all appear in the same bed sets. Buckland left a bed set containing 'j. paire of the best ffustyans' and 'j. payre of Shetis of Raynes' but no blankets to her son; several bed sets including 'Blankettes' and 'Shetes' but no fustians to various beneficiaries; a bed set containing 'a pair of the best blankettes' but no sheets or fustians to a parson, and left a bed set including 'j. paire fustyance' but no blankets or sheets in the Manor of Ochecote.[57]

Sheets served a similar function within the bed as they do today. There are two main distinctions between sheets: 'schetes' and 'schetes of Reynes', which were often described as 'fyne'. The latter refers to the particularly fine, plain-weave linen, produced in Rennes or like

---

[54] *Lincoln Diocese Documents*, ed. Clark, p. 39.

[55] K. Berenson, 'Tales from the "Coilte"', *V&A Online Journal* 2 (Autumn 2009) <http://www.vam.ac.uk/content/journals/research-journal/issue–02/tales-from-the-coilte/> [accessed 28 August 2012]; *Lincoln Diocese Documents*, ed. Clark, p. 135; *Paston Letters and Papers*, ed. Davis, I, 326, 212.

[56] *Lincoln Diocese Documents*, ed. Clark, pp. 40–1; Lincoln, Lincolnshire Archives, REG/20, ff. 55r–56r.

[57] Ibid.

the sheets produced in Rennes, and is thus the superior of the two.[58] Although the former's material is not usually specified, it is probably a type of linen. Sheets were measured in leaves, so that Joan Buckland bequeathed 'j. paire of fyne shetis of three levys', 'j. paire of fyne shetis of ij. levys & dim.' and 'j. paire of shetis of ij. levys and dim.' in her will, while in 1487 Elisabeth Poynings or Browne (née Paston) left 'iij payer of newe shetys of iij levis of iij ellys and an half long; and two payer of shetys of ij levis and an half long [...] and vj paiere of shetys ouer-worne of ij levis'.[59] Qualifying sheets in terms of the number of leaves is due to the fact that linen was woven into thin lengths. Clark suggests that it was 'usual practice' to rotate three leaves of linen, so that when the middle leaf became worn, it could be moved to the edge in order to make the sheet last longer.[60] I find no evidence of this practice at the time, though it is possible that a damaged leaf may have been replaced to save discarding the whole sheet.

Fustians and blankets served similar functions to each other and were interchangeable, as evidenced by Roger Flore's bequest of two beds to his son: 'I wull he haue to þe oone a peyre fustyans, and to þe oþer a peyre blankettis, and to ilk of þe too beddis too peyre shetys goode'.[61] The choice between blankets or fustians may have depended on worth, status or use of the bed. An inventory of Elizabeth Syward-by's goods in York in 1468 values 'two pairs of fustians' at '6s. 8d.', 'two pairs of blankets' at '4s.' and 'two other pairs of blankets' at '3s.'.[62] An inventory of Henry Bowet, Archbishop of York, in 1423 suggests that 'fustians' were basically blankets made out of fustian, while 'blankets' could be made out of fustian or some other material: records '£2 re-ceived for three used pairs of blankets of fustian' and '5s. received for three worn blankets of white cloth'.[63] A useful way of thinking about the relationship between blankets and fustians might be to compare the term 'fustian' with the use of the term 'nylons' to refer to stockings

---

[58] A. C. Moule, 'Linen of Rens', in *Quinsai, with Other Notes on Marco Polo* (Cambridge, 1957), pp. 67–9; 'cloth of raynes', Phyllis G. Tortora and Ingrid Johnson, *The Fairchild Books Dictionary of Textiles*, 8th edn (New York, 2013), p. 128.

[59] *Lincoln Diocese Documents*, ed. Clark, p. 42; Lincoln, Lincolnshire Archives, REG/20, ff. 55r–56r; *Paston Letters and Papers*, ed. Davis, I, 212.

[60] *Lincoln Diocese Documents*, ed. Clark, p. 37.

[61] *Fifty Earliest English Wills*, ed. Furnivall, p. 56.

[62] *Probate Inventories*, ed. and trans. Stell, p. 626.

[63] Ibid., 536–7.

made out of nylon.[64] The higher price given to fustians is indicative of their higher cultural value, as suggested by Joan Buckland's bequest of fustians for her son and blankets for a parson and servants, as well as the presence of 'Fustian and shetis' in John Russell's description of the king's bed in his *Book of Nurture*.[65] The 'honest bede' of 'Bonum lectum' has blankets but no fustians, nor does it have a featherbed. Fustians, like featherbeds, might therefore be considered luxury items, whereas blankets are the standard option.

Sheets, blankets and fustians are always mentioned in pairs in wills, inventories and conduct books, which explains why the word 'pair' is as large as 'bed' in Fig. 1, and 'paire' and 'peyre' are very large in Fig. 3. References to single or odd numbers of these items within the context of bedding are remarkably few, as if a single sheet, blanket or fustian was simply unheard-of. Literary evidence shows that the pairs of sheets, blankets and fustians sandwiched the bed's occupants. In Malory's *Morte Darthur*, written by 1470, when Tristam is wounded in battle and then goes to bed, he 'bebledde bothe overshete and the neyther-shete', the qualifying adjectives implying that the sheets are intended to go over and under the bed's occupant.[66] Similarly, 'Bonum lectum' mentions 'þe two blanketis of þi beed', 'þe neþer schete' and 'þe ouer schete'.[67] The instructions on making the King's bed in the Household ordinances of Henry VII shed light on how to order the pair of sheets and the pair of fustians. After the featherbed, the 'yeoman of the stuff' is instructed to 'take a fustian and take the assaye and cast it upon the bedd […] and the sheet on the same wise […] then lay on the other sheete […] then lay on the over fustian above'.[68] As blankets and fustians were interchangeable, it is probable that blankets would have similarly surrounded the sheets. Where there were both fustians and blankets in the bed set, pairs of blankets and fustians may have been swapped out when the bed was changed, or they may have formed an extra layer either side of the bed's occupant.

---

[64] My thanks to Nicholas Perkins for this suggestion.

[65] Lincoln, Lincolnshire Archives, REG/20, ff. 55r–56r; Russell, *The Boke of Nurture*, p. 179.

[66] T. Malory, *The Works of Sir Thomas Malory*, ed. E. Vinaver, rev. P. J. C. Field (Oxford, 1990), p. 394.

[67] 'Bonum lectum', ed. Doyle, p. 187.

[68] *A Collection of Ordinances*, pp. 121–2.

Coverlets

After the 'over fustian' or top blanket, the next layer of the bed is the coverlet. With many beds, this would be the top layer of covering. John Russell instructs his audience to 'kover with a keuerlyte clenely þat bed so mannerly made', as if a well-presented coverlet signifies a well-made bed, fit for a king.[69] A similar idea is found in *Cursor Mundi, c.* 1300, where Christ's bed at the nativity is described as humble: 'was þar na riche geres graithed/ Was þar na pride o couerled'.[70] Rather than referring to a certain type of fabric, the term 'coverlet' denotes any useful upper layer of bedding, literally covering the rest of the bed. This is most obvious in 'Bonum lectum', where the coverlet 'coueriþ þe multitude of synnes' and represents a love of God 'ouer alle þinge'.[71] As the top layer, it was often richly wrought or decorated. For example, an inventory of heirlooms at Stonor from around 1474 includes a 'rede coverlet wyth grene chapelettes' and 'a grene coverlett wyth pottes and Estrych ffeþurs', while a Paston inventory from around 1465 reports the theft of 'vj couerlytys of werkys of dyuers colourys'.[72] In 1452, William Duffield's belongings included a coverlet 'with a crowned lion in the middle' and two coverlets 'of tapestry work with heads of serpents'.[73] In 1400, the inventory for the chamber of Thomas Dalby, Archdeacon of Richmond included 'a red coverlet with wheels and grey dragons', valued at two shillings, and 'a coverlet with plunket griffins', valued at one shilling and sixpence.[74] Although they are the most decorative items of bedding in his chamber, they are not the most expensive items: much more could be got for a mattress (3s. 4d.) or a canvas (10s.) from the same chamber.[75] Patterns for coverlets sometimes include heraldic or religious motifs, flowers, stripes and animals.[76]

---

[69] Russell, *The Boke of Nurture*, p. 179.
[70] *Cursor Mundi (The Cursur o the World): A Northumbrian Poem of the XIVth Century in Four Versions*, ed. R. Morris (London, 1893), ll. 11238–9.
[71] 'Bonum lectum', ed. Doyle, p. 187.
[72] *Stonor Letters and Papers*, ed. Carpenter, p. 147.
[73] *Probate Inventories*, ed. and trans. Stell, p. 595.
[74] Ibid., p. 499.
[75] Ibid.
[76] The significance of some such decorations will be discussed in ch. 2, pp. 64–9.

Bankers

Unlike coverlets, which are often included in bed sets in wills and are described as being physically on the bed, bankers are more difficult to define. Their appearance in Russell's instructions on making the king's bed, between the instructions for the coverlet and the pillows, suggests that they were considered to be part of the bed: 'kover with a keuerlyte clenely þat bed so mannerly made;/ þe bankers & quosshyns, in þe chamber se þem feire y-sprad,/ boþe hedshete & pillow also, þat þey be saaff vp stad'.[77] However, bankers do not form part of the 'Bonum lectum' and are not part of every bequest of beds, so are not essential to the bed. In 1395, Lady Alice West left her son 'costers and bankers, of sute of that forseyde bed'.[78] While at first glance it seems that the bankers must go on the bed, in Russell's description it is made clear that the bankers should be 'feire y-sprad' about 'þe chamber', and in Alice West's will it is not clear whether the bankers are for covering the bed, hanging with the costers or simply matching the 'sute' with which the bed is made. In other contexts, it is clear that bankers were displayed horizontally: the 1463 will of John Baret of Bury refers to 'a banker of grene and red lying in [his neice's] chambyr' and around 1410, Nicholas Love in *Mirror of the Blessed Life of Jesus Christ* (*c.* 1400) describes how 'oure lord Jesu sitteth downe … on the bare grounde, for there had he neither banker ne kuschyne'.[79] The *MED* suggests that the term comes from the Old French 'banquier', which has resonances of benches and seating.[80] The implication is that the banker's primary function is for sitting on, rather than lying under, which agrees with Love's use of the term in his *Mirror*. That being said, as mentioned above, Lady Alice West's will and Russell's instructions suggest that the banker was considered to belong to the bed. As such, it is likely to have been some sort of cushion or stuffed covering, which could be used to sit on the floor or displayed upon a bed.

Pillows, bolsters and headsheets

The next step in making the bed is the placement of the bolster and/or pillows. While it is commonly asserted that people in the late Middle

---

[77] Russell, *The Boke of Nurture*, 179.
[78] PROB 11/1/82; *Fifty Earliest English Wills*, ed. Furnivall, p. 5.
[79] *Wills and Inventories*, ed. S. Tymms, p. 23; N. Love, *The Mirrour of the Blessed Lyf of Jesu Christ*, ed. L. F. Powell (Oxford, 1908), p. 98.
[80] 'banker, n.', *MED*.

Ages slept sitting up, there is little evidence that this was the case in late medieval England.[81] Indeed, Henry VII's Household Ordinance instructs the esquires to 'lay [the pillows] on, as it pleaseth the King best, highe or lowe'.[82] Wills tend to refer to 'j. pillow' in each bed set, which suggests that it was normal to have a single pillow to a bed, although some sets contained two.[83] Some bed sets contained both a pillow and a bolster, for instance Dame Joan Buckland left Sir Robert Carleton 'j. good bolster, j. good pyllow' and Jacob 'a bolster, j. pillow'.[84] Where the two exist on the same bed, 'Bonum lectum' makes it clear that pillows belonged on top of the bolster, as it describes 'þe bolster þat þe pilowes schul be onne' and 'þe pilowes þat þe hede schal be onne'.[85] Bolsters and pillows had similar functions, in that they are both used to provide support under the head, though they were made from different materials and were of different sizes. The Mystery of Upholders' complaint, discussed above, implies that bolsters were supposed to have been stuffed with feathers, while pillows were supposed to be stuffed with down.[86]

On top of the pillow (or the bolster, if there is no pillow) lies the headsheet. The *MED* suggests that a 'hedshete' is a pillowcase, which correlates with references in wills to 'hedshetes' before or after referring to pillows.[87] However it is, in fact, a sheet of cloth wound around the pillows, rather than an enclosed case. The Ordinance instructs that the esquire:

> take a head sheete of raynes and lay thereon [on top of the pillows], and put the one side of the sheete under the pillowes, and lett the other side lie still; then take a head sheete of ermines and lay it above the pillowes on the other side of the sheete, and lay it over all them.[88]

---

[81] The assertion that people slept sitting up is often made, but not backed up with evidence. See, for example, J. Pile, *A History of Interior Design*, 2nd edn (London, 2005), p. 115; Worsley, *If Walls Could Talk*, pp. 7–9, and countless online blogs and forums.

[82] *A Collection of Ordinances*, p. 122.

[83] *Lincoln Diocese Documents*, ed. Clark, pp. 40–2; *Paston Letters and Papers*, ed. Davis, I, 387.

[84] *Lincoln Diocese Documents*, ed. Clark, p. 41; Lincoln, Lincolnshire Archives, REG/20, ff. 55r–56r.

[85] 'Bonum lectum', ed. Doyle, p.188.

[86] See above, p. 27; *Calendar of Letter-Books*, ed. Sharpe XI.

[87] 'hed-', *MED*.

[88] *A Collection of Ordinances*, p. 122.

While it could be argued that the king is a special case (unlike most beneficiaries in wills, for instance, he has two headsheets), Margaret Paston's will of 1482 suggests that a similar method was used with her bed. She left 'ij peir of [her] fynest shetes ich of iij webbes' and 'a fyne hedshete of ij webbes' to her daughter, Anne.[89] It is very unlikely that a pillowcase would have required two-thirds of the amount of material used to make a sheet, while a headsheet wrapped around one or two pillows or a bolster (curiously, neither pillows nor bolsters are bequeathed to Anne, so we cannot say) would have required a larger amount of material. Headsheets are often mentioned in wills straight after a pair of sheets, which suggests that they were considered to have something in common with the sheets. It is likely that the same type of fabric is used for both.

Canopies and curtains

Many beds belonging to aristocratic and bourgeois people had an overhead component, which often included curtains. In some cases the bed sets included 'Silour, the Testour, three Curteyns & the hylling'.[90] The tester was 'at þe heede', and takes the form of an extended head-board.[91] The term 'hilling' is used in other contexts to mean a shelter. For instance, Richard Rolle's commentary on the Psalter uses the term to mean shelter afforded by God, and the Ordinances of Worcester of 1466 refers to certain 'Tylers' as 'hillyers'.[92] Within the context of a bed, it is likely that the hilling would have been a canopy or roof-like structure to the bed. The silour was also a type of canopy, described as being 'ouer þi bede' in 'Bonum lectum'.[93] It sometimes comes with the adjective 'hool' in wills, as in 'a bed of Lyn wit a hool silour', in Thomas Tvoky's will of 1418, which suggests that some silours were not always whole, perhaps only covering half of the top.[94] The difference between

---

[89] *Paston Letters and Papers*, ed. Davis, I, 387.

[90] *Lincoln Diocese Documents*, ed. Clark, p. 39.

[91] 'Bonum lectum', ed. Doyle, p. 188.

[92] R. Rolle, *The Psalter, or Psalms of David and Certain Canticles*, ed. H. Ramsden Bramley (Oxford, 1884), p. 219. Rolle translates 'velamento' as 'hillinge'; *English Guilds: The Original Ordinances of more than One Hundred Early English Guilds: Together with The Olde Usages of the Cite of Wynchestre; the Ordinances of Worcester; the Office of the Mayor of Bristol; and the Costomary of the Manor of Tattenhal-Regis*, ed. J. Toulmin Smith (London, 1870), p. 398.

[93] 'Bonum lectum', ed. Doyle, p.188.

[94] *Fifty Earliest English Wills*, ed. Furnivall, p. 36.

silours and hillings is unclear from the documentary evidence, but as they can occur within the same bed set, as in the one above, it is likely that they have separate uses. It is probable that a hilling is sturdier than a silour, which could be strung up underneath a hilling or by itself. This is suggested by the etymology of the two terms – as a roof or shelter is more solid than the sky or the heavens – and by their contexts in literary and pragmatic sources: silours in bed sets that did not contain hillings are sometimes listed next to other methods of support, suggesting that they are not self-supporting. 'Bonum lectum' refers to 'þe corde þat þe siller schal be tied vp wiþ to þee rydels', again suggesting that a silour needed support to stay up.[95] In John Paston I's inventory of Fastolf's goods, eight silours are listed, six of which are listed in the sequence 'j traunsom. Item j selour'.[96] As 'traunsom' is usually used in the context of beams of wood or construction materials, as in the 'lx trasons' that make up a chapterhouse floor in Stamford and the 'v quarteres for traunsones' for the roof of a house, it seems likely that a transom in the context of beds refers to some sort of cross-beam, for holding up a canopy.[97] For beds with canopies, therefore, there were either hillings, which were sturdy and probably attached to the tester, or silours, which may have been made of cloth or a sturdier material, which were supported on rails or beams.

In bed sets containing curtains, the curtains would normally cover the three sides of the bed that are not covered by the tester. 'Bonum lectum' refers to 'þe courteyne one þe riȝt side', 'þe curteyne onne þe left side' and 'þe curteyne at þe feet'.[98] Where there is a tester and hilling or silour, the curtains are attached around the edge or below the canopy. Where there was no canopy, a rail was often attached to the walls or ceiling. Several extant English illustrations of beds show the curtains hanging from a rail, which I would argue is what the author of the 1324 romance *Bevis of Hampton* means to signify with the term 'raile tre', from which Josian hangs her husband.[99] Curtains would add

[95] 'Bonum lectum', ed. Doyle, p. 188.
[96] *Paston Letters and Papers*, ed. Davis, I, 108–14.
[97] '1445E101/504/19 Cambridgeshire Indenture', in *An Anthology of Chancery English*, ed. J. H. Fisher (Knoxville, 1984), p. 298; *London City Church*, ed. Littlehales, p. 138.
[98] 'Bonum lectum', ed. Doyle, p. 188.
[99] See, for instance, BL, Harley MS 3487, f. 121v; *Bevis of Hampton*, in *Four Romances of England*, ed. R. B. Herzman, G. Drake, and E. Salisbury (Kalamazoo, 1999), l. 3217; See ch. 6 below, p. 205.

warmth to the bed, as they would stop draughts, and would allow a degree of privacy for the occupants.

The bedstead

As this chapter has shown, the broader sense of the Middle English term 'bed' is the composite structure made up of materials. However, it can also refer to the bedstead which, when mentioned in wills and inventories, is usually paired with a qualifying adjective, which describes either the material or use of the bed. To name a few, in 1387 Robert Corn left his nephew a 'bed of tree' (a wooden bed); an inventory of heirlooms at Stonor in 1474 refers to a 'truckle bed' (a moveable bed that fits under another bed, so that a servant literally 'truckles' to their superior); in 1482 Margaret Paston refers to a 'trussyng bedde' (a portable bed) in her will, and an inventory of John Asserby's goods in 1527 refers to 'on bordeynd bed stede' (a bedstead made of boards).[100] The term 'bedstead' existed at this time, but is seldom found in extant records. Rare examples include the church records of St Mary at Hill, London, which refer to payments for four bedsteads between 1498 and 1527, and John Lee's will of 1533, which stipulates that 'bedstedes in the chambers stond as erelomys to my son harry and his heyres'.[101] The bedstead is rarely mentioned in literary descriptions or in wills and is not usually a feature of visual representations of beds, but their presence in inventories and accounts suggests that bedsteads were part of the bed as a whole. The fact that bedsteads are often left out of wills, as in Roger Flore's 1424 summary of a 'bed, þat is to say, couerlide, tapite, blankettis, too peyre schetes, matras, and canvas', could be for several reasons.[102] It is possible that bedsteads are not often mentioned as part of bed sets in wills because they are not very moveable – perhaps, like John Lee, will-makers often wished to let the bedsteads 'stond' – or it could have been assumed that the beneficiaries would not need or want another bedstead, whereas soft furnishings become worn and

---

[100] London, Metropolitan Archives 9171/1 (Courtney Register), f. 198v; *Fifty Earliest English Wills*, ed. Furnivall, p. 2; *Stonor Letters and Papers*, ed. Carpenter, p.147; *Paston Letters and Papers*, ed. Davis, I, 387; *Lincoln Diocese Documents*, ed. Clark, p. 134.

[101] *London City Church*, ed. Littlehales, pp. 232, 244, 293, 340; *Lincoln Diocese Documents*, ed. Clark, p. 163.

[102] TNA PROB 11/3/174, ff. 70r–73v (f. 71r); *Fifty Earliest English Wills*, ed. Furnivall, p. 57.

need to be replaced.[103] Where beds are described in terms of aesthetics rather than in order to create an inventory such as in literary texts, it is likely that the bedstead was unlikely to have been seen underneath the covers and surrounding curtains, and so was not part of the scene. On the other hand, it could be argued that bedsteads were not usually seen to be important enough to describe because they were merely the base upon which the rich bedclothes would be presented, in the same way that wall hangings are described but the walls themselves are not.

The complete ensemble

In this study I have listed the many layers that could have comprised the typical late medieval English bourgeois or aristocratic bed. As archaeological evidence of such beds from this time is scarce, it can be difficult to imagine how the structure stayed upright, particularly given that the tester and canopy would have added some height to the ensemble. In this respect, the construction of the 'honest bede' in 'Bonum lectum', while metaphorical, is invaluable to our understanding of how beds were put together, as, in an attempt to give allegorical meaning to each component of the bed, it details how the bed structure is held up:

> lat þes tuo courteynes [the left and right] renne one tene ringgies of þe tene comandementis and loke no rynge be broken. for if þei be broken þe curteynes wille sagge downe. [...] lat [the curtain at the foot of the bed] renne one vij ringgis of þe vij werkis of mercy [...] Lat þe corde þat þe siller schal be tied vp wiþ to þee rydels be made of dowbel silke or twyne [...] þe hokes þat þe rydelis schul be tyed vp with [...] must be smyten in wiþ into þe foure wallis of þi chambour. [...] þis beed ȝut must be borded lest þe streye wille falle ouȝt. [...] & þanne naile togeder þes bordes at þe foure corneris.[104]

The various layers that could comprise the late medieval English bed are as shown in Fig. 4.

'A bed couenable for her estat'[105]

This figure shows the layers that could have been part of the bed, except for the bankers and cushions that seem to have been understood to belong to the bed, but did not have a fixed place on the bed itself.

---

[103] *Lincoln Diocese Documents*, ed. Clark, p. 163.
[104] 'Bonum lectum', ed. Doyle, pp. 188–9.
[105] *Fifty Earliest English Wills*, ed. Furnivall, p. 6.

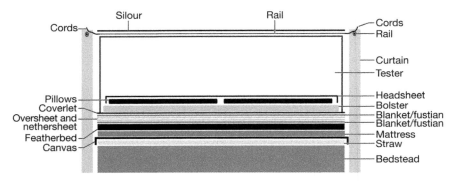

Figure 4: The stratigraphy of a bed, shown from the foot of the bed, comprising each item discussed, excluding the bankers, cushions and third curtain for clarity.

However, even within bourgeois and aristocratic circles, beds varied according to the status of their occupants, and not all beds would have contained every layer. An analysis of the frequency of individual terms, supported by the relative sizes of the terms in Fig. 3, suggests that the most common articles of bedding – the minimum of materials that may have made up a bed in a bourgeois or aristocratic house – are those shown in Fig. 5.

Figure 5: A stratigraphy of the minimum layers required to make a late medieval English bourgeois or aristocratic bed, shown from the foot of the bed.

The bed is an indication of status. This is made very clear in Alice West's will, where she leaves her children richly wrought bed sets, containing her 'beste', 'secunde best' and 'thridde-best' featherbeds, as well as rich trappings containing her ancestors' arms, her 'beste pilwes', silk covers, celures and curtains.[106] She then continues to bequeath other bed sets to beneficiaries, according to their status: Beatrice Waryn receives 'a bed couenable for a gentel womman',

[106] Ibid., p. 7; TNA PROB 11/1/82.

and several of her servants receive beds 'couenable for [their] estat'.[107] What is interesting about her will is that she does not specify which of her beds would be 'couenable' for her beneficiaries; the lack of stipulation implies that it was obvious to her executors. It seems to have been widely recognised that beds were symbols of status. Such an assumption is evident in some romance texts. For instance, in the late thirteenth-century romance *Havelok the Dane*, the narrator laments that the Earl did not give Havelok and his sisters a bed worthy of their royal status, listing this grievance alongside those relating to food and clothing: 'he hem clothede right ne fedde,/ Ne hem dede richelike bedde'.[108] The adverb 'richelike' indicates that it is not the absence of a bed that is the problem, but instead that it is not of a high enough quality. The juxtaposition of this concern with ones relating to food and clothing implies that the wrong sort of bed is a huge mistreatment of the young prince and princesses, as much so as starving them and dressing them in rags. This idea is played out in the reverse later in the narrative. When Grim is made aware of Havelok's identity, he gives the boy food, then 'whan he havede eten and was fed,/ Grim dede maken a full fair bed, / Unclothede him and dede him ther-inne' (ll. 658–9), meeting all of the needs that Havelok was previously denied. His 'full fair bed' both contrasts with his previous, unsatisfactory bed and is a direct response to Grim's knowledge about Havelok's background. Similarly, in *Amis and Amiloun*, written around the same time, the leprous Amiloun is placed in Belisaunt's 'bedde […] with clothes riche and wele ywrought', an action which both signifies that Amiloun is worth more than his ragged leprous appearance would suggest and comments on the prosperity of Amis and Belisaunt.[109]

The idea of the bed and chamber

Texts such as the Royal Household ordinances, Russell's *Boke of Nurture* and 'Bonum lectum' are invaluable sources of information that explain in great detail how to make a bed and prepare the chamber. However, the most interesting and intriguing aspect of each text is not

[107] Ibid.

[108] *Havelok the Dane*, in *Middle English Verse Romances*, ed. D. B. Sands (Exeter, 1986), ll. 420–1.

[109] *Amis and Amiloun*, in *Amis and Amiloun, Robert of Cisyle, and Sir Amadace*, ed. E. E. Foster, 2nd edn (Kalamazoo, 2007), ll. 2110–11.

the meticulous description *per se*, but the fact that it is written in the first place, as its existence highlights the importance of the bed and chamber in the late medieval English consciousness. Jeremy Goldberg's study of late medieval inventories supports this view. He found that bourgeois householders spent proportionately more on beds and bedding than their peasant counterparts, and attributed this to 'a rather different system of values', in which beds were deeply significant.[110] This concern is equally noticeable in wills, when we consider the care taken to bequeath specific articles of bedding to individuals, implying that meanings have been ascribed to the bedding by their owners. For example, Alice West's bequest to her son of 'a bed of tapicers werk, with alle the tapites of sute, red of colour, ypouthered with chapes and scochons, in the corners, of myn Auncestres armes' indicates that the bed is rich in meaning.[111] The presence of her 'Auncestres armes' on the bedding suggests that she, or her predecessors, considered the chamber to be an appropriate space in which to remember her ancestors and have a visual representation of her bloodline. By bequeathing the bedding to her eldest son, she passes on a souvenir of his maternal bloodline.[112]

The cultural value placed on beds meant that they merited respect. Russell's instructions for making the king's bed in the *Boke of Nurture* displays an understanding that the bed of a royal person should be treated with a similar level of respect as the sovereign himself or, conversely, that the bed was understood to be a metaphor for service. The sense of importance and ritual is also found in Russell's instructions for 'The Warderobeʒ', in which the manner of putting the king to bed for a digestive nap is written meticulously, deferentially and almost lovingly:

> his bed y-spred þe shete for þe hed þe pelow prest þat stounde,
> þat when youre souereyn to bed shall go to slepe þere saaf & sounde,
> The curteyns let draw þem þe bed round about;
> se his morter with wax or perchere þat it go not owt.[113]

The bed is described as a 'saaf & sounde' place in which the king should be able to sleep. It seems that a properly made bed offers not

---

[110] Goldberg, 'Bourgeois Domesticity', p. 128.

[111] TNA PROB 11/1/82; *Fifty Earliest English Wills*, ed. Furnivall, p. 5.

[112] For further discussion on Alice West's 'Auncestres armes', see ch. 6 below, p. 186.

[113] *Boke of Nurture*, ed. Furnivall, p. 182.

just somewhere to lie down, but also a degree of care. The adjective 'prest' conveys the dual sense of being ready for use and ready to be at someone's service. This idea of bedclothes being ready to provide the king with safety and protection, combined with the idea that the occupant has the right to a certain quality of bed that reflects his or her status, implies that the bed is in some way subservient to its occupant: the more important the occupant, the higher the level of service the bed should offer. On the other hand, the practice of sprinkling 'holy water on the bedd' and the instructions for 'all other that were at the making of the bedd' to 'drinke altogether', as found in the Household Ordinances, suggests that it is the bed itself that warrants respect.[114] The 'honest bede' mentally constructed by both the writer and audience of 'Bonum lectum' is a further indication of the pervading idea of the bed in late medieval England. Not only is the audience expected to be able to recall the different components of the bed, regardless of their own status, in order that the mnemonic device holds up, but the bed itself is considered a worthy object 'in þe wiche oure lorde iesu crist will haue likinge to reste inne'.[115]

The difference between the components that are discussed in texts such as 'Bonum lectum', courtesy books and romances, and those that comprise the bare essentials of a bourgeois or aristocratic bed, indicates that the idea or Saussurian *signifié* of the term 'bed' is vastly different from the everyday reality. Similarly, the chamber in literary texts is almost always private, and for the sole use of the protagonists. In reality, as houses containing chambers only had one or two chambers and significantly more occupants, the chamber would often be at best an occasional thoroughfare and at worst more like a dormitory. This discrepancy between imagined and experienced beds is the inspiration for the primary research question of this book: what are the cultural meanings of the bed and chamber, and how do they relate to actual practice?

Arising early

Let us return to the boy narrator of the Magdalen schoolbook *vulgaria*. He misses his childhood bed not only because it was so comfortable and his chamber was so pleasing to look at upon waking, but because

---

[114] *A Collection of Ordinances*, p. 122.
[115] 'Bonum lectum', ed. Doyle, p. 186.

'nowe at fyve of the clocke by the monelyght I most go to my booke and lete slepe and slouthe alon'.[116] Elsewhere in the schoolbook, the boyish narrator laments his cold and early wakening, 'wherfore if I myght have myn owne wyll I wolde not cum oute of my bede before the sone wer upe'.[117] However, as he and his youthful audience appear to grow up (indicated by the increasing difficulty of the translation assignments) he begins to find joy in early mornings:

> It is a worlde to se the delectacioun and pleasur that a mann shall have which riseth erly in thies summer mornynges, for the very dew shal be so confortable to hym that it shal cause hym inwardely to rejose [...] Who wolde than lye thus loterynge in his bedde, brother, as thou dost, and gyve hymself only to slepe, be the which thou shalt hurt greatly thyself and also short the tyme of thy lyff? It shall cause the furthermore to be dull and voide of connynge, withoute which lyff and deth be both onn.[118]

The message to the schoolboys is clear: as one approaches manhood, one must not only arise early, but take delight in doing so. As there is so much value placed on sleeping in a well-made bed suitable for one's social status, it seems almost incongruous that the intended (male) audiences of the schoolbook and the Book of Brome precepts are instructed to 'arysse erly'.[119] However, the bed's relationship to sleep is an interesting one, as it is very clear that in the late medieval mindset, it is improper and un-manly to sleep in a bed during the day. In the 'Arise Early' precepts, it is implied that sleeping in is just not done, whereas the schoolbook *vulgaria* is less subtle, suggesting that one would become stupid or even die if one did not wake before dawn.

The need to arise early is clearly gendered.[120] In the early four-teenth-century romance *Ywain and Gawain*, it is suggested that it is un-knightly to lie in bed – when Ywain tarries with his wife, he is rebuked:

> that knight es no thing to set by
> That leves al his chevalry
> And ligges bekeand in his bed.[121]

---

[116] *A Fifteenth Century School Book*, ed. Nelson, p. 2.

[117] Ibid., p. 3.

[118] Ibid.

[119] McDonald, 'Fragments of *(Have Your) Desire*', pp. 254–5.

[120] See ch. 6 below, pp. 177–8.

[121] *Ywain and Gawain*, in *Sir Perceval of Galles and Ywain and Gawain*, ed. M. Flowers Braswell (Kalamazoo, 1995), ll. 1457–9.

In the roughly contemporary *Sir Degaré*, the morning after Degaré falls asleep in a lady's chamber, he is rudely awakened by the lady:

> Amorewe whan hit was dai-light,
> Sche was uppe and redi dight.
> Faire sche waked him tho:
> 'Aris!' she seide, 'graith* the, an go!'   *get ready
> And saide thus in here game:
> 'Thou art worth to suffri schame,
> That al night as a best sleptest,
> And non of mine maidenes ne keptest.'
> 'O gentil levedi,' seide Degarre,
> 'For Godes love, forgif hit me!
> Certes the murie harpe hit made,
> Elles misdo nowt I ne hade […]'[122]

The lady appears to be shocked that Degaré is still asleep at 'dai-light', while Degaré's reaction suggests that he knows he has behaved badly by doing so. A modern audience might find such an exchange bemusing, as it does not appear to us that Degaré has behaved out of turn. The narrative relies on this exchange primarily as a bridge for the lady to recount her story, so the rebuke itself is not treated as exceptional. Indeed, the lady's explanation is treated as obvious, that as a man he should have guarded the women in the castle (or at the very least, have paid close attention to one of the nine women). The comparison of the sleeping Degaré to 'a best' (l. 854) brings home the point that men – as opposed to women or animals – do not sleep in. This idea is inherent in the fifteenth-century *The Wedding of Sir Gawain and Dame Ragnelle*, in which Arthur and his knights fear for Gawain's life when he stays in bed with his wife 'tylle middaye': '"Aryse", sayd the Kyng to Sir Gawen;/ "Why slepyst thou so long in bed?"'.[123] While the knights have no problem with Dame Ragnelle (a woman with animal-like qualities) staying in bed all morning, such behaviour is so unlike a man that they fear for his life. As discussed in Chapter 6 below, problems do, indeed, occur for men who sleep in. In *Sir Gawain and the Green Knight*, Gawain's purity and courtesy are threatened when he is first allowed to lie in while the men go out hunting in a gory display of

---

[122] *Sir Degaré*, in *The Middle English Breton Lays*, ed. A. Laskaya and E. Salisbury (Kalamazoo, 1995), ll. 848–59.

[123] *The Wedding of Sir Gawain and Dame Ragnelle*, in *Sir Gawain: Eleven Romances and Tales*, ed. T. Hahn (Kalamazoo, 1995), ll. 721, 731–2.

masculinity; when the boy of the Magdalen schoolbook tries to sleep through his master's cries, he is 'troublede with marveliouse visions', and abusive husbands who do not wake up before their wives are in potential danger of being killed in their sleep.[124]

This chapter has explored the physical and imagined chamber and the components that make up the sort of bed the contemporary audience of late medieval literature might have imagined, as well as the sort of bed that bourgeois and aristocratic people would have been more likely to have in their own chambers. Now that an understanding of the chamber and the bed has been constructed, in the words of 'Bonum lectum' we must arise from it to make room for Jesus 'to abide & reste'.[125]

---

[124] *Sir Gawain and the Green Knight*, ed. Tolkien and Gordon, Passus III; *A Fifteenth Century School Book*, ed. Nelson, p. 2; the bed as a gendered space will be further explored in detail in ch. 6 below.

[125] 'Bonum lectum', ed. Doyle, p. 190.

2

'Serve Thy God Deuly'

Behold thou art fair, my beloved, and comely. Our bed is flourishing.

Song of Songs 1.15[1]

The main function of 'Bonum lectum', as mentioned in the previous chapter, is allegory, explaining to its audience how to prepare the 'chambour of þi soule' and 'an honest bede […] in þe whiche oure lorde iesu criste wille haue likinge to reste inne'.[2] The text explains that this bed 'is þe bede þat oure lorde iesu crist speikeþ of in his boke of loue and seiþ <Canticorum primo Lectulus noster iam floridus est> oure bede is ful of floures'.[3] This reference to the Song of Songs illustrates that 'Bonum lectum' is the product of a long tradition of thought and reflects contemporary theology. As argued by Daniel Frank, the 'frank eroticism' of the Song of Songs required allegorisation, in order that Christians could be reconciled to its place in the canon.[4] Medieval commentaries on the Song of Songs placed great emphasis on its allegorical nature, sparking a renewed appreciation of allegory throughout the Middle Ages.[5] The bed in the Song of Songs is

---

[1] All Bible references in English are from the Douay-Rheims version of the Vulgate Bible, unless otherwise stated. <www.drbo.org>.

[2] 'Bonum lectum', ed. Doyle, p. 186.

[3] Ibid., p. 189. The Latin text within the chevrons is interlinear.

[4] D. Frank, 'Karaite Commentaries on the Song of Songs from Tenth-Century Jerusalem', in *With Reverence for the Word: Medieval Scriptural Exegesis in Judaism, Christianity, and Islam*, ed. J. Dammen McAuliffe, B. D. Walfish and J. W. Goering (Oxford, 2010), pp. 51–69 (p. 51).

[5] Frank, 'Karaite Commentaries'; E. A. Matter discusses how medieval commentaries of the Song of Songs 'tell a story of the triumph of the allegorical'

treated in medieval commentaries as a metaphor for the relationship between the two speakers and between the believer and God, as well as a physical space in which the soul seeks the bridegroom Christ.[6] This chapter will address the pervasive idea that the bed is a suitable space in which to meet with God, and the ways in which this idea is played out in late medieval England. It begins with an exploration of religious encounters and prayer in bed, before moving on to look at evidence of devotional practice in the chamber. Finally, it explores the ways in which the relationship between faith and beds extends beyond the walls of the chamber.

Encountering God in bed

The verse referring to the bed in the Song of Songs is usually translated into a female voice, which commentaries often take as a representation of the believer or the Church as the bride of Christ, or as the Virgin Mary.[7] Conversely, 'Bonum lectum' attributes the Bible verse to Christ, so that the 'honest bede' is 'þe bede þat oure lorde iesu crist speikeþ of'.[8] This attribution has the effect of making the bed God-sanctioned, as if God were waiting for the believer in the bed, rather than the other way around. The result is that the act of making the bed becomes an act of devotion. The mnemonic nature of 'Bonum lectum' lends itself to this method of devotion. Within the text, the bed is assembled piece by piece, reflecting the acquisition of the readers' godly attributes. While the text itself is an allegory, its attention to detail and the way in which the physical attributes of the bed's components relate to their symbolic meanings make the bed seem very real. For instance, the coverlet is 'charite' because 'charite coueriþ þe multitude of synnes', while one must be careful that none of the 'tene ringis of þe tene comandementis [...] be broken. for if þei be broken þe curteynes wille sagge downe

---

and posits that pre-Reformation commentaries of the text had much more appreciation of allegory than those post-Reformation. See E. A. Matter, *The Voice of My Beloved: The Song of Songs in Western Medieval Christianity* (Philadelphia, 1990), pp. 3–16.

[6] *The Glossa Ordinaria on the Song of Songs*, ed. and trans. M. Dove (Kalamazoo, 2004), p. 194; Gregory the Great, *Gregory the Great on the Song of Songs*, trans. M. DelCogliano (Collegeville, 2012), p. 116; William of Saint Thierry, *Exposition on the Song of Songs*, trans. C. Hart (Kalamazoo, 1970), pp. 77, 82.

[7] Matter, *The Voice of My Beloved*, pp. 151–77.

[8] 'Bonum lectum', ed. Doyle, p. 198.

and þanne þe enmy þe fende may loke ouer into þe bed of iesu'.[9] These very physical descriptions would allow a medieval reader meditating upon the text to recall the components of his or her own bed and ascribe the respective attributes to each one. Furthermore, the text would make very fitting bedtime reading.[10] A person reading 'Bonum lectum' in bed or lying awake in bed after reading it might have contemplated their bed in light of the text. In such a case, running through the text in one's mind would have led to the spiritual act of 'shaking out' sins and replacing them with the 'wille to amend thee' and 'bisy and deuouȝte praier', adding 'bittur sorowe for [their] synne', as it is unlikely that one would have made the effort to remember a set of pious instructions without carrying out the instructions themselves.[11] Biblically, repentance is key to salvation, so it makes sense for the audience of 'Bonum lectum' to act upon the advice.[12] The boundary between the allegorical bed, in which godly attributes are contained, and the physical bed, in which the instructions are carried out, is thus blurred until the physical bed becomes a religious object with a similar function to a set of rosary beads, with different components as physical reminders to perform a certain pious act.[13] A mnemonic device centred on the bed, where one usually spends time relatively undisturbed every night, is likely to be remembered, in particular as at least some copies of the text are likely to have belonged to religious houses, in which the art of *memoria*, as Mary Carruthers argues, 'formed the core of monastic life'.[14] The proliferation of 'Bonum lectum', which according to Doyle had a 'longer and wider circulation' than the number of extant manuscripts reflects, implies that the bed's use as a mnemonic device and a physical space in which one could contemplate God was both known and well-received by a large number of people.[15]

---

[9] Ibid., pp. 187–8.

[10] For a discussion on reading in bed and the relationship between beds and books, see ch. 4 below, pp. 123–30.

[11] 'Bonum lectum', ed. Doyle, pp. 186–7.

[12] For Biblical teaching on the direct link between repentance and salvation see, for example, 1 Kings 8.46–51; Isaiah 30.15; Ezekiel 18.30–2; Matthew 3–4; Mark 1.15; Luke 15; Acts 3.19; 2 Corinthians 7.10.

[13] M. Carruthers, *The Book of Memory: A Study of Memory in Medieval Culture* (Cambridge, 1990), p. 99.

[14] 'Bonum lectum', ed. Doyle, pp. 179–86; Carruthers, *Book of Memory*, p. 154.

[15] According to Doyle, 'Lectulus Noster Floridus', pp. 179–86, the text survives in seven manuscripts: Cambridge, St John's College, MS G. 8, ff. 49v–52r; Oxford, Bodleian Library, MSS Douce 302, ff. 32v–33v, Laud Misc. 19, ff. 22v–30v, Laud

'Bonum lectum' is part of a wider tradition of locating God in bed. Other late medieval devotional texts and commentaries indicate that the bed was considered to be a place in which one would meditate on one's relationship with God. Hugh of Saint-Victor's twelfth-century *De Archa Noe* refers to God 'in the soul as the bridegroom in the wedding-chamber' and refers to those who love God as 'His house, to the intent that He who made you may also dwell in you'.[16] In the thirteenth century, nuns' visions in Helfta 'include images of God's grace as a bed with pillows', while Ida of Neville refers to the 'spiritual dormitory'.[17] The fifteenth-century text *The Doctrine of the Hert* uses the metaphor of 'the hous of þin hert', with a bed by which 'thow shalt undirstonde pees and rest of conscience'.[18] This symbolism is similar to Gregory the Great's seventh-century portrayal of the Church as a house, which has 'an entrance', a 'staircase of hope', 'banquet halls' of 'charity' and 'the bedchamber of the king':

> lest anyone exalt himself and fall into pride when he comes to know the secrets of God, when he scrutinises God's hidden commandments, when he is raised up to the lofty heights of contemplation, it is said that he enters 'the bedchamber of the king'. In other words, the more a soul is brought to the knowledge of his secrets, the greater the reverence that should be shown.[19]

Misc. 99, ff. 123r–124r, Eng. Theol. C. 57, ff. 131v–132v; Oxford, Jesus College, MS 39, pp. 560–2 and Oxford, University College, MS 123, ff. 74v–75v. **U**, **S**, **D** and **M** are separate versions and do not derive from any others. **J**, **E** and **L** have significant variations but sometimes agree with **D**, 'pointing to a common parent nearer the original' (p. 186). There are some linguistic links between **U** and **S**, **S** and **D**, **D** and **M**. These suggest that the text was widely disseminated over a fairly long period of time.

[16] Hugh of Saint-Victor, *Noah's Ark*, in *Hugh of Saint Victor: Selected Writings*, ed. and trans. A. Squire (London, 1962), pp. 49–50.

[17] Cited in M. Oliva, 'Nuns at Home: The Domesticity of Sacred Space', in *Medieval Domesticity: Home, Housing and Household in Medieval England*, ed. M. Kowaleski and P. J. P. Goldberg (Cambridge, 2008), pp. 145–61 (p. 145); R. Voaden, 'All Girls Together: Community, Gender and Vision at Helfta', in *Medieval Women and Their Communities*, ed. D. Watt (Toronto, 1997), pp. 72–91 (p. 74); J. Hamburger, *Nuns as Artists: The Visual Cultural of a Medieval Convent* (Berkeley, 1997), p. 145.

[18] *The Doctrine of the Hert: A Critical Edition with Introduction and Commentary*, ed. C. Whitehead, D. Renevey and A. Mouron (Exeter, 2010), pp. 8–9.

[19] *Gregory the Great on the Song of Songs*, trans. DelCogliano, pp. 128–9; Matter, *The Voice of My Beloved*, p. 96.

Gregory's use of the 'bedchamber of the king' is interesting because it equates the chamber with a certain level of intimacy and knowledge, arguing that the Church has reached the spiritual level of 'bedchamber' (after the entrance, staircase and banquet hall) due to being 'already filled with and rooted in the mysteries of God', reaching 'the lofty secrets and even penetrat[ing] them'.[20] It also implies that the most appropriate space for 'reverence' is the 'bedchamber'.[21] As chambers became more frequent in the later Middle Ages, their owners may well have recalled such teaching.

Richard Rolle, writing in the fourteenth century, specifically locates prayer in bed. In his commentary on the Psalter, he equates 'my bed-dynge' to 'the nether party of my saule' in reference to Psalm 6 and suggests, in reference to Psalm 62, that meditation on God in bed is necessary because 'for he that nought thinke on him in reste, in his warke he holdes nought his thought in him'.[22] Interestingly, Rolle interprets Matthew 6.6, 'intra in cubiculum tuum & clauso ostio ora Patrem tuum' (enter into your chamber, and having shut the door, pray to your Father), metaphorically rather than literally: '"Entre, he sais, þi bed", þat is, call þi hert hame, "& þen stake þi dore", þat is, hald þi wittis in þe, þat nane wend out'.[23] This reading recalls texts such as *The Doctrine of the Hert* and implies that the bed and chamber are obvious symbols for the heart in relationship with God.

In *The Book of Margery Kempe*, probably written in the late 1430s, there are several occasions where Margery encounters God in bed. [24]

---

[20] *Gregory the Great on the Song of Songs*, trans. DelCogliano, p. 128.

[21] Ibid., p. 129.

[22] Rolle, *The Psalter*, pp. 23, 219. Rolle's Psalm 62 is numbered 63 in modern Bible editions; Rosamund Allen points out that there are over twenty extant manuscripts of Rolle's commentary, attesting to its popularity. *Richard Rolle: The English Works*, ed. R. Allen (Mahwah, 1988), p. 66.

[23] R. Rolle, *English Prose Works of Richard Rolle: A Selection*, ed. C. Horstmann (London, 1896), p. 142.

[24] Much scholarship has been devoted to the authorship of Margery Kempe, whether the protagonist can be seen to be an accurate representation of the 'real' Margery Kempe, whether the events in the narrative took place and whether it was actually dictated by a woman of that name. For the purposes of clarity, I use 'Kempe' to refer to the author(s) and 'Margery' to refer to the protagonist. For a discussion on the authorship of Margery Kempe, see, for example, J. C. Hirsch, 'Author and Scribe in the *Book of Margery Kempe*', *Medium Ævum* 44 (1975), 145–50; C. W. Atkinson, *Mystic and Pilgrim: The Book and the World of Margery Kempe* (Ithaca, 1983); J. M. Mueller, 'Autobiography of a New 'Creatur': Female Spirituality, Self-hood, and Authorship in *The Book of Margery Kempe*', in *Woman*

It is clear that the bed is not the only space in which God is physically present to Margery: God reportedly tells Margery that 'whan thow gost to chyrch, I go wyth the; whan thu syttest at thi mete, I sytte wyth the; whan thow gost to thi bed, I go wyth the; and, whan thu gost owt of towne, I go wyth the'.[25] However, it is apparent throughout the *Book* that Kempe understands the bed to be a particularly appropriate space in which to spend time with God. For instance, after the birth of her first child, Margery 'went owte of hir mende' (l. 149) for over six months. She attributes her recovery to a bedside visit from Jesus:

> as sche lay aloone and hir kepars wer fro hir, owyr mercyful Lord Crist Jhesu, evyr to be trostyd, worshypd be hys name, nevyr forsakyng hys servawnt in tyme of nede, aperyd to hys creatur, whych had forsakyn hym, in lyknesse of a man, most semly, most bewtyuows, and most amyable that evyr mygth be seen wyth mannys eye, clad in a mantyl of purpyl sylke, syttyng upon hir beddys syde, lokyng upon hir wyth so blyssyd a chere that sche was strengthyd in alle hir spyritys, seyd to hir thes wordys: 'Dowtyr, why hast thow forsakyn me, and I forsoke nevyr the?' (ll. 167–73)

Margery had been restrained in bed due to her sickness, so if a vision of Jesus were to appear at any time, it would have had to have been in her chamber. However, the link between the bed and heavenly visitations does not stop there. The description of Christ 'syttyng upon hir beddys syde' emphasises the bed as the locus of this visitation. Later on in the narrative, as she 'lay in hir bedde wyth hir husbond' (l. 241), she hears heavenly music. Elsewhere in her *Book*, perhaps more famously, Margery literally marries God, as 'the Fadyr toke hir be the hand in hir sowle' (ll. 2027–8) before the other two members of the Trinity, Mary, the saints, apostles, holy virgins and angels and declares, 'I take

in the Middle Ages and the Renaissance: Literary and Historical Perspectives, ed. M. B. Rose (Syracuse, 1986), pp. 155–72; D. Lawton, 'Voice, Authority and Blasphemy in "The Book of Margery Kempe"', in *Margery Kempe: A Book of Essays*, ed. S. J. McEntire (London, 1992), pp. 93–115; C. Glenn, 'Author, Audience, and Autobiography: Rhetorical Technique in the Book of Margery Kempe', *College English* 54.5 (1992), 540–53; L. Staley Johnson, 'The Trope of the Scribe and the Question of Literary Authority in the Works of Julian of Norwich and Margery Kempe', *Speculum* 66.4 (1991), 820–38; S. Beckwith, 'Problems of Authority in Late-Medieval English Mysticism: Language, Agency, and Authority in *The Book of Margery Kempe*', *Exemplaria* 4 (1992), 172–99.
25 *The Book of Margery Kempe*, ed. L. Staley (Kalamazoo, 1996), ll. 704–6.

the, Margery, for my weddyd wyfe' (ll. 2030–1). He then discusses the physical consummation of that marriage in bed:

> For it is convenyent the wyf to be homly wyth hir husbond […] thei must ly togedir and rest togedir in joy and pes. Ryght so mot it be twyx the and me […] Therfore most I nedys be homly wyth the and lyn in thi bed wyth the. Dowtyr, thow desyrest gretly to se me, and thu mayst boldly, whan thu art in thi bed, tale me to the as for thi weddyd husbond, as thy derworthy derlyng […] And therfor thu mayst boldly tale me in the armys of thi sowle and kyssen my mowth, myn hed, and my fete as swetly as thow wylt. (ll. 2097–2108)

The details of the production of *The Book of Margery Kempe* have been hotly disputed. Regardless of the authorship, intention or accuracy of this report, what is important to this book is that 'the Fadyr of Heven' is described giving instructions specifically for 'whan thu art in thi bed' and suggesting that a tangible presence of God can be (and must be) present within the bed. While the fact that Margery is repelled by many of her contemporaries within the text implies that her experiences are not necessarily the norm, the placement of God within the bed is concurrent with contemporary writings and reminiscent of the flourishing bed in the Song of Songs. Early thirteenth-century texts such as *Ancrene Wisse* and *Hali Meiðhad*, following Jerome, suggest that virginal women were deemed by far superior to both 'widewen' and 'weddede'.[26] As such, it makes sense that Christ fills the space in bed, which a husband would otherwise occupy, after she has taken her vow of chastity. Like the author of 'Bonum lectum', Kempe puts forward the abstract idea of meditating on God, by using physical characteristics associated with the physical bed. The 'Bonum lectum' author uses the physical construction of the bed; Margery Kempe uses its recognised role as a space for sex.[27] The mixed life followed by both Rolle and Kempe means that their ideas are only representative of a

---

[26] *Ancrene Wisse*, ed. R. Hasenfratz (Kalamazoo, 2000); *Hali Meiðad*, in *Medieval English Prose for Women: Selections from the Katherine Group and* Ancrene Wisse, ed. B. Millett and J. Wogan-Browne (Oxford, 1990), pp. 2–42 (ll. 28–9); St Jerome, 'The Perpetual Virginity of Blessed Mary. Against Helvidius', in *The Principal Works of St Jerome*, ed. and trans. W. H. Fremantle, G. Lewis and W. G. Martley (Edinburgh, 1892), pp. 334–46; St Jerome, 'Against Jovianus', in *The Principal Works of St Jerome*, trans. W. H. Fremantle, G. Lewis and W. G. Martley (Edinburgh, 1892), pp. 346–86.

[27] For the chamber's role as the only appropriate space for legitimate sex, see ch. 5 below.

small growing minority, but that their texts reached out to a number of people. The proliferation of Rolle's manuscripts indicates that his ideas were well-respected, so it is probable that some of his instructions were followed by some of his audience.[28] Similarly, while *The Book of Margery Kempe* exists in only one manuscript, it had at least four early readers, probably at Mount Grace Priory, so it was deemed worthy of study within a religious institution.[29] Both writers assume that praying in bed is normal.

The idea of the bed as a meeting place for God and the believer is not only articulated through explicitly religious writings. There are a significant number of examples in Middle English romance in which encounters with God, heavenly voices and angelic apparitions often occur within the chamber, which shows that the idea of the bed as a meeting place for God was widespread and not exclusive to those in religious positions, as Middle English romances were consumed by a mostly secular audience. In many cases, the characters are passive, encountering God or God's works without initiating prayer. For example, in *Le Chevelere Assigne*, probably composed in the late fourteenth century, 'an Angelle come to þe hermyte & askede if he slepte'.[30] The role of a hermit is to remove himself from the world in order that he is in constant communication with God, and yet the divine message still arrives while he is in bed, which suggests that the bed is a locus particularly suited to communing with the supernatural. Similarly, in *Havelok the Dane*, the only instance in which a 'voyz' of an angel is heard is when Havelok and Goldeboru are in bed together.[31] In addition, the brightly shining 'noble croiz' (l. 1264) that marks Havelok as a king anointed by God is only witnessed in the chamber, first by Goldeboru and then by soldiers peering into his 'bowr' (l. 2094). In the early fourteenth-century romance *The King of Tars*, the maiden has a dream in which she is almost ravaged by hounds twice, but is saved 'þurth Ihesus Cristes passioun'.[32] One of the dogs is then transformed

---

[28] For details of each of Rolle's manuscripts, see R. Hanna, *The English Manuscripts of Richard Rolle: A Descriptive Catalogue* (Exeter, 2010).

[29] London, British Library, Additional MS 61823; 'Introduction' to *Margery Kempe*, ed. Staley; for a hand description of the four readers see 'Introduction' to *The Book of Margery Kempe*, ed. S. Brown Meech (Oxford, 1940), pp. xxxv–xlv.

[30] *The Romance of the Cheuelere Assigne*, ed. H. H. Gibbs (London, 1868), l. 193.

[31] *Havelok the Dane*, ed. Sands, l. 1265.

[32] *The King of Tars: A Critical Edition*, ed. J. Chabot Perryman (Heidelberg, 1932), l. 443.

into a knight 'in white cloþes' (l. 451), who calls her 'mi swete wiȝt' (l. 452) and reminds her that 'þi lord þat suffred passioun/ Schal help þe at þi nede' (ll. 455–6). Upon waking up, 'on hir bed sche sat al naked' (l. 457) to pray to Jesus. Further divine encounters in bed occur in *The Siege of Milan*, written in the second half of the fourteenth century, Sir Alantyne prays to God both inside and outside of his chamber, but he only hears 'by hym on a walle/ Ane angelle' when he is in 'bed-de'.[33] Furthermore, 'the same nyghte' (l. 109), Charlemagne lies 'in his bedde' (l. 110) and has a dream in which an angel comes to him with a message from God. The angel gives him a sword, saying it is a gift from God:

When Charls wakenede of his dreme,
He sawe a bryghtenes of a beme
Up unto hevenwarde glyde.
Bot when he rose, the swerde he fande
That the angelle gaffe hym in his hande
Appon his bedde syde. (ll. 133–8)

Not only is it appropriate to communicate with holy beings in bed, but a physical manifestation of God's favour upon Charlemagne is delivered through the medium of sleep and the bed. Furthermore, in *Amis and Amiloun*, the chamber is an important locus of divine activity. Toward the end of the romance Amiloun, who has become leprous after sacrificing his honour in order to help his friend and sworn brother Amis, is cast out by his wife and eventually arrives at Amis' house, where it is assumed he will die. Shortly afterwards, 'an angel com fram heven bright/ And stode biforn [Amis'] bed ful right', before visiting the bed-ridden Amiloun in his dreams, explaining that Amis must sacrifice his children if he wishes to save Amiloun.[34] Carrying out the angel's instructions, Amis 'alon himself, withouten mo,/ Into the chaumber he gan to go,/ Ther that his childer were' (ll. 2281–3), anointing Amiloun 'in bed' with the children's blood and covering him with rich bedclothes (ll. 2343–6). God restores Amiloun and resurrects the children, both miracles taking place in bed. After Amis slays his children, 'he laid hem in her bed ogain' (l. 2311), then leaves the chamber, locks the door and hides the keys, even though he intends to blame

---

[33] *The Siege of Milan*, in *Three Middle English Charlemagne Romances*, ed. A. Lupack (Kalamazoo, 1990), ll. 85–91.
[34] *Amis and Amiloun*, ed. Foster, ll. 2200–1, 2222.

his children's death on a burglar (ll. 2314–20). While this deception would be more believable if the door remained unlocked, the writer highlights the fact that the chamber is locked and the key hidden from human eyes. This fact is important, as it emphasises that the resurrection of the children occurs inside a locked chamber, as Jesus was resurrected in a sealed tomb.[35]

One reason why many divine encounters in romances occur in the chamber is that messages from God and visions are more credible if given through the medium of a dream, avoiding any accusations that the author is putting words in God's mouth. However, it is clear that there is more to the chamber in relation to encounters with the divine in late medieval literature than simply being the place in which a character falls asleep. Dreams do not account for the resurrection of Amis and Belisaunt's children within a locked chamber, nor for occasions where romance characters specifically decide to pray within a chamber. For instance, in *Sir Eglamour of Artois*, written around 1350, Eglamour wishes to marry the Earl's daughter and prays in bed for the marriage:

[…] tyll his bed he gas
That rychely was wroght.
Both his handys he cast up sone,
To Jhesu Crist he made his bone,
To the Lord that us bowt.[36]

There is a trope of heartsick characters taking to their beds but unlike many lovelorn characters, Eglamour does not throw himself on the bed in order to soliloquise on his sorrow.[37] Instead, he deliberately chooses to pray in bed. Similarly, the fifteenth-century romance *Sir Gowther* emphasises the importance of the chamber as a space for domestic piety. Originally a wild, evil child spawned from a demon, Sir Gowther eventually repents and carries out his penance in an emperor's castle, where he is treated like a fool, remaining mute and only eating food that has been given first to the dogs. His use of a chamber as a space in which to pray can be seen to be an important step towards salvation, as it is far removed from the orchard in which

---

[35] John 20.

[36] *Sir Eglamour of Artois*, in *Four Middle English Romances: Sir Isumbras, Octavian, Sir Eglamour of Artois, Sir Tryamour*, ed. H. Hudson (Kalamazoo, 1996), ll. 98–102.

[37] For characters deliberately entering chambers in order to be emotional, see ch. 4 below, pp. 130–6.

he was conceived and the physical and spiritual wilderness in which he committed his many sins. Upon hearing the news that the emperor's daughter is at risk from heathen invaders, 'Syr Gowther went to a chambur smart/ And preyd to God in his hart'.[38] The adverb 'smart' emphasises his conscious change of location: he did not pray straight away, but first went to the chamber. The chamber as the site for prayer is emphasised when the answer to his prayer arrives in the form of a horse and armour 'at his chambur dor' (l. 411), and when it disappears from within the 'chambur' (l. 439) after he has used it. After his prayers are answered a second time, Gowther chooses to lie in his chamber while the rest of the court celebrates 'in tho hall' (l. 529), in order that he can think about how he can achieve salvation: 'he had no thoght bot of is syn,/ And how he myght is soule wyn/ To tho blys that God con hym by' (ll. 538–40). As the chamber and hall are often used as binary opposites within the romance genre, the emphasis on Gowther 'in his chamber' (l. 532) and not 'in tho hall' (l. 529) marks the chamber out as a space specifically chosen by Gowther for prayer and contemplation. Because of the three occasions on which Sir Gowther literally puts on 'the armour of God' in his chamber, and the sincerity with which he strives for repentance in the chamber, he is absolved of all his sins.[39] The repeated reference to his 'chambur' suggests that the location itself played an integral part to his salvation, while his active role in seeking out the chamber in which to pray suggests that Gowther – and by extension the author and audience – understood the chamber to be a space for prayer.

Devotional practice in the chamber

So far this chapter has explored how the bed was considered to be a particularly suitable space in which to communicate with God and, by extension, how the chamber was considered appropriate for devotional activities. While, on the one hand, the chamber was used for prayer and expressions of piety because devotional texts and popular literature modelled such behaviour, on the other hand, it was done out of a sense of anxiety. The night was understood to be full of dangers. Rumours of ghosts, demons and satanic influences abounded,

---

[38] *Sir Gowther*, in *The Middle English Breton Lays*, ed. A. Laskaya and E. Salisbury (Kalamazoo, 1995), ll. 403–4.
[39] Ephesians 6. 10–17.

propagated by Christian teachings on the contrast between light and darkness as the difference between good (Christ as the light of the world) and evil (all who are against him).[40] Sleep had its own terrors, as a sleeper relinquishes control of his or her mental faculties. Such a problem was understood to allow the devil to get a foothold, as is seen in 'Bonum lectum': if the curtains of 'resoun' and 'þinne owne wille' sag down, þanne þe enmy þe fende may loke ouer into þi bed of iesu'.[41] Practically, night was when people were most at risk of crime or house fires, and when they were least equipped to protect themselves. For example, in the divorce case of Nesfeld vs. Nesfeld in 1396, Margery Nesfeld is reported to have told her husband that 'she could kill him in bed at night if she wanted'.[42] Because of the vulnerability associated with sleep, prayers upon sleeping and waking were intended to protect against spiritual and physical harm. For example, Rolle recounts the advice given to St Edmund by his apparition:

> þis is mi lordis name þat þou sees þus writen. Þis name I wil þou haf in mynde & prente it in þi saule; & croice þi fronte with þis name: or þou ga to slepe: & fra drecchings of þe fend: it sal þe 3eme þat night, & fra sodayn dede; & all þas þat bi night: croicis þaim þerwith.[43]

The two main horrors of the night, 'þe fend' and 'sodayn dede', are kept at bay through keeping the name of Jesus in mind and performing an act of devotion, in this case by crossing oneself.

We tend to associate acts of piety with the church or chapel, but what evidence do we have of devotional practice in the chamber? A good starting place is the 'Arise Early' advice upon which this book is structured. The addressee, having risen, is immediately instructed to serve God.[44] As many of the precepts begin with the active imperative 'goo' – 'goo be the wey', 'goo to thy met', 'goo to thy sopper' – we could take from the lack of the verb 'goo' in the precept that the addressee

---

[40] See D. Youngs and S. Harris, 'Demonizing the Night in Medieval Europe: A Temporal Monstrosity?', in *The Monstrous Middle Ages*, ed. B. Bildhauer and R. Mills (Toronto, 2003), pp. 134–54 (pp. 136–8).

[41] 'Bonum lectum', ed. Doyle, p. 187.

[42] P. J. P. Goldberg, *Women in England, c. 1275–1525* (Manchester, 1995), p. 142. See also ch. 6 below, p. 206.

[43] *English Prose Works of Richard Rolle*, ed. Horstmann, p. 152; 'drecchings' = trouble. '3eme' = to pay attention to (from 'yemen'), although here the sense is that Christ's name will protect from such 'drecchings'.

[44] McDonald, 'Brome Women at Play', p. 254.

is supposed to serve God where he is.[45] The juxtaposition between the command to arise, with its inherent connotations of the space in which one would arise, and the command to serve God suggests that some form of active devotion was expected of the addressee, immediately upon getting out of bed. Versions of these 'precepts in –ly' survive, with significant variation but each with the injunction to serve God immediately upon arising, across a large number of manuscripts and printed books, and one inscription in a painted chamber at 3 Cornmarket Street, Oxford (see Fig. 6).[46] Their popularity suggests that such a routine was at least condoned, if not emulated, by their audience. The presence of the inscription on a chamber wall is further indication that the instruction would be attempted: waking up to a lasting reminder to 'serue god Deuoutlye' might spur the reader to take action.

Figure 6: Detail from the mid sixteenth-century inscription in the Northern room on the second floor of 3 Cornmarket Street, Oxford.[47]

---

[45] See Introduction, p. 10.

[46] *DIMEV*, 560 cites thirteen manuscript witnesses and three medieval print witnesses, as well as the Oxford inscription.

[47] My thanks to the Oxford Preservation Society, for allowing me to view and photograph this room. Very little has been written on this chamber. See E.

While we cannot assume that each reader was able to spend every day working wisely, eating soberly or serving God devoutly, we can imagine that they would at least recognise a routine in which they would work, eat and pray. Those particular precepts are not alone in their instruction to serve God as soon as one wakes up. Lydgate's fifteenth-century *Dietary*, surviving in fifty-seven manuscripts as well as early printed books, includes the instruction, 'fyrst at thy rysing to God do reverens'.[48] Written around the same time, *How The Wise Man Taught His Son*, preserved in five manuscripts, has the wise man teach his son that his 'fyrst werke' is to 'go se thi God in form of bred/ […] Bot fyrst worschype God on the dey'.[49] The order of daily events reflected across such texts suggests that what the late medieval consciousness imagines to come next after waking up, in the daily order of things, is prayer.

Assuming that at least some people in late medieval England started their days by serving God in their chambers, the next issue to address is what exactly that means. How did one go about serving God in the chamber? Rolle instructs his audience to 'euer as þou wakyns: lift þi hert to god with som hali thought, & rise & prai to þi lorde þat he grante relesse of paynes to þe dead, & grace to þe quyk & lif with-outen ende'.[50] In *The Book of Margery Kempe*, Margery is described praying in bed: 'lying in hir bed the next nyth followyng, [she] herd wyth hir bodily erys a lowde voys clepyng "Margery". Wyth that voys sche awoke, gretly aferyd and, lying stille in sylens, sche mad hir preyerys.'[51] Interestingly, although the 'voys' is from God, Margery chooses to pray in bed in silence, which might be a reflection of everyday devout practice in bed.

There is very little concrete evidence of specific prayers said morning and night in the chamber, due to the fact that if they were said morning and night, they were likely to be either memorised formulae such as the *Pater Noster* or a spontaneous prayer for God to grant a

T. Leed., 'A Second Elizabethan Mural Painting in No. 3, Cornmarket Street, Oxford', *Journal of the British Archaeological Association* 37 (1932), 144–50; W. A. Pantin, 'The Golden Cross, Oxford', *Oxoniensia* 20 (1955), 46–89 (pp. 49–50).

[48] J. Lydgate, *Item 31, The Dietary*, in *Codex Ashmole 61: A Compilation of Popular Middle English Verse*, ed. G. Shuffleton (Kalamazoo, 2008), p. 44.

[49] *Item 3: How the Wise Man Taught His Son*, in *Codex Ashmole 61: A Compilation of Popular Middle English Verse*, ed. G. Shuffleton (Kalamazoo, 2008), ll. 19–25.

[50] *English Prose Works of Richard Rolle*, ed. Horstmann, p.152.

[51] Staley, ed., *The Book of Margery Kempe*, ll. 3090–2.

specific boon or afford protection, such as we find mirrored in romance. A more tangible form of devotional practice is the act of reading devotional material. As suggested above, 'Bonum lectum' would make particularly appropriate bedtime devotional reading. The idea of reading religious material in the chamber is not unprecedented, as evidenced by the fact that reading devotional texts in the chamber is part of the Virgin Mary's medieval iconography. For example, in *Mirror of the Blessed Life of Jesus Christ*, Love suggests that on the night of the Annunciation, Mary was 'in here pryue chaumbure that time closed […] perauentur redyng the prophecie of ysaie, touchyng the Incarnation'.[52] Although there is no scriptural tradition in which Mary was in a private chamber at the time of her visitation, the late medieval imagination makes sense of her solitude by placing her in a chamber, and of her role as exemplary devout woman by making her read Scripture. The prevalence of Flemish art and artists representing the Annunciation in late medieval England could well have affected the English view of the Annunciation, and thus altered the model of how women or anyone wishing to emulate the Virgin should conduct themselves within the chamber. In illustrations of the event, Mary is often represented reading next to her bed, visually linking devotion with the chamber.[53]

Cecily Neville's will of 1495 indicates that she spent some time praying and reading in her private domestic space.[54] She bequeaths books of various bindings, as well as a 'masse boke' and 'sauter' described in her will as 'for the closett'.[55] Royal household ordinances shed some light on her devotional activity:

> She useth to arise at seven of the clocke, and hath readye her Chapleyne to saye with her mattins of the daye, and mattins of our lady; and when she is fully readye she hath a lowe masse in her chamber [… After dinner she …] sleepeth one quarter of an hower, and after she hath slepte she contynueth in prayer unto the first peale of evensonge […]

---

[52] N. Love, *Nicholas Love's Mirror of the Blessed Life of Jesus Christ: A Critical Edition Based on Cambridge University Library Additional MSS 5478 and 6686*, ed. M. G. Sargent (New York, 1992), p. 21.

[53] See, for example, H. Memling, 'The Annunciation' (1465–75) in The Metropolitan Museum of Art, New York.

[54] C. A. J. Armstrong, 'The Piety of Cicely, Duchess of York: A Study in Late medieval Culture', in *England, France, and Burgundy in the Fifteenth Century*, ed. C. A. J. Armstrong (London, 1983), pp. 135–56.

[55] TNA PROB 11/10, q. 25 (1495).

one howre before her goeing to bed, she taketh a cuppe of wyne, and after that goeth to her pryvie closette, and taketh her leave of God for all nighte, makinge ende of her prayers for that daye: and by eighte of the clocke is in bedde.[56]

While the ordinances are clearly an idealised representation of actual practice, they do suggest that private devotion was an important part of Cecily's routine. Her chamber clearly played a role in her devotional practice. The reference to the 'Chapleyne to saye with her mattins' before 'she is fully readye' implies that she said her prayers immediately upon getting out of bed, as she was still 'in her chamber' for 'lowe masse', once ready. The note that 'after she hath slepte she contynueth in prayer unto the first peale of evensonge' suggests that the writer of the ordinances, if not Cecily herself, understands a link between sleep and prayer and also implies that Cecily could hear the bells chiming the hours from her chamber, and used them to ring in her devotional activity.

Cecily Neville was not alone in observing religious practices in her chamber. Joan Clifland's deposition in Margery Baxter's trial for heresy in 1429 claims that William Baxter would read the Bible to his wife Margery in her chamber at night, and that Margery invited Joan and her maids to join her.[57] Although it was the Lollard Bible being read, we can assume from Margery's actions that the chamber was not chosen in order to retain secrecy, but instead because it was the most appropriate place within the house in which to learn scripture. As Margery invited others to join her and her husband, the chamber was not being treated as a private chapel for quiet contemplation, but instead an intimate space in which to learn about God.

Evidence for a close relationship between the bed and the study and contemplation of religious material is found in the visual arts. A miniature at the beginning of the first Psalm of Henry VIII's Psalter from

---

[56] *A Collection of Ordinances*, p. 37.

[57] *Heresy Trials in the Diocese of Norwich, 1428–31*, ed. S. McSheffrey and N. Tanner (London, 1977); P. J. P. Goldberg, *Women in England*, pp. 290–5; 'Account of the Heresy Trial of Margery Baxter', in *The Broadview Anthology of British Literature: Concise Edition, Volume A*, ed. J. Black (Peterborough ON, 2011), pp. 396–8 (p. 397); R. Copeland, 'Why Women Can't Read: Medieval Hermeneutics, Statutory Law, and the Lollard Heresy Trials', in *Representing Women: Law, Literature, and Feminism*, ed. S. Sage Heinzelman and Z. Batshaw Wiseman (Durham NC, 1994), pp. 273–86 (p. 272); J. C. Ward, *Women in England in the Middle Ages* (London, 2006), p. 193.

Figure 7: Miniature depicting Henry VIII reading in a chamber, *c.* 1540–1 © The British Library Board. BL Royal 2A.XVI f. 3r.

around 1540 (Fig. 7), depicts the King in a chamber reading the Psalter or, according to the British Library *Catalogue of Illuminated Manuscripts*, 'praying in his bedchamber'.[58] Rather than depicting only the Psalter

---

[58] 'Royal 2 A XVI f. 3 Henry VIII', in British Library, *Catalogue of Illuminated Manuscripts* <http://www.bl.uk/catalogues/illuminatedmanuscripts/record. asp?MSID=8719&CollID=16&NStart=20116>.

itself, there are two books piled next to the figure of Henry, suggesting that the chamber is the location in which Henry VIII wishes to be shown reading. The bed is an important part of the picture, taking up more than a quarter of the space. The curtain nearest the head of the bed rests on the red covering rather than hanging at the side, a position that is reflected by the blue book resting at right angles on the red book beneath it. The bed curtain's position is unusual in this miniature, as most illustrations of beds show curtains either hanging down or fixed up. Its unusual position, combined with the parallel in colours between the bed clothes and book covers, is a deliberate visual link between the bed and the devotional literature. The line of sight created by the angles in the picture causes the books to lead on to the bed, while the bed curtain in disarray and the books piled on the floor give the impression of use and familiarity, as if the use of the bed and books is a frequent activity within this chamber.

The relationship between devotional reading and the chamber is further implied by the gaze of the figure of Henry VIII. As the miniature is in his personal Psalter, the audience of the book would be himself. In the miniature, instead of reading the book that is in his hands, he is portrayed gazing out towards the reader. The gaze creates an intriguing relationship between the owner, the book and the chamber. If we take the book being held by Henry in the picture to be representative of the Psalter in which the illustration resides, as is usually the case in depictions of the owner within presentation copies and devotional books, the real Henry would sit in his chamber holding the Psalter, looking at the representation of himself sitting in his chamber holding the Psalter, looking back at him. This circularity makes the Psalter, the chamber and the act of reading devotional texts inextricably connected. The direct gaze at the audience could also serve as a sort of visual self-correction, conveying the impression that Henry watches himself perform devotional activities, self-consciously monitoring his expressions of piety.

The lack of security in the chamber, illustrated by the open door leading to an outside space, makes it clear that the chamber in the miniature is not an accurate representation of Henry VIII's sleeping quarters.[59] It is possible that the open door to a courtyard is meant to

---

[59] While the King's chamber may have been more public than the Queen's, Henry VIII's chamber would have been in a deep space. See A. Richardson, 'Gender and Space in English Royal Palaces', pp. 131–65.

represent the inner court at Nonsuch, as according to Amanda Richardson, 'the gatehouse leading into the inner courtyard represented entry into a cultured Renaissance world to which the court aspired'.[60] It is not evident whether the illustration depicts a real chamber but, as will be explored in Chapter 3, it was not unusual for a bed of estate to be present in a chamber which would not be used as a sleeping room. One could take the open doorway as an insight into Henry's imagination, as in the representation of Mary of Burgundy in her Book of Hours.[61] The two devotional books are similar in that both require their owners to gaze upon representations of themselves reading the book in which they are depicted. However, while Mary of Burgundy can visualise herself attending the Virgin Mary, the open doorway behind Henry frames nothing but scenery. The well-worn path leading to an unseen destination might be the spiritual path the reader should tread while contemplating the Psalms. Whether the room is real or conceptual, the artist deemed it important to portray Henry with his books and a richly decorated bed, which could suggest that the artist knew that some of Henry's devotional reading was carried out in a chamber. The miniature could also be the artist's attempt to curry favour with the King, by suggesting that he is thought of as someone so devout that he must read his Psalter in solitude, rather than merely as a public performance of piety in the church or chapel. The bed, as the most intimate space, suggests his intimate relationship with God. Taking the bedding in slight disarray as indicative of its frequent use, we can infer that Henry starts and ends his day in prayer and contemplation of scripture.

Evidence of religious imagery and devotional objects in the chamber is further indication that the chamber was seen to be a space for devotion. That is not to say that the church and the chapel were not, but that contemplation of God extended into the chamber, as is fitting given the cultural links between the bed and a relationship with Christ. John Baret, who made his will in Bury St Edmunds in 1463, certainly understood both the bed and chamber as spaces to remember God and the Virgin Mary, as can be seen in his instruction to his executors:

> I yeve and bequethe to dame Margarete Spurdaunce, of Norwiche, my crucifix, whiche is in my white chambyr; and the selor of cloth on loffte,

---

[60] Ibid., p. 157.
[61] Vienna, Österreichische Nationalbibliothek, Codex Vindobonensis 1857, ff. 14v–15r.

with the valaunce of scripture abowte the ymage, be nat remevyd ne
had awey; and I wil there be maad onn my cost such anothir crucifix, to
be set vp in the white chambir wer the tothir crucifix was. [62]

As Diana Webb comments, this action is 'as if to say that *a* crucifix
was an indispensable feature of this chamber'.[63] It indicates that the
crucifix itself was not of utmost importance, but the white chamber
was understood to be a space which contained a crucifix, and would
have been lacking without. The silour, containing a (presumably religious) image and some Biblical text, is understood to belong so much
to that particular chamber that it cannot be given away or removed.
A similar silour belonged to the chamber in which John Baret's neice,
Jenete Whitwelle, slept at the time Baret's will was made: he gives
her 'the selor and the steynyd clooth of the Coronacion of oure lady,
with the clothes of myn that longe to ye bedde that she hath loyen in'.[64]
In this case, the bedding containing the religious imagery was given
away, but as it was given to his niece, who was given free access to
the chamber in which she resided for as long as she lived, the effect
was that it remained in the same place. Although the wording of the
bequest suggests that the 'selor and the steynyd clooth' could be separated, the bequest makes it very clear that the Marian image remains
with the bed. Baret so much associated religious iconography with the
bed, that he took a bed containing a Marian image on his travels: he
bequeathed to his boy, John Aleyn, 'a tester with ij. coster[es] smale
palyd of bukram blew and bette blew, with an ymage of oure lady in
gold papyr, that I vsed to trusse with me […] and the selour longyng
therto'.[65]

John Baret was not alone in his penchant for chambers containing
religious iconography. In 1526 William Nelson left his son 'a coveryng
of a bed with ymagery'.[66] Cecilie Lepyngton's will of 1526 includes her
'best over-see bed called the Baptest', which presumably refers to an
image of John the Baptist on the bed.[67] A 'bedde called the maydens

---

[62] *Wills and Inventories*, ed. Tymms, p. 36.
[63] D. Webb, 'Domestic Space and Devotion in the Middle Ages', in *Defining the Holy: Sacred Space in Medieval and Early Modern Europe*, ed. A. Spicer and S. Hamilton (Aldershot, 2005), pp. 27–48 (pp. 42–3).
[64] *Wills and Inventories*, ed. Tymms, p. 23.
[65] Ibid., p. 34.
[66] *Testamenta Eboracensia: A Selection of Wills from the Registry at York*, ed. J. Raine and J. Clay, 6 vols. (London, 1869), V, 200.
[67] Ibid., p. 224.

bedde' is left by William Gybbyns to his son in 1535.[68] Given that the bed is not left to a 'mayden', and in conjunction with the bequest of his soul 'to our ladye saynte marye' and the bequest of 'iij s. iiij d.' 'to our ladye light in the chauncell', it can be assumed to be a bed representing the Virgin Mary. More specific evidence of religious imagery in the chamber is found in reference to some dormitories in monastic institutions, possibly because there was a higher number of beds and chambers than in secular households, so it was necessary to be more specific in inventories. Dormitory hangings in Cheshunt priory featured the image of St Giles.[69] In the convent at Minster, Sheppey, there was 'a table of the crucyfyx payntyd' in 'Dame Ursula Gosborne Superior's Chamber' and 'a table with a crucfyx of wod payntyd, and an Image of oure Lady, payntyd' in 'Dame Anne Clifford's Chamber'.[70] Lillechurch Priory owned several bed hangings of saints and a red coverlet with an image of Christ, while the prioress had a chamber hanging containing a prayer to the Virgin Mary.[71] The bedding in St Mary's Priory, Langley included one coverlet of crosses and roses and one of Mary as Queen of Heaven.[72]

The 'chaumbur of love' in the early fifteenth-century romance *Sir Degrevant* is richly decorated with paintings, text and statues representing secular and religious characters and stories, and sheds some light on the perceived possibilities of religious décor in the chamber.[73] The description of the chamber indicates that there is a fine line between decorations understood to belong to the church and the chamber, and that the two can overlap. Arlyn Diamond uses the models of the decorated chamber of Countess Adela de Blois, Westminster Hall, the King's painted chamber and the paintings of the Apocalypse in Westminster's Chapter House to argue that the stories represented in Melidore's chamber are designed to symbolise the 'interpenetration

---

[68] *Lincoln Diocese Documents*, ed. Clark, pp. 191–2.

[69] Oliva, 'Nuns at Home', pp. 149–52.

[70] M. E. C. Walcott, 'Inventories of St Mary's Hospital, Dover, St Martin New-Work, Dover, and the Benedictine Priory of S. S. Mary and Sexburga in the Island of Shepey for Nuns', *Archaeologia Cantiana* 7 (1868), 272–306 (p. 297).

[71] J. E. Cussans, *A History of Hertfordshire* II: *Hitchin, Hertford, and Broadwater* (London, 1870–1), p. 268; R. F. Scott, *Notes from the Records of St John's College* (Cambridge, 1913), pp. 404–7.

[72] Walcott, 'Inventories', pp. 121–2.

[73] *Sir Degrevant*, ed. Kooper, ll. 1439, 1441.

of spheres' in *Sir Degrevant*, and in chambers on the whole.[74] While I agree with this interpretation to an extent, the description of the chamber does more than simply blur the boundaries between the public and private. The lack of archaeological evidence of chambers means that we cannot possibly claim, like Diamond, that no-one, not 'even the Pope', had such decorations in their chambers.[75]

While Melidore's chamber and its contents may seem overtly hyperbolic, with a crystal floor, marble walls and cords of 'meremaydenus hare' (l. 1520), they are not, for the most part, beyond the realms of possibility. For instance, it is possible to use the vocabulary of *Sir Degrevant* to describe Isabeau of Bavaria's room, as depicted in London, British Library, Harley 4431 (Fig. 12), which contains 'pyllorus', 'square wyndowus of glas', 'gaye gablettus and grete' of red and green, a floor possibly 'paved overal/ With a clere crystal', 'overkeveryd with a pal'.[76] The 'bede […] With testur and celure,/ With a bryght bordure/ Compasyd ful clene' has upon it the Queen's 'owun banere' and one could well claim that 'was nevere bede rychere/ Of empryce ne qwene'.[77] The wall hangings could be described as 'fayr schetus of sylk', 'of aszure' and containing 'mony a rede gold' fleur-de-lys.[78] If such aspects of Melidore's chamber are found elsewhere, it is likely that its religious iconography mirrored that of other chambers.

The chamber is so full of meaning-laden iconography that a close reading is essential in order to unpack the resonances embedded within the description. First, we are told that the ceiling contains:

> Arcangelus of rede golde,
> Fyfty mad of o molde,
> Lowynge ful lyghth.
> With the Pocalyps of Jon,
> The Powlus Pystolus everychon,
> The Parabolus of Salamon,
> Payntyd ful ryghth. (ll. 1450–6)

---

[74] A. Diamond, '*Sir Degrevant*: What Lovers Want', in *Pulp Fictions of Medieval England: Essays in Popular Romance*, ed. N. McDonald (Manchester, 2004), pp. 82–101 (pp. 95–6).

[75] Ibid., p. 95.

[76] See Fig. 12, p. 114; *Sir Degrevant*, ed. Kooper, ll. 1458, 1473, 1478, 1485–8.

[77] Ibid., ll. 1489–92, 1502–4.

[78] Ibid., ll. 1505, 1489, 1515.

The fifty red-gold archangels on the ceiling are reminiscent of the fourteenth- and fifteenth-century roof angels decorating the ceilings of churches, particularly those in East Anglia but also found in Westminster and York.[79] The effect is to break down the distinction between church and chamber, reflecting the semantic links between the spaces. Similarly, the presence of Biblical texts on Melidore's ceiling suggests that the chamber is considered to be a space for Biblical consumption. The late medieval preoccupation with the Apocalypse is clear from the many Doom paintings in medieval churches and monastic institutions and the significant number of apocalyptic texts and works of art, particularly in the thirteenth and fourteenth centuries.[80] There is evidence that Margaret of York owned a personal copy of the *Apocalypse*, which contained many illustrations.[81] It is thus not unheard-of for a woman to privately contemplate a pictorial representation of the Apocalypse, and so we must not rule it out as possible chamber decoration. I agree with Diamond that some of the texts represented on the ceiling 'may exist as text rather than image – the wording is ambiguous', particularly 'Powlus Pystolus', as it is unlikely that a pictorial representation of 'everychon' of his epistles is possible: most illustrations of Pauline epistles simply show him preaching or writing a letter.[82] The narrator

---

[79] C. Cave, *Roof Bosses in Medieval Churches: An Aspect of Gothic Sculpture* (Cambridge, 1948), p. 48; Michael Rimmer's Angel Roofs project contains an extensive gallery of roof angel images. Michael Rimmer, *The Angel Roofs of East Anglia* (2012) <www.angelroofs.com>.

[80] A comprehensive study of the circulation and reception of Apocalypse literature in England is outside the intentions of this book and is done elsewhere. See, for example, R. K. Emmerson and S. Lewis, 'Census and Bibliography of Manuscripts Containing Apocalypse Illustrations, ca. 800–1500', *Traditio* 41 (1985), 370–409; S. Lewis, *Reading Images: Narrative Discourse and Reception in the Thirteenth-Century Illuminated Apocalypse* (Cambridge, 1995); P. Szittya, 'Domesday Bokes: The Apocalypse in Medieval English Literary Culture', in *The Apocalypse in the Middle Ages*, ed. R. K. Emmerson and B. McGinn (Ithaca, 1992), pp. 374–97; Peter K. Klein, 'Introduction: The Apocalypse in Medieval Art', in *The Apocalypse in the Middle Ages*, ed. R. K. Emmerson and B. McGinn (Ithaca, 1992), pp. 159–99; L. LeBlanc, 'Social Upheaval and the English Doomsday Plays', in *End of Days: Essays on the Apocalypse from Antiquity to Modernity*, ed. K. Kinane and M. A. Ryan (Jefferson, 2009), pp. 87–102.

[81] New York, Pierpoint Morgan Library, MS 484; S. Lewis, 'The *Apocalypse* of Margaret of York', in *Margaret of York, Simon Marmion, and* The Visions of Tondal, ed. T. Kren (Princeton, 1992), pp. 77–98 (p. 77).

[82] Diamond, 'What Lovers Want', p. 96. See, for example, London, British Library, Royal MS 1 E V, f. 5r.

goes on to describe carvings and statues in the room, urging the audience to listen, not to the narrator, but to the decorations themselves:

And the foure gospellorus
Syttyng on pyllorus
Hend*, herkeneth and herus,   *beautiful/ strong/ smooth
Gyf hyt be youre wyll.
Austyn and Gregorius
Jerome and Ambrosius,
Thus the foure doctorus
Lysten tham tylle. (ll. 1457–64)

The imperatives 'herkeneth and herus'; 'lysten tham tylle' are ambiguous. On the one hand, they emphasise the authority of the writers' works, and can be read as a warning to Melidore and Degrevant that they should pay attention to the evangelists and philosophers, in order to be judged favourably in the Apocalypse described above. On the other hand, 'herkeneth and herus' can be read as a plea to the 'gospellorus' to listen to our prayers. If they are able to listen, the presence of the evangelists renders the chamber especially equipped as an appropriate space for prayer. It suggests that representations of holy figures in the chamber, such as John Baret's images of the Virgin Mary, are not merely for decoration or contemplation, but also as a medium by which one's prayers are conveyed to God.[83]

The recently discovered frame of the fifteenth-century Paradise Bed, thought to have been presented to Henry VII and Elizabeth of York for their marriage ceremony in 1486, contains richly layered religious imagery.[84] The triptych arrangement on the tester portrays Adam and Eve as agents of the Fall of Man (Fig. 8). This scene, with its resonances

---

[83] *Wills and Inventories*, ed. Tymms, p. 34.

[84] Research is ongoing with the so-called Paradise Bed. The oxidation of the timbers and shrinkage cracks along with evidence of whittling rather than lathe-turning suggest that it is pre-seventeenth-century. Jonathan Geach and Bernd Degen identify the wood as Eurasian White Oak, compatible with medieval sources of timber, probably from Germany. Helen Hughes' analysis of paint fragments found traces of sulphuric sea-coal primer, found in the finishes of fifteenth-century buildings and rarely used after 1650. The dimensions of the bed and carvings on the posts match those of the Thomas Stanley bed, dated *c*.1500. Iconography pertaining to Henry VII and Elizabeth of York and the presence of single, rather than Tudor, roses point towards a date of 1486. My thanks to Jonathan Foyle, for sharing this information and his ongoing research, and to Ian Coulson, the current owner, for allowing me exclusive access to the bed.

of both creation and temptation, reminds its audience that the bed is a site of procreation and temptation. At the same time, the figures of Adam and Eve, who arguably also represent Henry and Elizabeth, are shown to be transmuted through the cross of Christ's sacrifice into Jesus and the Virgin Mary, as figures of redemption. They are pictured holding an apple and rejecting the serpent's fruit, as they flank the Tree of Life, promised in Revelation, which grows several different types of fruit, which could represent the fruits of the Spirit.[85] The two figures are encircled in a scroll that presumably contained scripture, now replaced by later script.[86]

Figure 8: Detail from the tester of the Paradise Bed, *c.* 1486. Photograph credit: Ian Coulson.

---

[85] Revelation 22.2; Galatians 5.22.

[86] Paint analysis revealed evidence of secondary graining, where the current lettering, which reads 'The sting of death is sinne: The strength of sinne is the law', is incised. Jonathan Foyle suggests that the original lettering was raised and was planed off, though it could also have been painted on.

69

The visual representation of the creation story is reminiscent of royal genealogies, in which the family line is traced back to Adam and Eve.[87] In addition, the image's connotations of the balance of good and evil conveys the impression that the occupant knows how to judge justly, flattering the king and inspiring his followers to place confidence in him. In addition to the carvings of Adam and Eve, the representations of Christ and symbols of fertility, the bed frame has carvings of seven stars referencing the message of healing and conciliation between peoples in Isaiah as well as the stars in Christ's right hands in the book of Revelation.[88] The occupiers of this bed, whether they were the royal couple or not, would be visually situated in the middle of the story of the world, from Creation to the Apocalypse, so that they were literally lying at the centre of God's plan.

The chamber in the church and street

The cognitive link between beds, chambers and God in the late medieval English collective mindset is obvious from evidence of religious imagery within the chamber to the late medieval understanding that God could literally communicate with a believer in bed. However, evidence of this cultural connection does not stop at the chamber door. The idea of the bed and chamber as religious space also manifested outside of the chamber.

The rise in the number of chantry chapels is arguably linked with the idea of the 'chambour of þi soule'.[89] As John McNeill argues, a chantry chapel is 'an intermediate place, neither entirely within the church nor without'.[90] The so-called 'stone-cage' chantry chapels are architecturally reminiscent of domestic chambers: they are usually around the same height as a domestic chamber, closing off the space above with screens, canopies or lower vaulted ceilings, rather than reaching to the church's full height; the screens and lockable doors make them private

---

[87] S. Anglo, 'The *British History* in Early Tudor Propaganda, With an Appendix of Manuscript Pedigrees of the Kings of England, Henry VI to Henry VIII', *Bulletin of the John Rylands Library Manchester* 44.1 (1961), 17–48; In particular, London, British Library, Harley Rolls C. 9 begins with an illustration of the temptation of Adam and Eve.

[88] Isaiah 30. 26; Revelation 1.16.

[89] 'Bonum lectum', ed. Doyle, p. 186.

[90] J. McNeill, 'A Prehistory of the Chantry', *Journal of the British Archaeological Association* 164 (2011), 14.

spaces.[91] Similarly, chantry chapels built into choirs and naves close off the space, making them into a space of 'architectural intimacy' akin to chambers.[92] The use of textiles within the chantry chapel makes the chantry chapel look, from the inside, not aesthetically dissimilar from a chamber.[93] The descriptions in wills and inventories of textiles of various cloths used for vestments in chantry chapels, some containing heraldic devices and iconography, is very similar to the ways in which bedding is described. The enclosed space, decked out in cloth chosen by the owner or donor of the chapel and used by members of the owner's household, brought the domestic into sacred space. In addition, chantry chapels containing tombs could have been viewed as perpetual chambers for those enclosed within the tombs. This blurring of the sacred and the secular was emphasised by the propensity for sculptors to portray the deceased asleep or reclining on tomb chests. Luxford suggests that the rise of the chantry chapel correlated with a growing interest in the spiritual power of small architectural spaces, particularly monastic cells.[94] I agree, but do not think monastic cells are the only spiritually charged enclosed spaces. As explored above, the chamber was increasingly considered to be and used as a sacred space within the secular home.

Like chantry chapels and monastic cells, anchor holds could be seen to be neither the church nor the chamber, but made up of the two. Liz Herbert McAvoy describes the setting of Julian of Norwich's visions as 'almost certainly a domestic one – that of Julian's own bedchamber'.[95] Similarly, Elizabeth Robertson posits that an anchor hold might have

---

[91] S. Roffey, *Chantry Chapels and Medieval Strategies for the Afterlife* (Stroud, 2008), pp. 70–7; J. M. Luxford, 'The Origins and Development of the English "Stone-Cage" Chantry Chapel', *Journal of the British Archaeological Association* 164 (2011), 39–73; S. Roffey, *The Medieval Chantry Chapel: An Archaeology* (Woodbridge, 2007), p. 43.

[92] Luxford, 'English "Stone-Cage" Chantry Chapel', p. 64.

[93] K. Heard, 'Such Stuff as Dreams Are Made On: Textiles and the Medieval Chantry', *Journal of the British Archaeological Association* 164 (2011), 163–5 describes the kinds of textiles left specifically for use within the chantry.

[94] Luxford, 'English "Stone-Cage" Chantry Chapel', p. 66.

[95] L. Herbert McAvoy, '"Ant nes he him seolf reclus i maries wombe?" Julian of Norwich, the Anchorhold and Redemption of the Monstrous Female Body', in *Consuming Narratives: Gender and Monstrous Appetite in the Middle Ages and the Renaissance*, ed. L. Herbert McAvoy and T. Walters (Aberystwyth, 2002), pp. 128–43 (p. 130).

been attractive to a woman because it was 'a room of her own'.[96] The small size of some of the anchor holds, combined with their lack of escape, could be said to recall chambers. It is more likely, however, that late medieval chambers were considered in light of assumptions about the purity of anchor holds, rather than the other way around.

The donation of bedding to the church demonstrates an intrinsic understanding of the link between the domestic and the divine. For instance, William Thomson's wife bequeathed her 'best coverlet of arras work' to All Hallow's church, Barking, in 1471 without explicit instructions, but the nineteen altar cloths, of various materials and patterns, mentioned in the church's 1506 inventory might suggest that the coverlet was used to cover an altar.[97] What was once used as part of the donor's bed was transformed into a resting place for the Eucharist and could be considered to be under the protection of one of a number of saints, to whom the altar was dedicated. Such bequests of bedding were made with the implicit understanding that it would be beneficial for the donors' souls: the priest using the bedding might think upon the donor and offer up a prayer in remembrance. Items of bedding used as altar cloths were powerful objects as they would not only aid the memory of the priests but also support the transubstantiated body of Christ. As Eamon Duffy argues, the bequest of bedding for use as altar cloths was 'a gesture clearly designed to bring their domestic intimacies into direct contact with the Host'.[98]

The practice of displaying bedding in churches for its own sake, as found in Holy Trinity church, Kingston-upon-Hull, shows that the beds themselves were considered to have some religious meaning. The parishioners of Holy Trinity bequeathed bedding to the church in order that they were used in remembrance of the donors on specific days and also displayed more generally on St George's day. Thomas Wood's will of 1490 contains detailed instructions for the church's use of his bedding:

> To the Trinitie church one of my best beddes of Arreys werk, upon this condicion suying, that after my decesse I will that the same bedd shall

[96] E. Robertson, *Early English Devotional Prose and the Female Audience* (Knoxville, 1990), pp. 13–30 (p. 30).

[97] L. J. Redstone, *Survey of London* 12: *The Parish of All Hallows Barking* (London, 1934), pp. 33, 76–7.

[98] E. Duffy, *Stripping of the Altars: Traditional Religion in England 1400–1580*, 2nd edn (New Haven, 2005), p. 96.

yerely cover my grave at my *Dirige* and *Masse*, doone in the said Trinite churche w^t note for evermore; and also that I will that the same bedd be honge yerely in the said churche at the feste of Seynt George Martir emong other worshipfull beddes; and, when the said beddes be taken downe and delyvered, then I woll that the same bedd be re-delyvered in to the revestre, and ther to remayne w^t my cope of golde.[99]

This bequest is similar to that of the priest Richard Peke, who left a 'blew bed to remayn to the Trinitie chirch at Hull for ever' in 1481.[100] The repetition of 'beddes' throughout Wood's bequest suggests that the articles of bedding were still considered to be beds, rather than altar cloths or sepulchre hangings, after their donation to the church, and the phrase 'other worshipfull beddes' implies that such a bequest was common practice, while the beds themselves were valued as objects of worship. Kate Heard argues that the inclusion of personal symbols or insignia on vestments bequeathed to the church encouraged remembrance of the donor and inspired frequent prayer for their soul.[101] As the church was instructed to use the bedding on remembrance days associated with the donors, the church would have been required to have a record of which bed belonged to which donor, so it is possible that something similar is happening here. However, as Wood does not specify which of his 'best beddes' should be given to the church, and Peke's bed is only 'blew', neither item is personalised, so would not necessarily inspire prayer for their individual souls among the parishioners.

Considering these beds within the literary context in which texts such as 'Bonum lectum', commentaries on the Song of Songs and even romances teach their audience that the bed is at the heart of one's soul's relationship with God, we can read each of these beds as a representation of its owner's soul. As Jenny Kermode points out, Wood's intention to store his earthly bedding until resurrection 'raises interesting theological questions'.[102] While it is not clear from his will whether Wood expected to make use of his bed upon or after judgement day, it might suggest that beds were understood to play a part in the Apocalypse, as is implied by the *Pricke of Conscience* window in All Saints'

[99] *Testamenta Eboracensia*, ed. Raine and Clay, IV, 60.
[100] Ibid., p. 61.
[101] Heard, 'Such Stuff as Dreams Are Made On', pp. 157–68 (p. 164).
[102] J. Kermode, *Medieval Merchants: York, Beverley and Hull in the Later Middle Ages* (Cambridge, 1998), p. 140.

North Street, York, in which even during the Apocalypse, people die in beds and have the last rites performed.[103] If the bed was a physical symbol of one's soul, Wood's 'worshipfull bed' might be kept safe for God's inspection. It is clear that, for the merchant community of Holy Trinity church, Hull, beds played an important part in the church's calendar. As such, parishioners, not yet deceased, witnessing these church practices, would have understood their late acquaintances' beds in terms of their religious meaning. This understanding, in turn, would have affected the way in which they regarded their own beds and the chambers in which they were contained.

The act of publicly displaying beds in a (albeit temporary) religious space was practised in sixteenth-century York 'for the honour of godd & worship of this Citie'.[104] According to the York *House Books* of 1544, during the feast of Corpus Christi:

> it is further agreyd by the sayd presens that for the honour of god & worship of this Citie […] the Morro after Corpuscrysty day […] that every howseholdr that dwellith in the hye way ther as the sayd pro- cession procedith, shall hang before ther doores & forefrontes beddes & Coverynges of beddes of the best they can gytt […] for the honour of godd & worship of this Citie and this to be fyrmely kepte hereafter vppon payn of every man that he dothe the contrary this agrement shall forfait & pay to the Common Chambre of this Cite iijs iiij d.[105]

The repetition of 'for the honour of godd & worship of this Citie' and the need to impose a fine on those who did not comply suggests that the public display of bedding was not instigated by the owners of the beds themselves, and therefore was not only a competitive demon- stration of personal wealth, although it is probable that a display of the city's collective wealth was one of the factors in the decision. Like Wood's will, it is specifically beds and bed coverings that are men- tioned, rather than any other type of hanging or decorative cloth, indicating that beds had a certain meaning, in the cultural imagina- tion, which made them appropriate and necessary decorations for the event. Lining the Corpus Christi procession route with bedding effectively kept the body of Christ and everyone taking part in the

---

[103] *Pricke of Conscience* Window, All Saints North Street, York, *c.* 1420. My thanks to Jessica Knowles for sharing her research with me.

[104] Cited in *Records of Early English Drama: York,* ed. A. F. Johnston and M. Rogerson, 2 vols. (Toronto, 1979), I, 283.

[105] Ibid.

event between bedclothes, placing God and his worshippers in bed together. The practice also mirrored the plays themselves: just as the mystery plays sought to bring out the secrets and wonders of the gospels, which were otherwise hidden in Latin texts and read only by authorised priests, and allowed the citizens of York to identify with the humanity of Christ, the most intimate spaces and objects associated with the citizens' sense of self are turned inside-out, so that the beds are unhidden before the Corpus Christi.

The use of beds for specific religious occasions signifies their divine associations. In particular, the tradition of leaving beds to the church for the Easter sepulchre physically acts out what 'Bonum lectum' does symbolically: it wraps Jesus in the benefactor's bed. On Good Friday, parishioners would make their way to the cross on their knees and kiss it. The priest would then ceremonially wrap the cross, as a symbol of Jesus, or occasionally a more humanoid representation of Jesus, in rich fabric and place it inside a 'sepulchre', which was either part of the fabric of the church or, more frequently, a wooden structure draped in fabric.[106] It would be watched until Easter Sunday and then removed and placed on the high altar, to symbolise the resurrection. There is evidence of the use of bedding for either the sepulchre itself or the wrapping of Christ. For instance, in 1501, Richard Dampyr bequeathed 'to the church of Combe my best covering of a bed for Easter'.[107] The 1538 inventory of the Priory of St Mary, St James and Holy Cross, Castle Hedingham, includes 'a payer of shetes for the sepulcre', and in 1471–2 the church of St Ewen in Bristol received 'a grene couerlete of the yifte of Mawde Core that was wond to be sette aboute the Sepulcre'.[108] Cecilie Lepyngton's 'best over-see bed called the Baptest', discussed above, was left 'os an ornament to the sepulchre of oure Saviour Criste Jhesu at the fest of Easter' in 1526.[109] Its description, 'bed called the Baptest', suggests that the bed had explicit religious implications even while it was used as a bed, and could have been produced with its eventual use as part of the Easter celebration in mind. Bedding used in the sepulchre as a bed for Jesus would have been used, at different times, by the previous owners of the beds and

---

[106] For more detail on the Easter sepulchre, see P. Sheingorn, *The Easter Sepulchre in England* (Kalamazoo, 1987); S. Beckwith, *Signifying God: Social Relation and Symbolic Act in the York Corpus Christi Plays* (Chicago, 2001), pp. 72–89.

[107] *Somerset Medieval Wills*, ed. Weaver, p. 35.

[108] Sheingorn, *The Easter Sepulchre*, pp. 137, 150.

[109] *Testamenta Eboracensia*, ed. Raine and Clay, V, 224.

by a physical representation of Christ, so that they literally shared a bed with God. It might have been reassuring to those on their death beds that the same bed in which they were dying would become the bed in which Jesus – albeit merely a representation of Jesus – would become resurrected. Having the soon-to-be-resurrected Christ as one's bedfellow may well have lent weight to the hope of eternal salvation.

In bed with Jesus

This chapter has shown that there was a very clear link between the domestic and the divine in the late medieval collective psyche. The bed is widely understood to be the site of communication between the believer and Christ, as can be seen through the wide dissemination of devotional works and Biblical commentaries expounding this view. However, the idea of the bed and the 'chambour of þi soule' as the locus for divine encounter was not merely theoretical.[110] The use of devotional images and books within the chamber, the bequest of bedding for specific religious use and the repeated insistence that one must serve God immediately upon waking up all point towards an inherent understanding that the bed was a sacred space. With this idea in mind, Margery Kempe and her nocturnal encounters with Jesus may not have been as transgressive as they now appear to a modern reader. The ways in which the chamber was taken for granted as a space for worship, most often in romance but occasionally in documentary records, such as in the will of John Baret, which implies that a crucifix is a necessary item in his white chamber even after his death, are more telling than any didactic work.[111] Encounters with God happened in the chamber in late medieval English texts, because that was where God was understood to be. And if one made one's bed properly, He might even have had a little lie down.

---

[110] 'Bonum lectum', ed. Doyle, p. 186.
[111] *Wills and Inventories*, ed. Tymms, p. 23.

3

'Do Thy Warke Wyssely/ [...] And Awnswer The Pepll Curtesly'

Talking in bed ought to be easiest,
Lying together there goes back so far,
An emblem of two people being honest.

Philip Larkin, 'Talking in Bed'[1]

The previous chapter explored how communication with God was understood to happen most frequently in bed because of the tradition of the bed as a metaphor for the relationship between the believer and the divine. However, the bed as a space for honest, intimate communication was not reserved solely for encounters with God. In late medieval England, the bed was a symbol of power and intimacy. As such, the chamber's meaning as a space which was appropriate for a particularly deep level of communication unavailable elsewhere relies upon the physical or implied presence of the bed. The aim of this chapter is to analyse the bed's role as 'emblem of two people being honest', and how that affected the ways in which people used and thought about the chamber.

Being open in a closed space

The chamber's physical seclusion and the bed's connotations of intimacy lent themselves to a role as the centre for private discourse. As Felicity Riddy argues, within Middle English romance, the chamber is 'a feminine place of intimacy, love and a different kind of speech'.[2]

---

[1] P. Larkin, 'Talking in Bed', in *The Whitsun Weddings* (London, 1964), ll. 1–3.
[2] F. Riddy, 'Middle English Romance: Family, Marriage, Intimacy', in *The Cambridge Companion to Medieval Romance*, ed. R. L. Krueger (Cambridge, 2000),

This sense of intimacy and trust, though it is often expressed through romance narratives, is not confined to the romance genre. Instead it was present in a wider cultural understanding of the bed and chamber. The 'different kind of speech' to which Riddy refers is most apparent in romance when the conversation takes place in bed. Romance regularly demonstrates that the bed was seen to be a leveller in oral communication. Characters of different gender and social status are able to talk with a semblance of equality when they are in bed together. A very clear example is in *Havelok the Dane*, where the chamber and the bed give the protagonists the freedom to converse, which had hitherto been denied to them. Goldeboru, the rightful heir to the throne of England, is dominated by her evil guardian Godrich in the first half of the romance and her voice is never heard directly. The most forceful protest Goldeboru is able to make against Godrich is when he announces her imminent arranged marriage, during a public, staged celebration of her arrival in Lincoln. Even then, Goldeboru's retort is reported indirectly:

> She answerede and saide anon.
> By Christ and by Saint Johan,
> That hire sholde noman wedde,
> Ne noman bringen hire to bedde,
> But he were king or kinges eir,
> Were he nevere man so fair.[3]

While her opinion is clear, the indirect speech means that she remains physically voiceless to the audience and it makes no impact at all on Godrich's decision to marry her to Havelok. Havelok has some direct speech at this point in the narrative, though it is similarly ignored, yet there is no reported conversation between him and Goldeboru throughout the arranged wedding and subsequent move to Grimsby; indeed, the one hundred lines between his unheeded protest and their wedding night seem oppressively full of speech from everyone but the married couple.[4] As soon as the protagonists go to bed, however, a distinct change occurs. Goldeboru's passive, indirect voice and inability to defend herself and Havelok's silent acceptance of his situation are in stark contrast to their speech patterns once they are in their marriage

pp. 235–52 (p. 240). See ch. 6 below for an analysis of the chamber as a 'feminine' space.

[3] *Havelok the Dane*, ed. Sands, ll. 1111–16.

[4] Ibid., ll. 1147–1247.

bed. Rather than the consummation of marriage through sexual union
– which must occur eventually, as they produce fifteen children, but appears lacking at this point in the narrative – their previously repressed
voices commune in the marriage bed until the characters become one
in purpose. Their consummation is thus one of communication and,
like the conventional physical consummation of marriage, paves the
way for a new expression of affection between husband and wife.[5] The
first time Havelok speaks to Goldeboru directly, he asks her 'Lemman,
slepes thou?' (l. 1283). The term 'lemman' is used specifically to indicate love between the speaker and the interlocutor. Thus, with their
new-found communication in bed, Havelok accepts that Goldeboru
is his lover. He continues to describe his dream for twenty-nine con-
secutive lines, displaying more loquacity than at any other point in
the romance.[6] This episode is also the only instance in the romance in
which he speaks about his visions and feelings. He then asks Goldeboru directly for advice: 'Deus! lemman, what may this be?' (l. 1312),
allowing for interaction between the characters. Goldeboru's answer
is even longer, equally eloquent, and the first time she speaks aloud in
the text.[7] Her answer indicates prophetic abilities, proclaiming:

> Ne non strong, king ne caisere,
> So thou shalt be, for thou shalt bere
> In Engelond corune yet.
> Denemark shall knele to thy feet. (ll. 1316–20)

Goldeboru's rhetoric, making use of alliterative repetition of the negative, the future active tense and the powerful image of the whole of
Denmark kneeling at Havelok's feet, is very persuasive: a far cry from
the passive voice Goldeboru adopts outside of the chamber. She uses
the imperative four times in laying out the plan to recapture Denmark
and England, demonstrating military and political savvy as well as
a linguistic authority that was not present before this moment in the
chamber. Her command to 'do nou als I wile rathe' (l. 1335) is not rebuked by Havelok, suggesting that he does not consider her to be out
of place in giving counsel in bed. Instead, he follows her plans 'sone

---

[5] For the bed as the locus of the consummation of marriage, see ch. 5 below, pp.
146–56.

[6] Ibid., ll. 1284–1312.

[7] Ibid., ll. 1314–52. Goldeboru's answer is at least forty lines long, but possibly
more as some lines are missing. Sands comments that lines rhyming with 'joye'
and 'trone' are probably missing.

it was day' (l. 1354). It is interesting that the only other instance of direct speech for Goldeboru occurs at the moment her plan has come to fruition, when both Denmark and England are reclaimed. It is as if there is no need for her to say anything else, until her bedtime counsel has been followed.

The striking contrast in the characters' behaviour in and away from the bed reflects a trend within Middle English literature. There are similarities between Goldeboru and the emperor's second wife in the fourteenth-century text *The Seven Sages of Rome*. Like Goldeboru, we do not hear the empress' voice directly until after she and the emperor are married, and it is obvious that the emperor and empress had not communicated effectively before they were married, as she finds out from 'a seriant nyce', rather than her husband, that he already has a son and heir.[8] The first time we see them in bed together, after they have 'played', she immediately becomes vocal and dominates the conversation, explaining frankly that the emperor has done her a disservice and demanding to meet the child.[9] The empress declares that there should be no secrets between the married couple, emphasising the bed's role within marriage: 'ʒe made me Emperice of Rome,/ To be with ʒow at bed and borde,/ And wit ʒowre cownsail ilka worde'.[10] This reference to bed and board, found elsewhere in marriage vows and descriptions of marriage in legal separations, is juxtaposed with a reference to counsel.[11] As such, it is pertinent that this speech is made in bed. Like Havelok, as soon as it is morning, 'th' emperour gan rise,/ And clothed him in riche gise', in order to carry out his wife's instructions.[12]

As I shall explore later in Chapter 6, the bed and chamber are particularly empowering for female characters. The bed's function as an equaliser between the sexes, which makes the aforementioned conversations in bed possible, causes the women to go out of their way to

---

[8] *The Seven Sages of Rome*, ed. K. Campbell (Boston, 1907), l. 285. A 'seriant nyce' probably refers to a member of the family who is in the employ of the household.

[9] Ibid., ll. 317–44. See ch. 4 below, pp. 140–1 for the use of 'play' as a euphemism for sex. Weber's edition makes it very clear that they are 'in chaumbre togidere'. *The Seven Sages*, in *Metrical Romances of the Thirteenth, Fourteenth, and Fifteenth Centuries: Published from Ancient Manuscripts*, ed. H. W. Weber, 3 vols.. (Edinburgh, 1810), III, l. 271.

[10] Campbell, ed., *The Seven Sages of Rome*, ll. 326–8.

[11] See ch. 5 below, p. 147.

[12] Weber, ed., *The Seven Sages*, ll. 301–2.

manufacture a meeting in a chamber, in order to maintain authority. For instance, in *Sir Degrevant*, 'a chaumbur therby/ Busked was yare' in order that Melidor's maid can talk openly to Degrevant.[13] In *Sir Gawain and the Green Knight*, female voices are not heard at all outside of the chamber.[14] Guinevere has no reported speech and while it is clear that both Lady Bertilak and Morgan le Fay can speak elsewhere in Hautdesert – Gawain is entertained every day by 'two so dyngne dame,/ Þe alder and þe ȝonge' (ll. 1316–17) – we only have access to Lady Bertilak's direct speech in the chamber. Specifically, we hear her speak only in Gawain's bed. Her use of commands, such as 'ȝe schal not rise of your bedde' (l. 1223), her ability to steer the conversation and ultimately to persuade him to retain the girdle show that, like Goldeboru, Lady Bertilak is in control of the conversation. At the same time, the bed is the space in which Gawain is most honest about himself. While in the hall he tells Bertilak the barest details about his exploits; however, he talks freely with Bertilak's wife in bed.

Just as Lady Bertilak seeks out Gawain in his chamber because that is the space in which she is able to speak, in the late thirteenth-century romance *King Horn*, as Riddy points out, Rymenhild summons Horn to her chamber because 'heo ne mighte at borde/ With him speke no worde,/Ne noght in the halle'.[15] Nevertheless, within her own chamber she has the power to speak and does so, vociferously. Throughout the romance, Rymenhild's voice is heard in the chamber, especially in bed, while she remains quiet and passive whenever she leaves the chamber walls. Later on in the narrative, Rymenhild, like Havelok, recounts her dream to Horn 'in bure' (l. 699), and his interpretation of it shapes their subsequent actions in the wider world. The bed in *King Horn* is not merely a space in which Rymenhild's voice can be heard and effect real change in the wider sphere of their romance world, but where she knows that she and Horn can talk honestly to each other.

While talking in bed was more often associated with marriage, depictions of homosocial relationships in Middle English romance often suggest that the bed is the space most appropriate for private conversation. In *Eglamour of Artois*, for instance, Eglamour waits until

---

[13] 'A nearby chamber was made ready'. My translation. *Sir Degrevant*, ed. Kooper, ll. 803–4.

[14] *Sir Gawain and the Green Knight*, ed. Tolkien and Gordon.

[15] Riddy, 'Middle English Romance', p. 240; *King Horn*, in *Middle English Verse Romances*, ed. D. B. Sands (Exeter, 1986), ll. 253–5.

he is resting 'in chambour' before he confesses his love for Crystabell to his squire and demands counsel: 'belamy, and thou kowdest leyne,/ A counsell I wold to the sayne'.[16] Similarly, in Chaucer's 1385 poem *Troilus and Criseyde*, Troilus 'in his chaumbre sit and hath abiden [...]/ For Pandarus, and soughten hym ful faste'.[17] When Pandarus arrives, even though he and Troilus need to talk to each other, Pandarus suggests that they first 'go to reste' (l. 944), and so 'with al the haste goodly that they myghte/ They spedde hem fro the soper unto bedde' (ll. 946–7). It is not until they are both in bed that Troilus asks, 'frend, shal I now wepe or synge?' (l. 952). Although Pandarus warns Troilus to 'ly stylle and lat me slepe' (l. 953), he proceeds to give him 'counseil' (l. 1044), which Troilus accepts. While neither character explicitly articulates that they need to be in bed in order to talk, the characters and audience share the implicit understanding that the bed is ideal for such conversations.

Some Middle English romances indicate that the bed's associations with private, honest discussion extended to include a certain style of education. In the late fourteenth-century hagiographical romance *Le Bone Florence of Rome*, Florence teaches Beatrice, the daughter of her rescuer, 'to lerne hur to behaue hur among men'.[18] Rather than educating her on this subject 'among men', where she might have had practice, we are told that 'they lay togedur in fere,/ In bed togedur, wythoute lesynge' (ll. 1566–7).[19] Florence's teaching method is therefore to lie in bed and talk to Beatrice. The eponymous heroine of *Emaré* has a similar education: before she can walk, she is sent to a lady called Abro, who 'tawghte thys mayden small,/ Nortur that men useden in sale,/ Whyle she was in her bowre'.[20] The audience might connect the name 'Abro' with the French 'abri' (shelter), associating her with the sort of shelter that might be provided by a chamber. When Emaré grows up, she performs a similar role to Abro's, as Kadore 'sent aftur her certeynlye/ To teche [his] chylderen curtesye,/ In chambur wyth hem to bene' (ll. 424–6). Teaching in the chamber is not only a practice performed by women: in the alliterative *Morte Arture* dating from around 1400, Arthur refers to Mordred as 'my nurree of old,/ That I have chastied

---

16 *Sir Eglamour of Artois*, ed. Hudson, ll. 51–3.
17 Chaucer, 'Troilus and Criseyde', ii, ll. 935–7.
18 *Le Bone Florence of Rome*, ed. C. Falvo Heffernan (New York, 1976), l. 1565.
19 'in fere' = companionably; 'lesynge'= lying. Essentially, they shared a bed together and had an equal, honest relationship.
20 *Emaré*, ed. Laskaya and Salisbury, ll. 61–3.

and chosen, and child of my chamber', suggesting that the chamber is an important part of Mordred's education and that Arthur personally invested his time in bringing Mordred up in his chamber.[21]

The definite contrast between levels of marital communication in and out of bed, as well as the way in which characters deliberately go to bed before seeking counsel, demonstrates a wider understanding that a bed was in some way required in order to communicate honestly and intimately. As discussed in Chapter 1, the bed might have been the most intimate space available in the household but it would not have been private, being open to distractions and eavesdroppers, not to mention the fact that not everybody would have owned a permanently made-up bed. It is apparent, therefore, that the idea of the bed was enough to evoke a sense of intimacy and honesty, regardless of personal circumstance and material possession.

In the late medieval collective imagination, the bed, considered on its own, was the most appropriate space in which two people could talk as if on an equal footing. By extension, a chamber containing a bed was understood to be a space for honest, open communication. Cultural meanings of space are most evident when they are employed unquestioningly by writers for narrative effect rather than as extraordinary details. For example, the author of *King Arthur and King Cornwall*, the only copy of which survives in a fragmentary state in the seventeenth-century Percy folio, assumed that the audience would understand the implications of conversing in the chamber.[22] When Arthur and his knights, dressed as pilgrims, spend the night in King Cornwall's castle, Cornwall's servants enclose a sprite 'under thrub chadler' and set it 'by King Arthurs bedside/ To heere theire talke and theire cumunye', expecting that the visitors would reveal something about their identity in the chamber that they would not reveal in the hall.[23] The use of this supernatural bugging device suggests that King

---

[21] *Alliterative Morte Arthure*, in *King Arthur's Death: The Middle English Stanzaic Morte Arthur and Alliterative Morte Arthure*, ed. L. D. Benson (Kalamazoo, 1994), ll. 689–90.

[22] London, British Library, Additional MS 27879.

[23] *King Arthur and King Cornwall*, in *Sir Gawain: Eleven Romances and Tales*, ed. T. Hahn (Kalamazoo, 1995), ll. 123–6. The exact nature of a 'thrub chadler' is unknown. Child uses philology to suggest that it is a 'rubbish barrel', though this seems an unlikely object to place by a guest's bed. *The English and Scottish Popular Ballads*, ed. F. J. Child, 5 vols. (New York, 1884–98) I, 275–88 (p. 279). Hahn points out that the reference to 'the bunge of the trubchandler' (l. 173)

Cornwall knows the knights will talk freely within the chamber, yet the narrative would not work unless the author and audience had similar assumptions.

Outside of romance, there is evidence that the chamber was consciously sought after as a place in which to have private discussions, offer advice and pass judgement, and that the presence of the bed was of high cultural importance. *The Book of Margery Kempe* is punctuated with several very similar instances in which the characters deliberately move from a public place into a chamber in order to hold discussions and pass judgement on Margery. During Margery's visit to the Bishop of Lincoln, in which she asks him to provide her with the mantle, white clothes and ring associated with a vow of chastity, 'sche was set to mete wyth many worldly clerkys and prestys and swyers on the Bysshoppys, and the Bysshop hymself', all of whom asked her 'many hard qwestyons', which she 'answeryd so redyly and pregawntly'.[24] This conversation is necessarily in the hall, in order that she might prove her worth in front of a crowd, but afterwards the Bishop 'sent for this creatur into his chawmbyr' (ll. 795–6) to deliver his decision on her request. Similarly, later on in the narrative, when Margery is summoned to the steward of Leicester, she is first addressed in a public space, with 'many prestys stondyng abowtyn to here what sche schulde say and other pepyl also' (ll. 2648–9). As before, she is asked 'many qwestyonys' in front of the crowd, which she answers 'redily and resonabely that he cowde getyn no cawse ageyn hir' (ll. 2654–5). Just like characters in romance, the steward assumes that he will get a truthful answer in the chamber, for he 'toke hir be the hand and led hir into hys chawmbyr' (ll. 2655–6), where he proceeds to insult, question and frighten her into telling him about her spiritual gifts. He is 'al astoyned' (l. 2666), not only because of her insistence that her actions are the result of 'the Holy Gost and not of hir owyn cunyng' (ll. 2665–6), but because after questioning her in the chamber, he still does not know whether she is 'a ryth good woman or ellys a ryth wikked woman' (l. 2668). This indecision goes against the tendency in literature for a clear decision to be made after meeting in a chamber. This event may be the exception that proves the rule, as the surprise

---

indicates that it is a stoppered vessel of some kind. As it is next to Arthur's bed and later on the characters are able to read the words in a Bible, I would suggest that it was some sort of box or barrel used as a night-stand to hold a candle.

[24] *The Book of Margery Kempe*, ed. Staley, ll. 790–5.

expressed by the steward belies his assumption that he would be able to pass sound judgement within the chamber.

As *The Book of Margery Kempe* progresses, the chamber becomes more developed as a place of judgement, while it continues to be contrasted with the hall. When she visits York, Margery is made to eat and talk with 'many prestys and other men' (ll. 3135–6), before being led through the Archbishop's hall 'into hys chawmbyr evyn to hys beddys syde' (ll. 3138–9), a phrase which wonderfully conveys a sense of proximity and intimacy. Unlike in earlier chamber episodes, it seems that Margery has learned what is expected of her in chambers, volunteering to be examined by the Archbishop. The Archbishop of York's proximity to the bed while holding counsel is clearly significant. Whether the account is real or fictional, and whether the author meant that the Archbishop was in bed or next to it, the location of the conversation at the bed's side either made an impression on Margery, or was considered by the author to be a significant detail to fabricate. The presence of the bed is clearly designed to impress. Margery, upon being led to his bed's side, 'thankyd him of hys gracyows lordeschip' (l. 3139), indicating that she sees the bed's suggestion of intimacy as a token of honour on her part. However, there is a fine line between impressive and intimidating. Margery is in a chamber, complete with emphasised bed, with a number of powerful men, who are discussing her fate and to how much 'dawnger' (l. 3185) they should subject her. The implicit sexual threat will not be lost on an audience following Margery's struggle to remain chaste.[25] The Archbishop's choice to interrogate Margery from his bed, the emphasis on the bed in this passage combined with the fact that the reasons behind it are not explained or questioned confirms that the bed's place in this interaction is significant to a late medieval audience. The bed is both a symbol of power and a symbol of trust, designed to invite truth while making the Archbishop's judgement final.

The wider setting of the chamber had a relationship with counsel, which involved the sense of honesty and intimacy conveyed by the bed, combined with a sense of good judgement. As seen in *The Book of Margery Kempe*, the bed's physical or implied presence is essential to the veracity of the judgement. A fascinating portrayal of the chamber as locus for good judgement, with the bed at the centre, is found in *The Seven Sages of Rome*, in which the chamber and the bed are core to

[25] See ch. 5 below, pp. 140–6.

the emperor's son's education. The seven wise men build a specially designed 'halle […] with chaumbres sevene', in which they teach him the seven liberal arts, each in a different chamber.[26] The bed is central to his assessment, and so the passage is worth quoting in full:

Leues* thai tok, sextene,	*leaves
Of iuy, that were grene;	
Under ech stapel* of his bed,	*corner of the bed frame
(That he n'iste)* four thai hid.	*(when he was not in bed)
The child yede to bedde anight,	
And ros arliche amorewen, aplight.	
His maistres him bifore stode,	
Open hefd*, withouten hode.	*bare-headed
The child lokede here and tar,	
Up and doun, and everiwhar.	
Hise maistres askede what him was?	
"Parfai!*, he seide, a ferli** cas!	*by my faith! ** strange
Other* ich am of wine dronke,	*either
Other the firmament is i-sonke,*	*or the heavens have sunk
Other wexen is the grounde*	*or the ground has grown
The thickness of four leues rounde.	
So much, to-night, heyer I lai,	
Certes, thanne yisterdai."	
The maistres, tho, wel understode,	
He coude inow of alle gode.[27]	

The boy, once educated in the seven chambers, is wise enough to pass judgement in the chamber, even when the difference is no more than the thickness of four leaves. The fact that the bed is essential to the test of the boy's knowledge indicates that the bed is at the heart of all decisions in the chamber. The boy is able to judge the bed's position in relation to both 'the firmament' and 'the grounde', which is enough for the seven wise men to accept that 'he coude inow of alle gode'.

The idea of the council chamber as a site of truth and judgement, with the sense of trust and equality associated with one-to-one conversations in bed, is prevalent throughout late medieval English literature. Caxton's late fifteenth-century *The Four Sonnes of Aymon*, based on versions known in England from the thirteenth century, emphasises the importance of the chamber when official counsel is needed. When

---

[26] *The Seven Sages,* ed. Weber, ll. 175–7.
[27] Ibid., ll. 199–218.

King Yon receives the message that he is under attack by Charlemagne, he immediately goes:

> in to his Chambre, & eyghte erles wyth hym, and commaunded that the dores sholde be well shet and thenne they set theym all vpon a benche. And whan they were all set, the king Yon toke the worde & sayd in this maner 'Lordes, I beseche & require, vpon the feythe that ye owe to me, that ye gyve me good conseill to thonour of me not at my will, but bi rayson [...]'.[28]

Directly before this moment, the herald delivers his message orally in front of 'a ryght fayr company', so it is clear that the purpose of locking themselves in the chamber is not to avoid the court knowing about the impending attack.[29] Instead, they convene in the chamber in order to hold counsel. The use of the personal pronoun in 'his Chambre' suggests that this is not merely a room with a lockable door, but that it is specifically the king's chamber. The way in which the lords unquestioningly follow Yon into the chamber and arrange themselves upon a bench suggests that counsel in this manner has precedent, and is also reminiscent of courts of law. As no explanation is given, we can conclude that Caxton presumed an understanding of the implications of removing to a chamber with a few trusted followers. Linguistically, this counsel in the chamber is similar to another episode of counsel in the chamber in Caxton's works. In his 1489 translation of *Jason et Medée*, once Jason has performed all the feats required of him and returned to his chamber after an amorous encounter with Medea, he receives a visit from Hercules, Theseus, Mopsius and 'many other all of Grece'.[30] Like King Yon, King Oethes 'toke the wordes' and begins 'conceyle'.[31] After Jason's reply, in which he thanks Oethes for his 'conceyle', Mopsius 'toke the worde' to give further advice.[32] The similarities in vocabulary, repetition of 'toke the word' to indicate the order in which the characters are speaking, and the chamber as the site for 'conseill'/'conceyle' in both episodes indicate that Caxton recognised a semantic link between the chamber and counsel. The phrase 'toke the worde' appears occasionally in homilies and saints' lives, and usually

---

[28] *The Foure Sonnes of Aymon*, ed. Richardson, p. 204.

[29] Ibid., 203.

[30] R. le Fevre, *The History of Jason*, trans. W. Caxton, ed. J. Munro (London, 2004), p. 134.

[31] Ibid.

[32] Ibid.

refers to God's judgement. One example, from John Mirk's *Festial* from around 1380, is an instruction to the audience to 'take þe worde of þe iuges mowth'.[33] This emphasis on judgement is in keeping with the chamber setting.

The distinction between types of conversation in the hall and in the chamber is emphasised in the fourteenth-century romance *Octavian*. After Octavian's wife is wrongly accused of committing adultery, Octavian invites kings and dukes to a feast in the hall lasting seven days. During this time, 'there duellyn the kynges samen', feasting, singing and playing: everything but discussing the fate of the empress.[34] On the eighth day, 'the Emperoure to the chambir yode', surrounded by 'all the lordes' (ll. 211–12). 'All' implies that the same crowd of people who were feasting in the hall are now in the chamber. As the audience is the same, the choice of location is clearly important. Upon entering the chamber, Octavian asks directly for advice, emphasising the relationship between the chamber and counsel: 'I aske juggement of this with reson/ Of hir whate worthy were.' (ll. 218–19).

The socially acknowledged function of the bed as an important accessory to a chamber used as a meeting room is highlighted in an account by Agnes Paston, written around 1466. Agnes records the events following the death of her husband, in a document which Norman Davis describes as part of a draft will.[35] After William Paston I's death, Agnes sent for 'John Paston, William Bakton and John Dam', all beneficiaries mentioned in William's will.[36] What follows is an extraordinary example of how a chamber and bed form an important backdrop in a legal dispute, as edited by Davis:

> John Paston, John Dam, and I yode in-to the chambre whyche was Goodredys, and they desyred of me to see the wyll. I lete them see it, and John Dam redde it. And whan he had redde it John Paston walkyd vp and down in the chamer; John Dam and I knelyd at the beddys fete. […] Than the same tyme I lete them see the ded of yiffte which as I suppose was councell to all tho this dede was made on-to till I shewyd it

[33] J. Mirk, *Mirk's Festial: A Collection of Homilies by Johannes Mirkus*, ed. T. Erbe (London, 1905), p. 235.

[34] *Octavian*, in *Four Middle English Romances*, ed. H. Hudson, 2nd edn (Kalamazoo, 2006), ll. 187–204.

[35] London, British Library, Additional MS 34889, ff. 44v–45r.

[36] *Paston Letters and Papers*, ed. Davis I, 47; Ibid., pp. 45–6 describes the reading of the will while William was still alive, mentioning these three people as beneficiaries.

them. And soo they swore all sauf John Paston and John Damme. After that my sonne John Paston had neuer ryght kynde wordys to me.[37]

There are several significant aspects to this account. First, the people involved made a decision to go into a chamber to discuss the will, and specifically 'the chambre whyche was Goodredys'. 'Goodred' is probably the same 'Goodreed' referred to by John Paston III as 'the justys in my grauntfadyrs dayis', who was Justice of the King's Bench by 1434.[38] One explanation for the choice of chamber is that the will might have been left in Goodreed's chamber for safe-keeping. We know from probate inventories that goods were often stored in locked chests in chambers, and it would make sense for William Paston to have his will left with a fellow justice, disputes being likely to arise following the reading of the will.[39] Another reason is that the name 'Goodreed' has obvious connotations with 'good rede': good advice. It is evident that the people present at the meeting were not in agreement, as John Paston refused to speak kindly to his mother after the event. A chamber containing the bed of someone nominally associated with good judgement could well have been chosen deliberately for this 'councell', in an attempt to quell the dispute.

Secondly, the bed is conspicuously unoccupied. While there were more people present than those named in the chamber, as is clear from the comment that 'they swore all sauf Jon Paston and John Damme', the only people mentioned entering the chamber in the account are John Dam, John Paston and Agnes herself. Goodreed's silence in this account suggests that he was not present in the chamber. The absent presence of Goodreed is significant, given that the meeting was deliberately chosen to take place in a chamber associated with the justice, as it implies that they are treating the bed as a stand-in for the justice himself. The choice of setting for this meeting indicates that the chamber itself connotes a certain specific meaning. Their positions within the room show that the bed was significant to the participants: they go

[37] Ibid., pp. 47–8.
[38] Ibid., p. 561; *Original Letters Written during the Reign of Henry VI. Edward IV. And Richard III. By Various Persons of Rank and Consequence; Containing Many Curious Anecdotes, Relative to that Turbulent and Bloody, But Hitherto Dark, Period of our History; Elucidating, not only Public Matters of State, but Likewise the Private Manners of the Age: Digested in Chronological Order; with Notes, Historical and Explanatory; and Authenticated by Engravings of Autographs, Facsimiles, Paper Marks and Seals*, ed. J. Fenn. 4 vols. (London, 1789), IV, 435.
[39] See ch. 1 above, pp. 16–18.

out of their way not to sit on the bed, instead walking 'vp and down in the chamer' and kneeling 'at the beddys fete'. It is arguable that the reason why Agnes kneels at the foot of the bed may reside in the carvings or paintings on the bed, but the lack of detail here suggests that this is probably not the case. It could perhaps be a response to the will: Isabel Davis argues that elsewhere, kneeling is associated with being called.[40] There is perhaps the possibility that Agnes Paston and John Dam understand that they are being called for a particular purpose, as executors and beneficiaries, and kneeling befits the occasion. If so, the choice and specificity of the location of the act of kneeling – 'at the beddys fete' – is pertinent. If kneeling on the floor is simply a way to avoid sitting on the bed, one has to wonder why. One would imagine that if the chamber were a spare, and not really 'Goodredys' at all, there would be no qualms about sitting on the bed. The bed clearly had a high cultural value, in itself or in association with Goodreed. The lack of explanation for the choice of setting is testimony to the fact that the chamber is understood to be an obvious place for such an activity to take place.

Thirdly, the existence of the account itself emphasises Agnes' understanding of the bed and chamber as symbols of trust and good judgement. After consulting the original, I do not agree with Norman Davis' suggestion that it is part of a draft will, but instead read the account as one written purposefully as a record of events, setting it in a space associated with honesty and good judgement: literally 'gode rede'. Although it is about the reading of William Paston's will, it is not part of a will itself. Unlike many of the documents in the Paston collection, it is not a letter and shows no signs of having been sealed and sent to a recipient. It is a single leaf of paper containing only the account mentioned above, except for a note on the dorse, in a second hand, which reads 'p[ro] voluntate Will[elmi] Paston justiciarij'.[41] The key to the reason for the document's existence lies in the final few lines of the account. After the meeting had broken up and the body had been taken to Norfolk to be buried, John Paston, with John Dam, again tried to claim land which Agnes believed her husband wished to be given to someone else. Agnes then went to William Bakton and told him that she could not counter her husband's wishes. After this discussion,

[40] I. Davis, 'Calling: Langland, Gower, and Chaucer on Saint Paul', *Studies in the Age of Chaucer* 34 (2012), 53–97.
[41] Transcribed from BL, Additional MS 34889, f. 45v.

John Dam came to see her. Davis has transcribed the conversation as follows:

> After this cam John Damme and askyd me whyche of the justic[ys] my husbond trusted most, and sayde to me, 'Be ye not remembrid of suche a day my maister helde wyth Maryott at Norwych?' I sayd, 'Yis, for I was ther my-selfe'.[42]

Davis has changed 'the' in the original to 'ye' in his edition, and 'this' to 'Yis', arguing that the document is a copy of a now lost original, in which the graphs `þ' and `y' were not easily distinguished.[43] As editor he has also added punctuation, which is lacking in the original. The result is that the text is read as a word-for-word retelling of a conversation between Agnes Paston and John Dam, in which both speakers' voices are recorded. The word 'the' is a valid form of the second person singular pronoun, but it could have been a wrongly transcribed 'ye' or the result of eye-skip, as it is directly below 'this'. However, 'Yis' seems a far less likely intention: it is not a common spelling in the Paston vocabulary, and is equally not likely to be mistaken by a scribe for 'this' if it is a report of direct speech. [44] There are no speech marks in this document, though speech marks are used in other documents in the collection.[45] If we modify the punctuation added by Davis, the original 'this' makes more sense: 'John Damme […] sayde to me, "Be the not remembrid of suche a day my maister helde wyth Maryott at Norwych?". I sayde this, for I was ther my-selfe.'[46] In this way, we can read the document as a self-conscious attempt to record events: Agnes has caused this account to be written, in order to set the facts straight. Her description of the chamber and the bed within the account – given that the bed is understood to be a symbol of honesty and openness – and the specific position of Agnes in relation to the bed creates a sense of credibility. The centrality of the bed in this account, which was clearly written some time after the event, shows that Agnes clearly thought the bed had meaning within the context of the event. Agnes' remark that 'after that my sonne John Paston had neuer ryght kynde wordys

---

[42] *Paston Letters and Papers,* ed. Davis, I, 48.

[43] Ibid., p. 47.

[44] 'Yis' occurs once in a letter from John Paston II to John Paston III from 1471. London, British Library, Additional MS 43491, f. 16; *Paston Letters and Papers,* ed. Davis, I, 440.

[45] See, for instance, London, British Library, Additional MS 27445, f. 2v.

[46] My transcription, from London, British Library, Additional MS 34889, f. 45r.

to me' emphasises that such a meeting, held around a bed within a justice's chamber, has deep, long-lasting effects.

The bed and chamber's association with counsel, truth and trust is often played out in literature through the subversion of the socially constructed ideals, in order to provide narrative complications. This subversion highlights the extent to which the chamber had cultural meaning outside of everyday experience. For instance, the idea of the chamber as a recognised space for official counsel is highlighted and exploited in the mid fourteenth-century romance *Athelston*, which relies on the audience's understanding of the chamber as a space in which people are honest and give sound advice. There is an assumed understanding within the text that the chamber is the appropriate place for a certain type of counsel, as it is explained that Athelston often called his peer Egelond and his wife 'to boure and to halle,/ To counsayl whenne they scholde goo.'[47] As the editorial note points out, a distinction is being made here between public and private counsel.[48] The chamber's role as a space for private counsel is brought home when Wymound, the earl of Dover, uses the privacy of the chamber and its association with the truth to deceive Athelston:

> `Sere kyng,' he seide, `yiff it be thi wille
> To chaumbyr that thou woldest wenden tylle,
> Consayl for to here,
> I schal telle a swete tydande […]'
> […]
> And whenne that they were the chaumbyr withinne,
> False lesynges* he gan begynne   * lies
> On hys weddyd brother dere.[49]

Even though Wymound is already in conversation with Athelston, he insists that they remove to the chamber for counsel. While there is, up until this point, no obvious animosity between the characters, it is obvious that Athelston does not trust Wymound, as we are told that 'the kyngys herte than was ful woo/ With that traytour for to goo' (ll. 127–8). However, convention requires that he lead Wymound to his chamber and act upon his counsel, which leads to tragedy. After the conversation in the chamber, even though 'the kyng lovede

---

[47] *Athelston*, in *Four Romances of England*, ed. R. B. Herzman, G. Drake and E. Salisbury (Kalamazoo, 1999), ll. 77–8.
[48] Ibid., n. 77.
[49] *Athelston*, ed. Herzman et al., ll. 121–32.

[Egelond and his family] as hys lyff', while no reference is made to any particular affection between Athelston and Wymound, Athelston immediately desires that Egelond and his family be put to death, upon hearing Wymound's counsel.[50] The implication that the convention of retiring to the chamber for counsel is more powerful than the king's own authority and the fact that the conversation in the chamber is the motivating crisis of the narrative require the audience's existing knowledge that the chamber is a space for private, honest discussion, in order to be believable. A similar situation occurs in the prose *Brut*, when Constantine is visited by a Pict, who 'seyd þat he wolde speke with þe kyng pryuyly in Counceyl'.[51] Without delay, Constantine 'lete voyde his Chambre of þo men þat were with-Inne; & þo Abide þere nomo but þe king and þe Pohete, & made a Countenance as þey wolde speak to-gidere in his ere', at which moment he is stabbed to death and the murderer runs away.[52] In both tales, the convention of using a chamber for counsel is the downfall of the king, but in neither text is it suggested that the king made a bad decision in entering the chamber with a traitor. Instead, the incidents are treated as if there were no other option; the chamber is the obvious space for private counsel, and one must trust the advice given there.

The above episodes could be read as criticism of the secrecy that comes with conversing in chambers, perpetuating the anxiety which often arises around the chamber in other roles, such as in the role of the birthing chamber, often the location of secrecy and deceit in romance.[53] Underneath the narratives is the implicit argument that the chamber is not the ideal space for counsel while recognising the social expectations that it is so, calling into question the sagacity of making decisions within a closed chamber: should the conversation in *Athelston* have taken place in a more public space, Wymound's testimony could have been negated and if Constantine had not cleared his chamber, he might not have been defeated. Similar anxieties are present in *Octavian*, in which advice in the chamber is immediately acted upon, despite the wishes of all concerned and without any confirmation of the facts. As in *Athelston*, the characters are dismayed by the results of the counsel, as the king of Calabire unknowingly sentences his own daughter to

---

[50] Ibid., ll. 74, 170–4.
[51] *The Brut*, ed. Brie, p. 47.
[52] Ibid.
[53] See ch. 5 below, pp. 164–5; ch. 6 below, pp. 191–8.

death.[54] As discussed above, it is expected that fair judgement will take place in the chamber. *Octavian* highlights the fact that not all decisions made in chambers are wise, and warns against taking advice given in chambers at face value. Frequently in Middle English romance, the characters wrongly sentenced to death or exile are women and children or servants who are coerced by powerful characters to simulate evidence of a crime, often within a chamber.[55] Decisions made in the chamber by the ruler's peers in romances are often wrong, providing the complication in the narrative. This trope can be read as a comment on the ruling (and therefore judging) social elite, highlighting the problem with under-representation among those admitted into council chambers. The chamber, as the space in which decisions are often made in romance, physically separates people of different social strata.

The implicit arguments against counsel in the chamber are proof of the cultural understanding that the chamber and the bed are spaces for speech and sound judgement. The romances' wide audience suggests that this view was shared by people across society, so that even those who did not have a chamber of their own were aware of the chamber's association with free speech and the role of the bed in private and political discussion. As shall be explored in the following section, such an understanding informed and was informed by the public's understanding of royal administration.

The King's chambers

It is evident that the bed was a symbol of trust and intimacy, as the trope of two people talking in bed together was widespread in late medieval literature. The presence of the bed (whether actual, or implied by the name of the room) meant that the chamber was regarded as a space where a select group of people could talk in private and be honest. This understanding is also reflected in the way in which royalty and the public used the idea of the chamber, when in discourse with one another. I now explore the king's chambers, from the physical chamber in which the king slept, to the idea of the Privy Chamber and

---

[54] Hudson, ed., *Octavian*, ll. 220–31.
[55] See, for instance, *Le Bone Florence of Rome,* ed. Heffernan; *Erle of Tolous,* ed. Laskaya and Salisbury; *Octavian,* ed. Hudson; *Sir Tryamour,* in *Four Middle English Romances,* ed. H. Hudson, 2nd edn (Kalamazoo, 2006); *Le Chevelere Assigne,* ed. Gibbs; *Emaré,* ed. Laskaya and Salisbury.

the Chamber as a metaphor for a relationship between the sovereign and the state.[56]

The king's bed was at the very heart of late medieval English politics, both physically and metaphorically. A memorandum in the Close Rolls of March 1298 describing how John de Langeton, the chancellor, J. Drokenesford the keeper of the king's wardrobe and others met 'in camera Regus apud Sandwych' (Edward I's chamber at Sandwich), 'coram lecto [...] Regis' (before the king's bed), in the king's presence and by his order to deliver to the king's treasurer the seal that the king used in England when he was in Flanders under the chancellor's seal, to be kept in the treasury, and then Edward delivered his great seal that he had with him in Flanders to John de Langeton under 'sigillo suo manum sua': his privy seal by his own hand.[57]

This interaction took place the morning after Edward I's return from Flanders in order to plan a retaliatory campaign against William Wallace's Scottish army.[58] It is interesting that the King's chamber and bed are mentioned in the memorandum before we learn that Edward was also there. The focus placed on the chamber and bed in this account signifies the importance of the location: this exchange happened not only in the chamber, but at a specific place at the foot of the bed. The location of the event, in this case, is as important as the presence of King Edward himself. There was no doubt a practical aspect to the choice of location; there may have been a chest or strongbox at the foot of the bed, which could have travelled with Edward from Flanders, such as the one in Hieronymus Bosch's painting of *Death and the Miser*.[59] That being said, the account refers specifically to the bed, so it is clear that the bed is meaningful to the participants of the meeting. As seals were understood to carry the authority of their owners, the King would have had to have placed great trust in the keepers of the seals.[60]

---

[56] To avoid complication, I shall use 'chamber' to denote the physical room and 'Chamber' when referring to the royal administrative body.

[57] TNA C 54/115, m. 13; *CCR 1296–1302*, pp. 150–1.

[58] M. Prestwich, *Edward I* (New Haven, 1997), p. 479.

[59] H. Bosch, *Death and the Miser* (Washington: National Gallery of Art of the United States, *c.* 1485–90). Digitally reproduced at <http://www.nga.gov/content/ngaweb/Collection/art-object-page.41645.html> .

[60] There is some literature on the significance of medieval seals and their functions as signifiers of authority. See, for example, B. M. Bedos-Rezak, 'In Search of a Semiotic Paradigm: The Matter of Sealing in Medieval Thought and Praxis (1050–1400)', in *Good Impressions: Image and Authority in Medieval Seals*, ed. N. Adams, J. Cherry and J. Robinson (London, 2008), pp. 1–7; E. A. New, *Seals*

The use of the foot of the bed as the location for the exchange of seal matrices has several layers of meaning. First, the location of the event reflected the meaning of the activity. The exchange of seals signified that Edward is at home, as the seal 'used in England when he was in Flanders' was handed back and exchanged with the seal the King used in residence.[61] There was nowhere more indisputably 'at home' than in bed, so the foot of the bed served to emphasise Edward's return to rule, which was particularly important as the kingdom is under threat. Additionally, Edward's use of the Privy Seal to hand over the Great Seal reflects the setting, as the Privy Seal was intrinsically linked to the royal domestic sphere, in particular the chamber, by both its use and physical proximity.[62] The use of the Privy Seal to control the Great Seal mirrored the actions of the king in the chamber, controlling his household to ultimately control his kingdom. The king sanctioning the transaction by 'manum sua' with the Privy Seal in or next to his bed would have been no mean feat, as the wax would have had to have been heated to a specific temperature and the matrix applied with some force: an odd bedside activity unless the bed and chamber were considered particularly important within the transaction.[63]

The notional and physical beds associated with the king were treated with an enormous degree of respect. In the *Boke of Nurture*, John Russell's instructions for making the king's bed include a reminder to beat the featherbed 'without hurt', which implies a respect for the bed because its association with the king.[64] Similarly, instructions in the Household ordinances of Henry VII treat the bed as if it were standing in the king's stead. Every night, after several yeomen puts the bed together, an 'esquire for the body' sprinkles it with holy water, 'then shall the esquires and the ushers, and all others that were at the

and Sealing Practices (London, 2010); P. D. A. Harvey and A. MacGuiness, *A Guide to British Medieval Seals* (London, 1995); A. Compton Reeves, 'Bishop John Booth of Exeter', in *Traditions and Transformations in Late Medieval England*, ed. D. Biggs, S. D. Michalove, A. Compton Reeves (Leiden, 2002), pp. 125–44 (p. 133); the essays in *Seals and their Context in the Middle Ages*, ed. P. Schofield (Oxford, 2015).

61 *CCR 1296–1302*, p. 150.
62 A. R. Myers, 'Introduction: The Government of the Realm', in *English Historical Documents*, ed. A. R. Myers (Oxford, 1996), pp. 351–400 (pp. 372–5).
63 TNA C 54/115, m. 13; Cf. the ongoing research on sealing practices by Philippa Hoskin and Elizabeth New on the 'Imprint' project (University of Lincoln and University of Aberystwyth).
64 Russell, *Boke of Nurture*, p. 179.

making of the bedd, goe without the travers, and there to meete them bread, ale and wine; and soe to drinke altogether'.[65] The practice of sprinkling holy water on the bed was normally reserved for marital beds of newly-weds, or to heal the sick.[66] The sprinkling of the king's bed every night sanctifies the space, while suggesting that the bed is also a marriage bed, so that each night becomes a consummation of the marriage between king and state. The ritual eating and drinking following the making of the king's bed adds to the sense of ceremony. As discussed above, the bed was the socially constructed allotted space for communication and honesty between spouses. The king's bed was an extension of this: its use as a symbolic marriage bed suggests that decisions that the king makes in bed will be beneficial for both crown and state.

The so-called 'Paradise Bed' (Fig. 9), argued persuasively by Jonathan Foyle to be the marriage bed presented to Henry VII upon his marriage to Elizabeth of York, emphasises that the king's bed is a marriage bed between the sovereign and state, just as much as it is between husband and wife.[67] The French and English arms, displayed either side of the central Adam and Eve panel, and the red and white roses on either post at the foot of the bed show that their marriage is not only between Henry and Elizabeth, but also between France and England, York and Lancaster.[68] The Tree of Life on the tester, growing from Christ's cross flanked by supplicant representatives of evil (the lion and dragon) is a symbol of reconciliation after defeating the enemy.[69] Foyle suggests that the bed was made by German artisans, and may have been arranged by Anne of Beaujeu. Its provenance on the Continent further strengthens ties between the English crown and European politics, workers and traders.

---

[65] *A Collection of Ordinances*, p. 122.

[66] D. Wolfthal, *In and Out of the Marital Bed: Seeing Sex in Renaissance Europe* (New Haven, 2010), p. 3; Woolgar, *The Senses in Late Medieval England*, p. 44; G. Egan, 'Material Culture of Care of the Sick: Some Excavated Evidence from English Medieval Hospitals and Other Sites', in *The Medieval Hospital and Medical Practice*, ed. B. S. Bowers (Aldershot, 2007), pp. 65–76 (p. 74).

[67] My thanks to Jonathan Foyle, who has shared his ongoing research with me.

[68] See ch. 2 above, pp. 69–70.

[69] The image of a tree growing out of overthrown enemies is found in Psalm 91, which is the psalm read at Compline (bedtime).

Figure 9: The 'Paradise Bed', *c.* 1486. Photograph credit: Ian Coulson.

The bed's message of peace and reconciliation, combined with the idea of good judgement that is conveyed by the figures rejecting the serpent's fruit, would have made a strong impression on anyone who saw the bed, especially since it was brightly coloured and would presumably have supported bedclothes of equal grandeur. It would show the audience that the king's private relationship with his wife was inextricably linked with his public relationship with his kingdom. As the iconography suggests, the royal marriage bed was understood to play a part in the reconciliation of the warring factions. Bernard André, writing around 1500, describes the preparation of the event as follows:

A high council of all the best men of the kingdom was called, and it was decreed by harmonious consent that one house would be made from two families that had once striven in mortal hatred. Then wedding torches, marriage bed, and other suitable decorations were prepared.[70]

André's writing is notoriously embellished and unreliable but it is clear that the bed was understood to have been an important part of the preparation to unite two warring families.[71] The notion that 'all the best men of the kingdom' gathered together to plan the production of Henry VII's marriage bed indicates the dual nature of the king's bed: on the one hand, it is very private and intimate, designed for the consummation of the royal marriage and the conception of heirs; on the other, it is a matter of public discussion and political importance.

Written descriptions of an incident at the Tower of London in 1381 illustrate that the king's bed had a strong semantic association with authority. As discussed by Mark Ormrod, Jean Froissart's and Thomas Walsingham's somewhat contradictory accounts of the peasants' storm on the Tower of London are united in their indignation about the treatment of royal beds.[72] Whether the rebels 'entered into the chamber of the princess [of Wales] and broke her bed' or 'gained access singly and in groups to the chambers in the Tower, and arrogantly lay and sat on the king's bed while joking', it is clear that the beds were important symbols to both the rebels and the chroniclers.[73] The reported act of breaking into the Tower and gleefully jumping up and down on the royal beds is a powerful illustration of the wider understanding of the king's bed as a symbol of royal authority and intimacy. As Ormrod points out, the 'image of the broken bed therefore becomes a paradigm of the general attack on all tangible symbols of authority during the Peasants' Revolt'.[74] The bed's status as a tangible symbol of royal authority is thus reaffirmed by both the rebels and the chroniclers. I agree with Ormrod that the two chroniclers' use of the beds are political and, as they are somewhat contradictory, cannot be taken to be entirely true. However, it is fascinating that the bed should be portrayed as the victim in each of the accounts. Within the

---

[70] B. André, *The Life of Henry VII*, trans. D. Hobbins (New York, 2011), p. 34.

[71] D. Hobbins, 'Introduction' to André, *The Life of Henry VII*, p. v.

[72] W. M. Ormrod, 'In Bed with Joan of Kent', pp. 277–92; J. Froissart, *Oeuvres*, ed. J. B. M. C. Kervyn de Lettenhove, 25 vols. (Brussels, 1870–77), IX, 404; T. Walsingham, *Historia Anglicana*, ed. H. T. Riley, 2 vols. (London, 1863–4), I, 459; R. B. Dobson, *The Peasants' Revolt of 1381* (London, 1983), pp. 191, 171–2.

[73] Cited in Ormrod, 'In Bed with Joan of Kent', p. 278.

[74] Ibid., p. 281.

narratives, while Joan of Kent appears to emerge harassed but relatively unscathed by the rebels, her bed is broken to pieces.[75] The fact that
she has such a physical reaction to her bed being broken in Froissart's
account, swooning and remaining for a day and a night 'like a woman
half dead', implies that she has a strong connection with her bed.[76] As
shall be explored in Chapter 5, in late medieval English literature the
violation of the bed is symbolic of the violation of its owner or occupant.[77] As such, within the narrative Joan of Kent is symbolically, if not
physically, raped. Whether or not either account is true, the fact that
beds feature so prominently in both indicates the extent to which royal
beds were significant in their own right, and how deeply ingrained
that significance was in the late medieval psyche.

The presence of the bed in any chamber conveyed a sense of intimacy and openness, allowing meetings within the chamber to be
approached frankly and impressing upon those present that they were
respected enough to be admitted into the most intimate of spaces. The
bed thus allowed for the public performance of privacy within the
chamber, even if privacy itself was not available. There was a symbiotic relationship between the bed and chamber, in which the chamber
containing the bed made access restricted and lent it the appearance of
privacy, while the bed made the chamber intimate. Therefore, naming
a room 'chamber' implied that there was a bed within. As a result,
the term 'Chamber' began to be used to refer to council chambers that
did not contain beds. There are some references to council chambers
in documentary sources, such as the council chamber at Westminster,
mentioned in a grant made by Elizabeth Faucomberge in 1366, for example, a letter from Simon Stallworth to William Stonor in 1483, and
the council chamber discussed in the ordinances of Worcester.[78] The
sense of communication, trust and sound judgement was so strongly
affiliated with the term 'Chamber' that a physical chamber containing
a bed was not always necessary for the meaning to be evoked. One
example is the Court of the Star Chamber, named after the room with
the star-spangled ceiling, which qualifies the court in terms of the

---

[75] Froissart, *Oeuvres,* p. 404: 'Encore entrèrent cil glouton en la cambre de la
princesse et despécièrent tout son lit'.

[76] Ormrod, 'In Bed with Joan of Kent', p. 278.

[77] See ch. 5 below, pp. 157–69.

[78] *CCR, 1364–1369,* p. 310; *The Stonor Letters and Papers, 1290–1483,* ed. C. Lethbridge
Kingsford, 2 vols. (London, 1919), II, 160; *English Guilds,* ed. Toulmin Smith, pp.
377–409.

physicality of the chamber in which it meets, rather than the court's purpose.

The term 'Chamber' was used as a collective noun for the principal centre of administrative activity concerned with the personal needs of the king, regardless of the presence of any physical chamber.[79] It was also used within civic rhetoric to denote civic authority. For instance, the Council Chamber on Ouse Bridge, York, was used as the centre of local government in York. As is clear from fifteenth-century certificates of English parentage, it was referred to as the 'counsaill chambre upon Ouse brig', and the officials presiding were known as 'chamberleyns'.[80] Indeed, the term is still understood to signify 'a judicial, legislative, or deliberative assembly' or a 'large room used for the transaction of official business' today.[81] The King's Chamber did not have to be a room at all. However, its status as the administrative body most connected to the private life of the king clearly reflected the cultural meanings of its namesake.

It is apparent from royal household accounts that Henry VII's beds were made increasingly larger throughout his reign. While the Paradise Bed is 5 feet 6 inches wide, Wardrobe accounts of pillows and fustians suggest a bed at least six feet in breadth – if not twice that – by 1498.[82] Henry clearly thought that size mattered. As a bed signifies power it follows that the bigger the bed, the more the perceived power of its owner. It is also suggestive of a larger capacity for bedfellows: perhaps Henry's beds were expanding to accommodate a greater number of potential followers. People invited into his chamber

---

[79] The changing role of the administrative Chamber is outside the parameters of this book and analysed in detail elsewhere. See, for example, S. B. Chrimes, *An Introduction to the Administrative History of Medieval England* (Oxford, 1959), pp. 62–244; R. L. Storey, 'Gentleman-bureaucrats', in *Profession Vocation, and Culture in Later Medieval England: Essays Dedicated to the Memory of A. R. Myers*, ed. C. H. Clough (Liverpool, 1982), pp. 90–129 (p. 118); T. F. Tout, *Chapters in the Administrative History of Mediaeval England: The Wardrobe, the Chamber and the Small Seals*, 6 vols. (Manchester, 1933), I, 356.

[80] J. Raine, ed., *A Volume of English Miscellanies Illustrating the History and Language of the Northern Counties of England* (London, 1890), p. 43.

[81] *OED*, 'chamber', 4a and 4b.

[82] *The Great Wardrobe Accounts of Henry VII and Henry VIII*, ed. M. Haywood (Woodbridge, 2012), p. 5. Pillows are up to two yards long, while fustians are four and a half yards long. Allowing for fustians to be tucked in and depending on whether the bed had one pillow or two side by side, the bed would be either around six or twelve feet in width.

for counsel would thus be given the impression that the bed is ready and waiting. Although it displays a sense of intimacy, it also hints at sexual threat, asserting the king's dominance over his courtiers even while suggesting that they can speak equally to him. Accounts of his death indicate that the king's physical bed and chamber were inextricably linked with the running of the country and the idea of the king's Chamber. If we are to believe the illustration in Thomas Wriothesley's account of Henry VII's decease (Fig. 10), by the time Henry was dying,

Figure 10: Illustration depicting Henry VII on his death bed surrounded by courtiers, by Sir Thomas Wriothesley (d. 1534). © The British Library Board. BL Add. 45131, f. 54r.

his bed was large enough to fit fourteen people comfortably around it.

The presence of the three physicians still holding urine bottles for diagnosis, as well the depiction of William Fitzwilliam closing Henry's eyes, suggests that Henry is only just dead. This illustration emphasises the contrasting meanings of the king's chamber: on the one hand it captures an incredibly intimate situation in which the king dies in his own bed, in his own chamber, surrounded by followers raising their hands in respect to him; on the other, this deeply personal moment has a large audience of people physically present, as well as everyone who later saw the manuscript. The presence of the coats of arms identifying certain figures around the bed emphasises that this is a political event. Even in death, there is no peace in the king's bed.

Despite the number of people present at Henry VII's death bed, the chamber was secure enough and so culturally laden with the idea of keeping secrets that, once the king had died, the attendees managed to keep his death secret for around two days while they haggled over positions and got royal affairs in order before breaking the news to the wider court.[83] Wriothesley reports that, during this time, Richard Weston, Groom of the Privy Chamber, and the Lord Chancellor, Archbishop William Warham, attended the king's chamber as if to seek private counsel with him, emerging 'with good countenance'.[84] This public display of private counsel with the king befits the role of the king's chamber and also shows that nothing the king did in bed was truly private and intimate: even though he was dead, his reported actions within the chamber were still in the control of others, to maintain a public image of normalcy. The Groom of the Privy Chamber's role in this public deception is interesting, as it suggests that the king's Chamber continued to operate even when the king himself was unable to do so.

The Groom of the Privy Chamber and the Chamberlain are roles which recall how the royal chamber was used in early medieval England. From at least the tenth century, bedthegns and burthegns or hrægelthegns, like the *cubicularii* or *camerarii* of the Continent, were appointed to be in charge of the king's chamber, all valuables stored within it, and all administration connected to it.[85] While the late medieval roles extended beyond the walls of the chamber, they continued to be linguistically associated with the physical space.

As discussed in detail by Christian Liddy, the term 'Chamber' was adopted 'at certain critical moments' by the cities of London, York,

---

[83] The exact length of time Henry's death was kept secret is disputed. See S. J. Gunn, 'The Accession of Henry VIII', *Historical Research* 64.155 (1991), 278–88; Robert Hutchinson, *Young Henry: The Rise of Henry VIII* (London, 2011), pp. 100–4.

[84] London, British Library, Additional MS 45131, f. 52v; cited in Hutchinson, *Young Henry*, p. 101.

[85] Chrimes, *An Introduction*, pp. 8–9; Tout, *Chapters*, pp. 70–1; L. M. Larson, *King's Household in England before the Norman Conquest* (Madison, 1904), pp. 124, 128–33; R. L. Poole, *The Exchequer in the Twelfth Century* (Oxford, 1912), pp. 22–6.

Coventry and Bristol to articulate their relationship with the Crown.[86] London and York referred to themselves as the 'King's Chamber', Coventry called itself 'the Prince's Chamber' and Bristol fashioned itself as 'the Chamber of the queens of England'.[87] It is clear that, while neither royal administration nor the cities occupied a real, physical chamber, the cultural meanings of the chamber as a space of administration and a space in which particular working relationships were forged extended beyond the chamber walls. The term 'Chamber', in reference to an administrative body or a city, is interesting because the term is, to an extent, reflexive. The metaphor was perpetuated not only by the king, but also by those bodies seeking to identify themselves as 'Chamber': namely, members of the court and city officials. As such, the chamber was in the unusual position of having been given a voice, so that some aspects of what a chamber meant to late medieval society were articulated by those attempting to identify themselves as part of the Chamber. In an account of the day of Edward III's death in June 1377, John Philpot is described addressing Richard of Bordeaux (soon to be Richard II) 'on the behalfe of the Citizens, and City of London, that you will have recommended to your good grace, the City your chamber'.[88] The address outlines the role ascribed to the City, as the King's Chamber: existing for 'the will and pleasure' of the king, while citizens were willing to lay down their goods and lives. Richard, for his part, is asked to take up residence within London and to keep the peace between London and the Lancastrians. Regardless of whether Maidstone's report is an accurate representation of Philpot's address, we can infer from it that the Chamber was understood to have certain standards it must uphold, but that the occupant of the chamber must also play his part by remaining in occupancy. After all, what good is a chamber without its occupant?

The cities' attempts to fashion themselves as the royal Chamber indicate that the idea of the Chamber was much more powerful than any physical chamber alone. It was also an idea which was self-perpetuating, as it is expressed by dignitaries within the cities, rather than being forced upon them by the Crown. As Liddy discusses, the

---

[86] C. D. Liddy, 'The Rhetoric of the Royal Chamber in Late Medieval London, York and Coventry', *Urban History* 29.3 (2002), 323–49 (p. 324).

[87] Ibid., pp. 323, 349.

[88] J. Stow, *Annals of England to 1603* (London, 1603), p. 440; *Chronicon Angliae, ab Anno Domini 1328 Usque ad Annum 1388. Auctore Monacho Quodam Sancti Albani*, ed. E. M. Thompson (London, 1874), pp. 146–7.

desire to be the royal Chamber was expressed very publicly: on 21 August 1392, Londoners put on a series of pageants to welcome Richard II and his queen back to the city.[89] Upon entering the city Richard was met by the royal warden, who proclaimed that 'with genuine tears, the city prays unceasingly that the merciful king will return to his chamber [...] Let not the bridegroom hate the bridal chamber which he has always loved.'[90] This reference to the bridegroom is reminiscent of the Song of Songs and casts the king as Christ, 'the merciful king', while London is simultaneously the bride and the bridal chamber.[91] In addition, it recalls Psalm 18, in which the sun is described 'as a bridegroom coming out of his bride chamber'.[92] Within the Psalm, God's power is described using the vocabulary of kingship. With love for the bridal chamber comes a promise of impact stretching 'into all the earth [...] to the ends of the world', ruling all, providing wisdom and making sound judgements.[93] Maidstone's plea emphasises the relationship between crown and state. Just as the holy water sprinkled on the king's bed evoked a marriage bed, the king's chamber was a 'bridal chamber'.[94] The chamber was thus central in holding the relationship between Richard and the kingdom together. As discussed above, one of the roles of the marriage bed was considered to be as a space for intimate, honest and equal communication between husband and wife. As such, the city's adoption of bridal chamber vocabulary was designed not only to bring the city closer to the king, but also to have more political sway over the king and be privy to more information than other cities. Although the invitation to accept London as the king's chamber was a request, there was also an element of threat to it. This

---

[89] Liddy, 'The Rhetoric of the Royal Chamber', p. 332.

[90]   Hoc rogat assidue lacrimis madefacta deintus,
         Mitis ut in cameram Rex velit ire suam.
         Non laceret, non dilaniet pulcherrima regni
         Moenia, nam sua sunt, quicquid et exstat in hiis.
         Non oderit thalamum sponsus quem semper amavit,
         Nulla subest causa cur minuatur amor.

     R. Maidstone, 'De Concordia', in *Alliterative Poem on the Deposition of King Richard II; Ricardi Maydiston De Concordia Inter Ric. II et Civitatem London*, ed. T. Wright (London, 1838), ll. 142–6; translation from Liddy, 'The Rhetoric of the Royal Chamber', p. 333.

[91] See ch. 2 above, pp. 45–7.
[92] Psalms 18.6.
[93] Psalms 18.4–5, pp. 8–10.
[94] Maidstone, 'De Concordia', l. 145.

speech at the city gates calls to mind the *hortus conclusus*, 'a garden enclosed, a fountain sealed up', the implication being that the king will only have access to the benefits the City can offer if he is willing to reside inside the walls.[95] The public procession and pageantry would have ensured that it was noticed by all levels of London society, many of whom would not have had a chamber to call their own. In this way, even those who might not have encountered a chamber would have still become part of the king's Chamber.

The physical impact on the citizens of York when it fashioned itself as the king's Chamber in the early 1390s is evident from the Close Rolls of 30 May, 1392. The Rolls clearly show the extent to which members of the public would have been affected by the adoption of the term 'Chamber', as suddenly all 'causes affecting the king and the estate of the realm' moved to York to 'hold pleas summonses, accounts and processes, and to do other things to their office pertaining, and to the treasurer to send and have there at that day all pleas, records, processes, rolls, writs and memoranda of the exchequer'.[96]

Further writs summoned the justices of the Bench, the king's clerk and 'Roger de Saperton warden of the Flete prison', as well as 'all prisoners in his custody for whatsoever cause'.[97] By 1393, York was referring to itself as 'your city and Chamber of York'.[98] In this way, even though Richard was not often in residence in York during this time, the administrative members of the royal household were in residence in the self-styled Chamber of York, and their presence undoubtedly affected the citizens, as they physically took up space and had to be reminded not to take over canons' houses. There is some debate surrounding York's use of the term 'the king's chamber', whether it was symptomatic of York's growing self-confidence owing to its financial clout within the country at the time or resulting from York's political insecurities and its somewhat sycophantic desire to be more like London.[99] Regardless of its initial motives, its association with the crown

---

[95] Song of Songs 4.12.
[96] *CCR, 1389–1392*, pp. 464–76.
[97] Ibid.
[98] TNA, SC8/103/5147. Cited in Liddy, 'The Rhetoric of the Royal Chamber', p. 335.
[99] Ibid., p. 335; R. B. Dobson, 'The Crown, the Charter, and the City, 1396–1467', in *The Government of Medieval York: Essays in Commemoration of the 1396 Royal Charter*, ed. S. Rees Jones (York, 1997), pp. 34–55 (pp. 42–4); C. D. Liddy, *War, Politics and Finance in Late medieval English Towns: Bristol, York and the Crown,*

and its label 'the king's chamber' would ensure that the concept of the chamber was significant to those living in York in or outside of chambers.

City authorities characterising their city as royal Chambers at various points in political history were clearly doing so with the understanding that the king's chamber was a positive space with an intimate relationship with the king, and should be cultivated. They emphasise trust and support, while highlighting the symbiotic relationship between the king and his (physical and metaphorical) chambers: a chamber would offer protection and comfort to the king, but required his occupancy in order to do so. While the bed was obviously not present in this metaphorical Chamber, its presence was implied through the desire for mutual communication and faithfulness, such as the idea of a bed would offer.

In bed with the King

The relationship between the physical and metaphorical chambers was symbiotic, and relied on the cultural understanding that the chamber signifies intimacy. This chapter has shown that the bed's role as a space for honest, equal communication was vital to the roles of both physical and metaphorical chambers. It is clear from abundant literary sources that the bed was understood to lend voice to the voiceless. Its role within marriage as a space in which a couple could converse on equal terms is key. Its presence in the chamber meant that the chamber was understood to be a place ideally suited for private counsel and administration. The use of the bed as a locus for some official activities, such as Margery Kempe's inspection by the archbishop of York and the Pastons' dispute over William Paston I's will, indicates that the bed is an important component of the space, even in a chamber used mainly for counsel where the bed was not used for sleep. Such associations naturally meant that the king's chamber, while giving the impression of intimacy, was noticeably public and political, an idea which is reflected by the bed.

1350–1400 (Woodbridge, 2005), pp. 63–4; W. M. Ormrod, 'York and the Crown Under the First Three Edwards', in *The Government of Medieval York: Essays in Commemoration of the 1396 Royal Charter*, ed. S. Rees Jones (York, 1997), pp. 14–33 (pp. 31–3).

In addition to, and sometimes in the place of, a physical chamber, the king had a Chamber which shared the nuances and implications of the term 'chamber' without requiring a physical room containing a real bed. This metaphorical Chamber had a private relationship with the king similar to that of a real chamber, and provoked cities to adopt the term at certain political points in order to capitalise on a special relationship with the Crown. As each of these versions of chambers occurred simultaneously, they each affected the cultural meanings of each other, so that the increased status, trust and special relationships resulting from cities being called the king's Chamber increased awareness of the importance placed on the Chamber. In turn, the term 'Chamber' metonymically referred to the administrative bodies in charge of the finances and affairs associated with the king's own household and also increased the social value of its namesake, the physical chamber. The power conveyed through individuals' chambers was, therefore, partly the result of the political clout of the administrative Chamber. Because of this association, people such as the dignitaries in *The Book of Margery Kempe* and the beneficiaries of William Paston I conducted their affairs in chambers, as these were associated with a sense of trust, counsel and justice. Meetings in chambers thus signified validity, which could be a factor in the increased practice of meeting in chambers, in order that official interaction would be taken seriously. This practice, in turn, elevated the status of those with access to chambers.

While the addressee of the precepts upon which this book is structured might go out into the world in order to work, he will never really escape the chamber, as the king's chamber extended far out into the world. We find proof of this reach shown visually by the depiction of the death of Offa in London, British Library, Harley MS 2278 (Fig. 11). There is no narrative context for this outdoor scene. In fact, the corresponding illustration in London, British Library, Yates Thompson MS 47, f. 15r, shows a detailed interior of a chamber. Instead, the Harley depiction of Offa's last actions as king, handing over his signet ring from his bed in a manner reminiscent of Edward I's exchange of seals, inexplicably situated in a pastoral scene, sums up the cultural meanings of the bed and chamber in relation to politics and personal communication. Far from losing his power towards the end of his life, King Offa's influence upon the kingdom from his bed was far-reaching. While one might imagine that the thick walls of a king's chamber, located in the deepest space of a house, might prevent a king's voice from a sick-bed from being heard, the reverse appears to be true. The absence of chamber walls in this illustration makes the king's relationship with his chamber very clear: the whole kingdom was the king's chamber, and the bed was at its very heart.

Figure 11: Illustration depicting the death of King Offa, *c.* 1434–9. © The British Library Board. BL Harley 2278, f. 21r.

4

'Goo To Thy Bed Myrely/ And Lye Therin Jocundly'

As I discussed in the previous chapter, the chamber was understood by late medieval English society to be a space in which honest advice and counsel could be sought and which promoted communication between couples or between the main occupant of the chamber and those who worked in the space. This sense of trust and intimacy came from the physical or, in the case of some council chambers and administrative bodies, perceived presence of the bed. This assumption is due to the idea that people shed their outer trappings as they go to bed, and so were more truly themselves in the chamber than anywhere else. Associations with intimacy made the chamber a suitable space for serious discussion, but also for fun and relaxation. In this chapter I focus on the cultural understanding of the chamber as an intimate space for communal and solitary leisure.

Merry and jocund in the chamber

Elenge* is the halle, ech day in the wike,   *desolate/sad
Ther the lord ne the lady liketh noght to sitte.
Now hath ech riche* a rule – to eten by hymselve   *wealthy person
In a pryvee parlour for povere mennes sake,
Or in a chambre with a chymenee, and leve the chief halle
That was maad for meles, men to eten inne,
And al to spare to spille that spende shal another.[1]

---

[1] Langland, *Piers Plowman* x, ll. 96–102; 'al to spare to spille that spende shal another' suggests that with no supervision, the men in the halls will talk about matters ignorantly and influence each other.

Dame Studie's lament in *Piers Plowman* is a testament to the fact that the chamber was used increasingly in the later Middle Ages as a space for social activities with a select group of people, away from the hall and its associated social conventions. Not only does this passage indicate that high-status people preferred to eat in the chamber, but it also implies that the hall itself was 'elenge' (desolate and sad) every day of the week through lack of use. The reference to the hall as the space for 'men to eten inne', as opposed to the space designated for the lord and lady, reflects the growing number of chambers built in late medieval England and the social segregation which ensued.[2] The chamber's association with power and high status, which came from the householder having enough money and space to have a specific room which separated a permanent bed structure from the rest of the house, meant that any social gatherings within the chamber were done self-consciously, as a performance of power and social status, admitting guests into that semantically charged inner sanctum. In such situations, the bed would be on show in the chamber, serving as both a status symbol and a symbol of intimacy, conveying to the guests that they were trusted and valued enough to view the object most intimately connected to its owner's body and soul.

Though the hall was 'elenge', the chamber was a space for merriment, not only because it was a space separated from the rest of society, but because it was a space in which one spends time, according to the precepts, between supper and sex. Sex in late medieval England was considered most appropriate when it was in bed with one's spouse, resulting in the birth of a child.[3] Common understanding was that both parties should enjoy their sexual encounter in order to conceive. As such, the course of events dictated by the 'Arise Early' precepts require merriment at bedtime, given that the most appropriate time for sex was considered to be in the evening.[4] The adverb 'myrely' conveys both joy and timeliness. For instance, Chaucer uses 'murily' to connote the idea of a good and timely entrance: in 'The Shipman's Tale', 'morwe cam, and forth this marchant rideth/ To Flaundres-ward; his prentys wel hym gydeth;/ Til he came into Brugges murily'.[5] In his 'The Prioress's

---

[2] Emery, *Greater Medieval Houses of England and Wales*, p. 32; Grenville, *Medieval Housing*, p. 86; Sheeran, *Medieval Yorkshire Towns*, p. 149; Woolgar, *The Senses in Late Medieval England*, p. 248.

[3] See ch. 5.

[4] See ch. 5, p. 156.

[5] G. Chaucer, 'The Shipman's Tale', in *Riverside Chaucer*, ed. Benson, 201–8, ll. 299–301.

Tale', 'murily' is used to express joyfulness and sweetness: 'this litel child, as he came to and fro,/ Ful murily than wolde he synge and crie/ O Alma redemptoris everemo'.[6] 'Jocundly' carries with it a sense of joy and delight.[7] While it is obvious that not all merriment in the chamber was a precursor to sex, the sexual potential inherent in the chamber made it a particularly appropriate space in which to have fun.

It is clear from linguistic evidence that the chamber was understood to be a space for play. Just as our modern euphemism for sex, 'sleeping together', comes from the fact that the activity takes place in the space predominantly associated with sleep, so that one bedroom-related activity is exchanged with another, the use of the Middle English verb 'pleien' to refer to sex suggests that 'playing' is an acceptable chamber activity for a late medieval couple. To name but a few examples of 'play' used to denote sex, Robert of Gloucester's late thirteenth-century *Metrical Chronicle*, transmitted in several later medieval manuscripts, recounts that Locrinus 'so longe [...] pleide such game/ Þat hii adde an doȝter'; in the fifteenth-century *Prose Merlin*, Gyomar and Morgan le Fey 'fellen down on a grete bedde and pleyde the comon pley'; and in Chaucer's 'The Merchant's Tale', January tells May that 'it is no fors how longe that we pleye;/ In trewe wedlok coupled be we tweye/ [...] For we han leve to pleye us by the lawe'.[8] When it is not being used euphemistically, the verb 'pleien' is much like our modern verb 'to play', referring to games, gambling, joking, sports, dramatic or musical performance, entertaining and general merrymaking.[9] Its euphemistic usage in reference to sex strongly suggests that at least some of these activities were understood to take place in the chamber.

The idea of the chamber as both an appropriate space for socialising and a social space that was charged with meaning are conveyed through manuscript illumination. For instance, the presentation scene in Christine de Pizan's so-called *The Book of the Queen* shows the chamber as an intimate social setting (Fig. 12). This illustration was designed to give the audience the impression that the book containing it was presented to Isabeau in her own chamber, suggesting an intimacy between Isabeau and Christine de Pizan. It is clear that Isabeau's bed in this illumination is held in high regard, both by the artist and

---

[6] G. Chaucer, 'The Prioress's Tale', in ibid., 209–12, ll. 552–4.

[7] 'jocund(e)li (adv.)', *MED*.

[8] R. of Gloucester, *The Metrical Chronicle of Robert of Gloucester*, ed. W. Aldis Wright (London, 1887), p. 44; 'The Tournament at Logres; King Lots and His Sons; and Morgan and Gyomar', in *The Prose Merlin*, ed. J. Conlee (Kalamazoo, 1998), l. 86; Chaucer, 'The Merchant's Tale', ll. 1835–41.

[9] My thanks to Emma Martin, University of York, whose current Ph.D. research confirms this definition.

Figure 12: Miniature depicting Christine de Pizan presenting the book to Isabeau
of Bavaria, *c.* 1410–14. © The British Library Board. BL Harley 4431, f. 3r.

the figures seated in the chamber. It takes up almost a third of the
illustration and the chamber, and yet it is kept at a respectful distance
by everyone in the chamber. A smaller bed demands similar respect: it
is occupied by Isabeau, while all others present sit cramped in the space
between the two beds. While the attention is on Christine presenting
the book, a female figure wearing a dress co-ordinating with the beds
looks towards Isabeau's bed behind her, as if in awe of its presence.
She wears a similar headdress to Christine, which suggests that the
woman is part of Christine's party, rather than Isabeau's entourage,
who wear similar headgear to their queen. The link between the beds
and the visitors, both through colour and the woman's gaze, gives
the impression that they have been deliberately received in Isabeau's
chamber and are consciously aware of the implications of the choice
of space.

Literary evidence further suggests that the presentation of books
to patrons often took place, or was understood to take place, in the

patron's chamber. Jean Froissart's account of the presentation of a book of poems to Richard II in 1395 locates the event in Richard's chamber:

> [...] voult veoir le roy le livre que je luy avoie apporté. Si le vey en sa chambre, car tout pourveu je l'avoie, et luy mis sur son lit. Il l'ouvry et regarda ens, et luy pleut très-grandement [...] [Il] regarda dedens le livre en plusieurs lieux ey y lisy, car moult bien parloit et lisoit le franchois, et puis le fist prendre par ung sien chevallier qui se nommoit messire Richard Credon et porter en sa chambre de retraite.

> (The King wished to see the book I had brought him. So he saw it in his chamber, because I had laid it ready on his bed. He opened it and looked inside, and it pleased him very greatly [...] He looked inside the book and read it in several places, because he could speak and read French well, and then he gave it to one of his knights, named Sir Richard Credon, to carry it to his inner chamber.)[10]

As there is a reference to an inner chamber, the bed in this chamber is clearly a state bed, such as those discussed in the previous chapter, whose function is to be present in the receiving chamber to denote power and intimacy. Not only is the book presented in the chamber, but it is placed ready on the bed, as if the bed is the obvious place in which to read a book, and, like the colour matching in Fig. 12, that there is a relationship between the book and the bed. It is interesting that it is Froissart himself who places the book on the bed, delivering it straight to the space most intimately associated with the king. Richard then shows his approval of the book by causing it to be delivered to his inner chamber where, one can presume, he will read it in bed. The actions of both Froissart (who places the book ready on the bed) and Richard (who sends it to his inner chamber) are compelling evidence that there was a culturally understood link between beds and books. Andrew Taylor argues that the chamber was 'a realm of private solace in which dreaming and reading intermingle'.[11] The connection between reading and beds will be discussed later, but this idea does not fit entirely with what is happening in Froissart's description: the presentation is far from private and the meeting, at least from Richard's point of view, is work rather than rest.[12] However, the intimate setting

---

[10] Froissart, *Oeuvres*, xv, 167. My translation; See also Taylor, 'Into His Secret Chamber', p. 41.

[11] Taylor, 'Into His Secret Chamber', p. 42.

[12] See ch. 3.

of the chamber and the idea of reading from the bed conveys a sense of bedtime intimacy. Considering this description alongside Christine de Pizan's presentation and the miniature depicting Henry VIII reading his psalter in a chamber in London, British Library, Royal MS 2 A xvi (Fig. 7), we can also see a pattern of patrons wishing to be seen reading and receiving books in the chamber.[13] As well as flattering the writers, presentations within the chamber shape how people were to see the patrons. As the bed and chamber were considered to be spaces in which one sheds outside trappings at the door, being seen reading books in the chamber suggests that their appreciation of the literature was genuine, and that they engaged in worthwhile reading habits.

Social gatherings in the chamber were not only reserved for the presentation of books to royalty. As discussed in Chapter 1, part of the demand for richly decorated bedclothes came from the owners' knowledge that they would be on view to members of society of a similar social status. In some cases, such as illness or pregnancy, the chamber would become a reception room in which the expecting or afflicted would receive visitors from their beds.[14] For instance, Richard Bryan, in a letter of 1479, describes how he visited the sick bed of Betson, who 'made us gode chere as a sike man might by countenaunce notwithstanding', while John Paston II in 1472 thought that his mother would be received 'into my ladyes chambre' during her lying-in period.[15] However, entertainment in the chamber was not restricted to the infirm or the physically or socially incapacitated. The manuscript containing the version of the precepts upon which this book is structured contains evidence of word and dice games played in the household which would make the most sense if they were played in the chamber.[16] As Nicola McDonald argues, such games 'were remarkable for their deliberate disruption of order'.[17] The chamber was a space in which normal order was suspended, so the most appropriate place to play them would have been within the chamber. Indeed, the injunction to 'goo to thy bed myrely' in the middle of a double-page spread containing cipher puzzles on its left and the first eight rolls of a dice game

[13] See Fig. 12, p. 114; Fig. 7, p. 61.
[14] See ch. 6, pp. 192–4.
[15] *The Stonor Letters and Papers*, ed. Kingsford, II, 87; *Paston Letters and Papers*, ed. Davis, I, 454.
[16] New Haven, Yale University, Beinecke Library MS 365; see McDonald, 'Fragments of (*Have Your*) *Desire*'.
[17] Ibid., p. 239.

McDonald calls *Have Your Desire* on the right situates the games in the chamber: the only space set aside for merriment by the precepts.[18] McDonald argues that the anti-feminist ciphers function to allow women playing the game to challenge or subvert misogyny, while *Have Your Desire* aims to arouse and occasionally satisfy amorous desire. As such, given that the function of merriment within the chamber is part of the natural daily progression between sleep and sex, such games, disruptive though they may be, were not only allowed within the chamber, but necessary to the chamber's purpose.

Much of what we know about games and leisure activities comes from laws made to control or prevent them. We know from these laws that games played in one's own chamber were considered very differently to games played in more inclusive spaces. Public game playing was apparently met with disapproval and regular parliamentary efforts were made to prevent people from playing games of cards, dice, quoits and other similar pastimes.[19] For instance, the 1388 Statute of Cambridge forbade 'les jeues as pelotes silon a meyne come a piee, & les autres jeus appellez Coytes dyces gettre de pere keyles & autres tielx jeues importunes' (games involving throwing or kicking a ball, and other games called quoits, dice, casting stones, keyles and other such importune games) in favour of archery practice, which had been made compulsory for all boys and men in 1363.[20] It is clear that games were being played, as in April 1388, Robert Hykelyng was granted 4d. a day for maintenance, provided 'he play no more at dice or practice

---

[18] New Haven, Yale University, Beinecke Library MS 365, ff. 1v–2r; reproduced in McDonald, 'Fragments of (*Have Your) Desire*', p. 240.

[19] P. R. Caille, 'The Problem of Labour and the Parliament of 1495', in *The Fifteenth Century V: Of Mice and Men: Image, Belief and Regulation in Late-Medieval England*, ed. L. Clark (Woodbridge, 2005), pp. 143–56 (pp. 153–4); C. Dyer, *An Age of Transition? Economy and Society in England in the Later Middle Ages* (Oxford, 2005), p. 237; M. K. McIntosh, *Controlling Misbehaviour in England, 1370–1600* (Cambridge, 1998), pp. 96–107; For a simple overview of the types of games played, see C. Reeves, *Pleasures and Pastimes in Medieval England* (Stroud, 1995), pp. 73–80.

[20] *The Statutes of the Realm. IV (1377–1504)*, p. 57 (my translation); J. A. Tuck, 'The Cambridge Parliament, 1388', *The English Historical Review* 331 (1969), 225–243 (p. 228); M. E. Mate, 'Work and Leisure', in *A Social History of England, 1200–1500*, ed. R. Horrox and W. M. Ormrod (Cambridge, 2006), pp. 275–92 (p. 283); N. Orme, *Medieval Children* (New Haven, 2003), p. 183; M. Prestwich, 'Training', in *The Oxford Encyclopaedia of Medieval Warfare and Military Technology*, ed. C. J. Rogers, 3 vols. (Oxford, 2010), I, 272–3; C. J. Nolan, *The Age of Wars of Religion, 1000–1650: An Encyclopedia of Global Warfare and Civilisation* (Westport, 2006), p. 547.

art or deed of hazard'.[21] In 1439, a hosier in Southwark was fined for playing a game called 'le Closshe' in public.[22] In 1461, it was illegal for anyone of lower estate to undertake in 'dicyng or pleiyng at the cardes' except during the twelve days of Christmas.[23] Further proof that people continued to play games is found in the Parliament Roll of 1478, which states that 'after the lawes of this lond, no persone shuld use any unlawfull pleys, as dise, coyte, foteball, and such like pleys' as the pursuits distract people from archery practice, and bans 'closshe, keyles, halfbowle, handyn and handowte, and quekeborde', because 'by the means therof dyvers and many murdres, robberies, and other felonyes full heynous, oftetymes be commytted'.[24] By the late fifteenth century, the rules became more nuanced towards the aristocracy and domestic space. The statute of 1495 stated that 'noon apprentice nor servant of husbondry laborer or servaunt artificer pley at the Tables [...] ner at the Tenys Closshe Dise Cardes Bowles nor any other unlaufull game in no wise out of Cristmas, and in Cristmas to pley oonly in the dwelling house of his maister or where the maister of any of the said servauntes is p[re]sent'.[25] The same law was still in force in 1541–2.[26]

In almost all of these cases, the focus was on people of lower orders playing games, whether in public or in their masters' houses. As Marjorie McIntosh argues, while the laws were ostensibly to encourage archery practice, they also served to restrict gatherings of the young and poor, in an attempt to prevent further peasant uprising.[27] The anomalous law of 1478, that 'no persone shuld use any unlawfull pleys', was soon amended so that the wording again contained

---

[21] *CPR, 1385–1389*, p. 433.

[22] *CPR, 1436–1441*, p. 306.

[23] 'Edward IV: Parliament of November 1461, Text and Translation', ed. W. M. Ormrod in *The Parliament Rolls of Medieval England*, ed. C. Given-Wilson et al. (Leicester, 2005) <http://www.sd-editions.com/PROME> [accessed 25 July 2013].

[24] 'Edward IV: Parliament of January 1478, Text and Translation', ed. W. M. Ormrod in *The Parliament Rolls of Medieval England*, ed. C. Given-Wilson et al. (Leicester, 2005) <http://www.sd-editions.com/PROME> [accessed 25 July 2013].

[25] *Statutes of the Realm IV*, p. 569; 'Henry VII: Parliament of October 1495, Text and Translation', ed. W. M. Ormrod in *The Parliament Rolls of Medieval England*, ed C. Given-Wilson et al. (Leicester, 2005) <http://www.sd-editions.com/PROME> [accessed 25. July 2013].

[26] *The Statutes: Revised Edition* (London, 1870), I: *Henry III– James II. A.D. 1235/6– 1685*, p. 497.

[27] McIntosh, *Controlling Misbehaviour*, p. 98. For more on how rules on sport segregated society, see T. S. Henrick, 'Sport and Social Hierarchy in Medieval England', *Journal of Sport History* 9.2 (1982), 20–37.

reference to servants and agricultural workers, which suggests that it was impossible to restrict those of a higher estate playing games.[28] This amendment may have resulted in part from a lack of state concern about leisure activities carried out in personal residences, particularly within chambers.

Although more emphasis of legislation is placed on games played in public places, games were also being played within the domestic space, not least because the climate, especially in winter, and the number of daylight hours would often make outdoor recreational activities impossible.[29] On Christmas Eve, 1459, Margaret Paston wrote to John Paston I about the games allowed in the house of John Fastolf's widow, Lady Morley, the Christmas after his death. She reports that:

> þere were non dysgysynggys nere harpyng nere lvtyng nere syngyn, nere non lowde dysportys, but pleyng at tabyllys and schesse and cardys, sweche dysportys sche gave here folkys leve to play, and non odyr.[30]

This clarification suggests that normally it would be appropriate for loud games and performances within the household at Christmas time, as well as tables, chess and cards. Not all games played in the domestic space would be played in the chamber, but it was certainly the site of some recreation. The concern of this chapter is not to suggest that the chamber was the only space in which people would engage in recreational activity in order to be merry, but that the meaning of such activities was affected by their location within the chamber. Literary evidence locates game playing in the chamber and suggests that games played in the chamber had different nuances of meaning to games played elsewhere. In Chaucer's *The Book of the Duchess*, the narrator considers whether to 'playe either at ches or tables', when he cannot sleep, but does not show any desire to get out of bed.[31] *The Romance of Guy of Warwick* similarly suggests that the chamber is an appropriate space for game playing, when Morgadour suggests to Guy that they

---

[28] 'Edward IV: Parliament of January 1478', ed. Ormrod.

[29] Due to climate change, periods of extremely cold and wet weather occurred in England in the time period concerning this book. For instance, the Great Famine of 1315–19 was the result of almost constant downpour, while there were many extremely cold winters between 1419 and 1459. See B. Fagan, *The Little Ice Age: How Climate Made History 1300–1850* (New York, 2000), especially pp. 28–32, 80–4.

[30] Davis, ed., *Paston Letters and Papers* I, 257.

[31] G. Chaucer, *The Book of the Duchess*, pp. 330–46.

go 'into þe chaumber […]/ Among þe maidens for to playe;/ At tables to pleye, & at ches'.[32] In *The Court of Sapience*, the protagonist goes to bed, where he plays out a game of chess in his head before he goes to sleep, which suggests a conscious link between beds and games.[33] In *The Avowyng of Arthur*, Arthur places a knight and Baldwin's wife in bed together, to test Baldwin's claim that he will not be jealous. To pass the time, 'the Kyng asshet a chekkere,/ And cald a damesel dere;/ Downe thay sette hom in fere/ Opon the bedsyde', where they continue to play chess until morning.[34] Undoubtedly, the cultural understanding of chess as a game of love makes it ideally suited for the chamber, particularly in *The Avowyng of Arthur*, where a sexual trial is taking place alongside the chess players.[35] Jenny Adams argues convincingly that the chess game is symbolic of political control, emphasising that Arthur has control over the bodies of his subjects.[36] However, we could also see the chess game as a model of restraint, reflecting the couple in bed beside them. If chess is a game of love, Arthur playing chess with an unknown 'damesel' is just as full of potential as the knight and lady sharing a bed. Just as Arthur is looking on to ensure that the knight and Baldwin's wife remain chaste, the knight, 'quyle on the morun that hit was day,/ Evyr he lokette as he lay' (ll. 870–1), is arguably looking out for Arthur. Whether the characters have political or romantic agendas, the most striking aspect of the game is that it is not unexpected: the game of chess is treated as a viable way to pass the time in bed, and is undertaken without question.

Further evidence of playing in the chamber is found in an illustration in Louis de Baveau's *Le Roman de Troyle*, which depicts women playing stringed instruments and perhaps singing, while a man lies in bed with a book (see Fig. 13). The man's attitude, with his head resting on his hands, suggests sleep or despondency, but the book's presence on the bed and the companionable positions of the women convey the

---

[32] *The Romance of Guy of Warwick. The First or 14th-Century Version*, ed. J. Zupitza (London 1883), ll. 3175–7.

[33] *The Court of Sapience*, ed. E. R. Harvey (Toronto, 1984), ll. 85–91.

[34] *The Avowyng of Arthur* in *Sir Gawain: Eleven Romances and Tales*, ed. T. Hahn (Kalamazoo, 1995), ll. 861–4.

[35] For the political and cultural implications of playing chess, see J. Adams, *Power Play: The Literature and Politics of Chess in the Late Middle Ages* (Philadelphia, 2006).

[36] Ibid., p. 8.

idea that the chamber is a space for high-status people to play, read and socialise.

Figure 13: Illustration of Louis de Baveau's translation of Boccaccio's *Roman de Troïlus, c.* 1440–60 © Paris, Bibliothèque Nationale de France. MS Fr. 25528, f. 85v.

Such continental images might have inspired Chaucer, who employs both the story of Troy and motif of the book in the bed in his works as well as the concept of socialising and playing music in the chamber. In Chaucer's 'The Miller's Tale', the relationship between the bed and music has sexual overtones.[37] When Nicholas sits 'allone, withouten any compaignye' (l. 3204) 'at his beddes hed' (l. 3211) playing his 'sautrie […] a-nyghtes' (ll. 3213–14), he sings 'Angelus ad virginem', a song which both extolls the virtues of virginity and hints at the potential for conception. Immediately after sexual intercourse with his landlord's wife, Alison, 'he kiste hire sweete and taketh his sawtrie,/ And playeth faste, and maketh melodie' (ll. 3305–6). Similarly, the next time they share a bed, their time together is described as 'the revel and the melodye' (l. 3652). Elsewhere in literature, music is portrayed as entertaining and calming, though the sexual undertones remain. In the mid fifteenth-century romance *Eger and Grime*, the wounded Eger sleeps in a chamber in which a lady plays a 'souter' and 'sweetlye sange' with her 'two maydens'.[38] They show great concern for Eger and appear to play the music not for their own benefit, but for that of the wounded knight in bed. The music seems to be in some way connected to Eger's healing process. As healing is generally associated with sickbeds, it makes sense that the musical performance is within the chamber. Meanwhile, in *Sir Degaré*, the ladies entertaining Degaré deliberately move to the chamber in order to play music:

The levedis wessche* everichon	*washed
And yede to chaumbre quik anon.	
Into the chaumbre he com ful sone.	
The levedi on here bed set,	
And a maide at here fet,	
And harpede notes gode and fine;	
Another broughte spices and wine.	
Upon the bedde he set adoun	
To here of the harpe soun.	
For murthe of notes so sschille*,	*skilfully played
He fel adoun on slepe stille.[39]	

---

[37] G. Chaucer, 'The Miller's Tale', in *Riverside Chaucer*, ed. Benson.
[38] *Eger and Grime: An Early English Romance, Edited from Bishop Percy's Folio MS, about 1650 A. D.*, ed. J. W. Hales and F. J. Furnivall (London, 1867), ll. 265–9.
[39] *Sir Degare*, ed. Laskaya and Salisbury, ll. 833–47.

Such an episode hints at seduction, as the lady and the knight sit on the same bed while intoxicating spices and wine are consumed, until the knight falls asleep 'on here bed' (l. 836). The deliberate move from hall to chamber in order to play the harp implies that the chamber is the most appropriate place in which to play.

Beds and books

Some people had music in their chambers; others had books. Chaucer's narrator of *The Canterbury Tales* comments that the Clerk would:

> […] levere have at his beddes heed
> Twenty books, clad in blak or reed,
> Of Aristotle and his philosophie
> Than robes riche, or fithele, or gay sautrie.[40]

'At his beddes heed' brings to the modern mind some sort of Ikea integrated headboard shelving system, though Chaucer probably means that books and fiddles are both likely items to be within reach of the bed in a chamber.[41] Fig. 13 shows that books and music could be consumed in the chamber at the same time, but Chaucer sees them as distinct pastimes: one could don 'robes riche' and play music in the company of other people, or read books which, as they are plainly bound in 'blak or reed', may be meant more for solitary reading than for being read in a social situation.

Considering texts such as Boethius' *The Consolation of Philosophy*, catharsis was considered to be one of the functions of reading. Reading, as Joyce Coleman explores, was often public and communal in late medieval England.[42] It is evident that people read both individually and communally throughout the house, including in the chamber. For instance, as discussed in Chapter 2, Margery Baxter and her husband were accused of reading the Wycliffe Bible aloud to their companions in their chamber.[43] However, there was understood to be a special significance to reading books in bed. Andrew Taylor argues that the late

---

[40] G. Chaucer, 'General Prologue', in *Riverside Chaucer*, ed. Benson, ll. 293–6. A 'sautrie' is a stringed instrument, as played in the bottom left-hand corner of Fig. 13, so called as it was used to accompany the psalter.

[41] See ch. 1 for a representation of the physical structure of a bed.

[42] J. Coleman, *Public Reading and the Reading Public in Late medieval England and France* (Cambridge, 1996).

[43] ch. 2, p. 60.

medieval chamber was 'a realm of private solace in which dreaming and reading intermingle, […] both a symbol and a material condition of a certain kind of leisure reading we now take very much for granted'.[44] The chamber as a space to assert one's individuality made it a particularly appropriate environment for this mode of reading.

The mode of reading associated with the chamber is addressed in *The Regiment of Princes*. Hoccleve recommends to Prince Henry (later Henry V) that:

> […] if yow list of stories taken heede,
> Sumwhat it may profyte, by your leeve;
> At hardest, whan yee been in chambre at eeve,
> They been good for to dryve foorth the nyght;
> They shal nat harme if they be herd aright.[45]

Hoccleve acknowledges that he has no business advising the Prince about his reading habits and that he has probably already read his sources, but suggests that it might make good bedtime reading. If nothing else, it will 'dryve foorth the nyght'. This lesson indicates that the chamber was not the only place understood to be suitable for the reading of books, but that books had a specific role to play in bed.

In addition to the tradition of presenting books to patrons in the chamber as discussed above, literary and documentary sources point towards the storage and consumption of books in the chamber. For instance, in *Troilus and Criseyde*, Troilus finds, 'at his beddes hed/ The copie of a tretys and a lettre'.[46] John Paston's 1462 inventory of Sir John Fastolf's belongings includes 'bokes Frenshe, Latyn and Englyssh remaynyng in the chambre of the seid Fastolff'.[47] Similarly, Woolgar points out that the fifteenth-century Bishop Sandale had in his chamber 'bibles, works on canon law, Priscian on grammar, the confessional treatise *Summa de viciis* by William Peyraut, and five books of romances as well as liturgical works'.[48] The Wife of Bath's husband apparently had his 'book of wikked wyves' to hand in his chamber, as he read it

---

[44] A. Taylor, 'Into His Secret Chamber: Reading and Privacy in Late medieval England', in *The Practice and Representation of Reading in England*, ed. J. Raven, H. Small and N. Tadmor (Cambridge, 1996), pp. 41–61 (p. 42).

[45] T. Hoccleve, *The Regiment of Princes*, ed. C. R. Blyth (Kalamazoo, 1999), ll. 2138–42.

[46] Chaucer, *Troilus and Criseyde* ii, ll.1696–7.

[47] *Paston Letters and Papers*, ed. Davis, I, 109.

[48] C. M. Woolgar, *The Senses in Late Medieval England*, p. 217.

'nyght and day'.[49] Similarly, in the *Confessio Amantis*, Nectanabus 'his chambre be himselve tok,/ And overtorneth many a bok'.[50] The widespread location of books within the chamber suggests a relationship between books and beds.

Reading at night, or even in the day in chambers with little natural light, would have required an open flame in a space that was particularly flammable. Despite the health and safety issues around the use of candles on or near a structure made out of a combination of straw, cloth and loose hangings, it appears that reading by the light of a flame in the chamber was common practice among literate people, which might testify to a perceived association between books and beds. The growing popularity of the 'chambre with a chymenee' meant that some chambers were lit by firelight and so people, like Pandarus, could have conceivably read by the fire.[51] In addition, there are some references to reading lamps in contemporary sources, showing that people read by the light of a flame in the chamber. Isabeau of Bavaria's chamber accounts include a reference to 'la chandelle quant la Royne dit ses heures' and in *King Arthur and King Cornwall*, it is mentioned that at the side of King Arthur's bed is a 'thrub chadler' (presumably some sort of candle-stick or shelf), upon which is placed a candle.[52] Within the romance, candlelight in the chamber is bright enough to 'reed' (l. 207) part of a Bible to exorcise a demon, and to read a name written 'on the backside of the leafe' (l. 208).

The miniature at the opening of a Latin miscellany made in Tournai around 1260 (Fig. 14) shows St Martin propped up in bed, covered in a blanket and surrounded by open books, from which he is referencing or copying into a tablet. Although it is not an English illustration, the similarity of climates, daylight hours and resources indicates that it was possible to read in bed in late medieval England, or at least to imagine someone doing so. The image suggests that the bed was multi-functional in more ways than we might have previously thought, as the spare cloak cast over the rail tree and the proximity of the lectern to the bed makes it difficult to discern where sleeping ends and studying

---

[49] G. Chaucer, 'The Wife of Bath's Prologue', in *Riverside Chaucer*, ed. Benson, ll. 685, 669.

[50] Gower, *Confessio Amantis* vi, ll. 1955–6.

[51] Langland, *Piers Plowman* x, l. 100; Emery, *Greater Medieval Houses*, p. 32; Grenville, *Medieval Housing*, p. 86; Sheeran, *Medieval Yorkshire Towns*, p. 149; Woolgar, *The Senses in Late Medieval England*, p. 248.

[52] A. Vallet de Viriville, *Extraits des Comptes Authentiques du Règne de Charles VI, 1380–1422* (Paris, 1859); *King Arthur and King Cornwall*, ed. Hahn, l. 124. Thomas Hahn posits that a 'thrub chadler' is a stand for a candle. See ch. 3, p. 83, n. 23.

Figure 14: Illustration depicting St Martin writing in bed, *c.* 1260. © Paris, Bibliothèque Mazarine. MS 753, f. ixr.

begins. Similarly, the portrayal of Christine de Pizan's book in Fig. 12 suggests a relationship between books and beds.[53] There is a range of colour evident in the illustration and yet the illustrator chose to colour

[53] See p. 114.

126

the book, situated between the two beds in the picture, in exactly the same shade and hue as the beds, with trimmings which match the bed-covers. The bright red stands out against the blue of the ladies' dresses, just as the red of the beds stands out against the blue of the wall hangings. The illustrator's colour indicates a symbolic relationship between books and beds. Furthermore, records show that Isabeau took great pride and interest in the binding of her books, having re-covered a chapel psalter in 'black velvet with scarlet pimpernels' as well as commissioning the production of decorated page-markers and book-clasps engraved with her coat of arms.[54] It is probable, therefore, that the book cover was designed specifically to agree with the aesthetics of Isabeau's chamber.

If there are books designed to match beds, there are also beds with bookish tendencies. Coverlets containing a story, such as the one in Melidore's chamber in *Sir Degrevant*, telling the 'storye [...] of Ydoyne and Amadas', are not unknown: a fourteenth-century Italian quilt, now in the Victoria and Albert Museum, tells the story of Tristan and Isolde in both images and text.[55] Textual elements in some late medieval English tapestries and bedding reveal that the coverlet of *Sir Degrevant* was not merely a literary device, but was also a reflection of real-world accoutrements of the chamber. In some cases, the fact that they contained words was more important than what the words themselves meant. In some inventories the record merely states that there is a text, for example 'four piece costers with a French inscription of red worsted'.[56] Such articles of bedding further serve to blur the distinction between books and beds and also point to the bedding itself being used as a literary medium.

Chaucer's *The Book of the Duchess* indicates that there was, without doubt, a strong relationship between books and beds in the late medieval cultural imagination. The framed narrative of the dream vision illustrates this intricate relationship, blurring the distinction between the book and the bed. The narrator, with whom an audience can sympathise, cannot sleep:

> So whan I saw I might not slepe
> Til now late this other night,

---

[54] Paris, Archives Nationales MS Kk. 42, f. 48r; R.l C. Gibbons, 'The Queen as "Social Mannequin". Consumerism and Expenditure at the Court of Isabeau of Bavaria, 1393–1422', *Journal of Medieval History* 26.4 (2000), 371–95.

[55] *Sir Degrevant*, ed. Kooper, ll. 1493–4; 'The Tristan Quilt'. London, Victoria and Albert Museum, Medieval and Renaissance, Room 9, Case <http://collections.vam.ac.uk/item/O98183/the-tristan-quilt-bed-cover-unknown/>.

[56] Stell, *York Probate Inventories*, p. 91.

Upon my bed I sat upright
And bad oon reche me a book,
A romaunce, and he it me tok
To rede and drive the night away (ll. 44–9)

Here, a romance is being read in bed by a man who has 'suffred' (l. 37) from insomnia for eight years. Like Hoccleve, Chaucer understands that books 'been good for to dryve foorth the nyght'.[57] While the narrator continues to describe the story, it becomes clear that in the book the narrator is reading, Alcyone is 'broghten […] in bed al naked', after making a plea for sleep similar to the narrator's own.[58] The scene is vividly described but little plot is mentioned, so that the book in the narrator's hand contains Alcyone's bed as a chamber would, as well as remaining a physical book within the narrator's chamber. The book then goes on to become a chamber for the god of sleep and his heir, who 'lay naked in her bed/ And slepe whiles the dayes laste' (ll. 176–7). The book's role as chamber is reiterated through the narrator's longing to sleep. He offers Morpheus and Juno 'al that falles/ to a chambre' (ll. 257–8), if they would allow him to sleep, placing great worth on bedding:

Yif he wol make me slepe a lyte*,   *a little while
Of down of pure dowves white
I wil yive hym a fether-bed,
Rayed with gold and right wel cled
In fyn blak satyn doutremer*,   *from across the sea
And many a pilowe, and every ber
Of cloth of Reynes, to slepe softe-
Hym thar not need to turnen ofte-
And I wol yive hym al that falles
To a chambre (ll. 249–58)

This promise collapses the distinction between the real world and the book world, as the narrator attempts to provide real-world materials for a location within his book. It is as if his terms are accepted, as shortly after this proclamation, the narrator falls asleep 'ryght upon [his] book' (l. 274). At this point, the book is simultaneously on the narrator's physical bed and, in being slept upon, performing the function

[57] Hoccleve, *The Regiment of Princes*, l. 2141.
[58] Chaucer, *The Book of the Duchess*, l. 125.

of the narrator's bed.[59] Next the narrator, while sleeping on his book, dreams that he wakes up in a chamber, whose walls and windows are remarkably book-like:

> And sooth to seyn, my chambre was
> Ful wel depeynted, and with glas
> Were al the wyndowes wel yglased
> Ful clere [...]
> [...]
> For hooly al the story of Troye
> Was in the glasynge ywroght thus,
> Of Ector and of kyng Priamus,
> Of Achilles and of kyng Lamedon,
> And eke of Medea and of Jason.
> Of Paris, Eleyne, and of Lavyne.
> And alle the walles with colours fyne
> Were peynted, bothe text and glose,
> Of al the Romaunce of the Rose. (ll. 321–34)

In this episode, the chamber effectively becomes a book, which tells the story of the *The Siege of Troy* and *The Romance of the Rose*. The narrator informs us that 'bothe text and glose' are present on the walls. These terms are normally only applied to books, and so upon falling asleep on one book, the narrator has woken up inside another. Even the bed within the dream chamber has bookish qualities, as 'throgh the glas' containing the history of Troy, 'the sonne shon/ Upon my bed with bryghte bemes' (ll. 336–7), so that the bed would have been covered with shining stories.

It is when the narrator rises from his bed, which is still his book, and leaves the chamber, also a book, that the main text of the narrative finally comes into being. The final transformation occurs in the conclusion to the tale when the narrator awakes from his dream to find himself in bed with his book. At this point the book and the bed are once again separate items, although the reference to the 'goddes of slepyng' (l. 1328) within the narrator's book suggest that the bed is the book's rightful place. The narrator then resolves to write the dream down, thus completing the cycle. The end result is a book – *The Book of the Duchess* – containing in its text the narrator's chamber and book,

---

[59] The definition of a bed, as discussed in ch. 1, depends on its composition, function or both.

and all the beds and chambers contained within the narrator's account. In this way the book, the bed and the chamber are inseparable.

The dream vision, which constitutes the main story of *The Book of the Duchess*, is, like many dream visions, framed by a realistic setting in which an unremarkable narrator falls asleep. Chaucer's dream narrative frame is highly self-reflexive, with very little distinction between the author and narrator, so that the narrator's actions are plausible in the real world, as well as within the realms of the narrative.[60] Certainly Chaucer, living in one room at Aldgate tower, would have had little choice but to have books within reach of his bed.[61] At the same time, critics such as Barry Windeat have posited that Chaucer uses prologues, in particular those of dream visions, to explore underlying ideas and 'ineffable truths' throughout his works.[62] If we are to subscribe to this argument, the intricate relationship between books and beds was an 'ineffable truth' in the late medieval cultural imagination.

'Bywayling in his chambre thus allone'

The practices of playing games with a large group of people or sitting alone in bed with a book stemmed from the same understanding that the chamber was the most intimate space in the house and therefore allowed the owner of the chamber to shed some of the protective layers and social obligations that were required outside of the chamber door. As a result, visitors to the chamber understood that they were being given an intimate audience, and readers and writers understood texts to have particular significance when they were read in bed, a space which contains the dreamspace inhabited by a sleeper, and so was intimately connected with its owner's consciousness. The idea that social pretences are shed at the door meant that it was understood that within the chamber, one could be truly one's self. The idea of the chamber as an appropriate space to display a sense of self is evident in Middle English literature where, time and again, protagonists seek

---

[60] W. A. Quinn, '*The Book of the Duchess*: Introduction' in *Chaucer's Dream Visions and Shorter Poems*, ed. W. A. Quinn (New York, 1999), p. 114. See also K. L. Lynch, *Chaucer's Philosophical Vision* (Cambridge, 2000), p. 3; S. Delany, *The Naked Text: Chaucer's Legend of Good Women* (Berkeley, 1994), p. 33.

[61] For more on Chaucer's living conditions, see P. Strohm, *The Poet's Tale: Chaucer and the Year that Made* The Canterbury Tales (London, 2014), pp. 49–89.

[62] Lynch, *Chaucer's Philosophical Vision*, p. 39; B. Windeat, 'Literary Structures in Chaucer' in *The Cambridge Companion to Chaucer*, ed. P. Boitani and J. Mann (Cambridge, 2003), pp. 214–32 (p. 215).

out their chambers before displaying emotion. The audience of the 'Arise Early' precepts is instructed to go to bed 'myrely' because other moods (and other adverbs) are available in the chamber. For instance, evidence from late medieval English literature has shown that the bed was considered to be the refuge of the lovesick and heartbroken. For instance, in *Amis and Amiloun*, Belisaunt lies 'sike in bed' for 'care and lovemorning/ Bothe bi night and day', because of her unrequited love for Amis.[63] In *The Siege of Milan*, Sir Alantyne 'wente […] unto bedde/ For sorowe hym thought his hert bledde'.[64] Similarly, in *The Erle of Tolous*, the emperor 'fell in swowne upon hys bedde' when told that his wife is an adulteress.[65]

In many literary texts, characters deliberately go to their chambers in order to be able to physically succumb to their emotions, suggesting that there was a conscious understanding between the authors and audience that the most appropriate space for a physical outpouring of emotions was in the chamber. For example, when Herodis is snatched by fairies in the early fourteenth-century *Sir Orfeo*, 'the King into his chaumber is go/ And oft swooned upon the ston/ And made swiche diol and swiche mon/ That neighe his lif was y-spent'.[66] Similarly, in the fourteenth-century romance *The King of Tars*, the Christian king's messengers went 'to chaumber' because they had 'gret pite'.[67] When the king and queen are delivered their bad news, they wait until they enter a chamber before expressing their grief:

> Into chaumber þai went þo.
> When þai were togider boþe to,
> Þan wakened alle her care.
> Þe king was in sorwe bounde,
> Þe quen swoned mani a stounde*   *many times
> For her douhter dere
> […]
> Þus þe quen & þe king
> Liued in sorwe & care morning;
> Gret diol* it was to here. (ll. 358–69)   *suffering

[63] *Amis and Amiloun*, ed. Foster, ll. 486, 482–3.
[64] *The Siege of Milan*, ed. Lupak, ll. 85–6.
[65] *Erle of Tolous*, ed. Laskaya and Salisbury, l. 870.
[66] *Sir Orfeo*, in *Middle English Verse Romances*, ed. D. B. Sands (Exeter, 1986), ll. 172–5.
[67] *The King of Tars*, ed. Perryman, ll. 323–4.

The 'When […]/Þan' construction (ll. 359–60) suggests that the delay in expressing their grief was deliberate on the part of the characters, and the lack of explanation implies that this reaction would be considered normal by a contemporary audience. Even physical symptoms of their grief do not manifest themselves until the king and queen are in the chamber, including the queen's swoon, a reaction which one would think to be spontaneous. From her reaction, we can infer that the chamber was a space understood to be appropriate for the physical expression of emotion, and so it was unthinkable that the queen would react physically to bad news anywhere else.

Chaucer's *Troilus and Criseyde* can be read as a study of how the chamber changes the way in which people behave. As we have already seen, the chamber is used as a space for counsel to great effect in this text, but Troilus also spends much of the poem 'bywayling in his chambre […] allone'.[68] His response to lovesickness is to 'ley as style as he ded were' (i, l. 723), and Pandarus agrees that such a practice is possible and appropriate within the chamber, acknowledging that he 'mayst alone here wepe and crye and knele' (i, l. 806). In fact, Pandarus has a similar response to grief, taking himself 'in wo to bedde […] and evere lay/ Pandare abedde, half in a slomberynge' (ii, ll. 62–6). Later on in the text, Troilus again deliberately shuts himself in his chamber before allowing himself to express his emotions:

Unto his chambre spedde hym faste allone
[…]
And hastily upon his bed hym leyde.
[…]
He rist hym up, and every dore he shette,
And wyndow ek and tho this sorowful man
Upon his beddes syde adown hym sette,
Ful lik a ded ymage, pale and wan;
And in his brest the heped wo bygan
Out breste, and he to werken in this wise
In his woodnesse […] (iv, ll. 220–39)

The adverb 'allone' and the emphasis on barring every entrance to the chamber highlights Troilus' need to be by himself in order to express his pain, and the repeated reference to the bed emphasises that Troilus is specifically in his chamber. The bed is an integral part of Troilus'

[68] Chaucer, 'Troilus and Criseyde' i, l. 547.

emotional space. It is clear from the 'heped wo' that he had been bot-
tling up his feelings until he reached the chamber, and the verb 'bygan'
is telling, as it suggests that all expressions of emotion had been post-
poned until the appropriate time and setting. In the previous stanza,
Chaucer compares Troilus to a tree in winter, which has lost its leaves,
leaving only 'disposed wood' (iv, l. 230). Elsewhere within the text, he
uses 'woodnesse' (iii, l. 1382) in reference to love, meaning 'madness',
from the adjective 'wode'. Here, both meanings are employed, to reflect
Troilus' mental state. The result is that he emulates a wooden object.
Sitting down 'upon his beddes syde […] in his woodnesse', like 'a ded
ymage', he could be a carved figure upon the bed. He then proceeds to
perform a physical demonstration of his emotions, beating his chest,
hitting his head on the chamber wall, throwing himself to the ground,
sobbing, crying and shouting in a broken voice, before returning once
more to 'his bed' (iv, l. 256) to soliloquise on his misfortune. Not only
are the bed and chamber the appropriate locus for Troilus' grief, but
they are actively involved in its playing out

In an exploration of Sir Palomydes' emotional behaviour by a well
in a forest in Malory's *Le Morte Darthur*, Bonnie Wheeler comments
that 'grief in medieval texts is usually public, often communal. Here
we have the rare instance of a character who seeks privacy.'[69] I contest
this view, as, like Troilus, many medieval characters deliberately move
to the relative privacy of the chamber in order to express grief, even if
the idea of 'privacy' itself is not understood. For instance, in *The Squire
of Low Degree*, a romance probably dating from the mid fifteenth century, preserved in two sixteenth-century printed books, the squire 'to
no man durst he make his mone,/ But sighed sore himselfe alone./ And
evermore whan he was so,/ Into his chambre would he go'.[70] It is clear
from the context that the squire is capable of being 'alone' elsewhere,
but he deliberately moves to the chamber in order to be lovesick in
solitude. *Sir Isumbras* demonstrates similar agency: the protagonist
finds a mantel and some gold, which were with his wife and children
when they went missing, in a bird's nest. He hides the gold under his

---

[69] B. Wheeler, 'Grief in Avalon: Sir Palomydes' Psychic Pain', in *Grief and Gender:
700–1700*, ed. J. C. Vaught with L. Dickson Bruckner (New York, 2003), pp.
65–77 (p. 75).

[70] *The Squire of Low Degree*, in *Middle English Verse Romances*, ed. D. B. Sands
(Exeter, 1986), ll. 23–6; E. Kooper, 'The Squire of Low Degree: Introduction', in
Sentimental and Humorous Romances (Kalamazoo, 2005).

bed[71], and whenever he goes to see it, 'he thoughte on hys wyff and on hys chyldren thre,/ Hys song was "weylaway!"'.[72] It is evident that the site of Isumbras' sadness is the chamber, due to his placement of the emotive objects. One version of the text focuses on his grief, which manifests itself upon him having entered the chamber: 'and he were never so glad of mode/ And he ons to his chambyr yode,/ He wepyd after all dey'.[73] Another version is nuanced to emphasise Isumbras' public performance of contentment versus his private grief: 'Wer he nevere so blythe off mood/ Whenne he out off hys chaumbyr yood,/ He wepte siththen al day'.[74] It is obvious that he has his public face and his private emotions. It is also apparent from each version of the text that Isumbras deliberately goes to his chamber in order to express and perform grief in seclusion.

Such emotional episodes in the chamber are prolific in the Arthurian tradition. In *Sir Launfal*, Guinevere retreats to her chamber when she becomes angry with Launfal, who tells her he loves a woman more beautiful than she, 'and anon sche ley doun yn her bedde./ For wrethe, syk sche hyr bredde'.[75] Almost immediately after this response, Launfal 'was to hys chaumber gon/ To han hadde solas and plawe' (ll. 728–9). In acknowledging the existence of his fairy lover, he has caused her to be lost to him forever, has lost access to his riches and has scuppered his relationships at court.[76] The result is that both Guinevere and Launfal retire to their respective chambers 'unfawe'.[77] Likewise, in the alliterative *Morte Arthure*, Guinevere (known as 'Waynor' in the text), twice takes to her bed in grief. The first time, Arthur 'went unto chamber/ For to comfort the queen that in care lenges./ Waynor waikly weepand him kisses,/ Talkes to him tenderly with teres ynow'.[78] It is

---

71 It is not clear whether this means under part of the bed such as the featherbed, often called 'bed' in wills and inventories, or whether his bed was on a raised frame.

72 *Sir Isumbras*, in *Four Middle English Romances*, ed. H. Hudson, 2nd edn (Kalamazoo, 2006), ll. 329–33.

73 Oxford, Bodleian Library, Ashmole MS 61; *Item 5, Sir Isumbras*, in *Codex Ashmole 61: A Compilation of Popular Middle English Verse*, ed. G. Shuffleton (Kalamazoo, 2008), ll. 661–3.

74 Cambridge, Gonville and Caius College, MS 175; *Sir Isumbras*, ed. Hudson, ll. 634–6.

75 *Sir Launfal*, in *The Middle English Breton Lays*, ed. A. Laskaya and E. Salisbury (Kalamazoo, 1995), ll. 703–4.

76 The objects in his chamber were given to Launfal by his lover, and serve as a connection between them.

77 Ibid., l. 732; 'unfawe'= joyless.

78 *Alliterative Morte Arthure*, ed. Benson, ll. 696–9.

interesting that the chamber is mentioned as the space in which Arthur must comfort his wife, as if he assumes not only that she would be in the chamber, but that she would be visibly upset there.[79] Later on in the poem, Guinevere 'yermes and yeyes at York in her chamber,/ Grones full grisly with gretand teres' (ll. 3911–12). Both episodes involve the exaggerated performance of emotion, and are the only instances within the romance in which Guinevere's 'teres' are mentioned. A similar function for the chamber is found in the Stanzaic *Morte Arthure*. The Earl's daughter falls in love with Lancelot 'and to her chamber went she tho;/ Down upon her bed she fell,/ That nigh her herte brast in two'.[80] Towards the end of the poem, 'Gawain gan in his chamber him hold;/ Of all the day he nolde not out go', until 'So sore his herte began to colde,/ Almost he wolde himselfe slo' (ll. 1982–9). When Lancelot goes to Guinevere's chamber to take his leave, 'for joy the teres ran' (l. 739). Immediately afterwards, '"Wele-away," then said the queen [...]/ "I may wofully weep and wake/ In clay til I be clongen cold!"' (ll. 340–51). When Lancelot quits the chamber, 'the lady swoones sithes three;/ Almost she slew herselfe there' (ll. 774–5). Finally, when Lancelot leaves court, Guinevere is 'in her bed all naked,/And sore seke in her chamber lay' (ll. 812–3). Later on, after Guinevere is sentenced to be burned alive:

> The queen went to her chamber so;
> So dolefully mone gan she make,
> That nigh her herte brast in two;
> For sorrow gan she shiver and quake,
> And said: 'Alas and wele-a-wo! [...]' (ll. 1406–10)

Again, she physically moves to the chamber in order to perform acts of emotion, which is, perhaps, unsurprising, as her doleful moaning and violent shaking could hardly have been considered appropriate public conduct for a queen.

As we have seen, many characters exhibit physical manifestations of trauma which could be considered involuntary and spontaneous, such as swooning and shaking, once they have reached the confines of their chambers rather than, as one might expect, at the time of the traumatic event. Research has found that somatic responses to grief and trauma are in some ways regulated by social constructs and constraints, so

---

[79] For the idea of the chamber as a woman's rightful place, see ch. 6 below.

[80] *Stanzaic Morte Arthur*, in *King Arthur's Death: The Middle English Stanzaic Morte Arthur and Alliterative Morte Arthure*, ed. L. D. Benson (Kalamazoo, 1994), ll. 186–8.

that even involuntary physical displays of negative emotions can be delayed until the most socially appropriate time and setting.[81] As the trope of characters expressing their emotions within their chambers is a reflection on cultural practice and social expectation, we can conclude that late medieval people who had access to chambers used them as spaces in which to express and control their emotions.

'Goo to thy bed myrely'

This chapter has shown that the chamber and bed had a powerful sway over what late medieval English society determined to be appropriate. As we have seen from the 'Arise Early' precepts, actions and events were deemed acceptable or appropriate depending on the time and place in which they took place. In this chapter I have recognised that games and music were not exclusive to the chamber and, more crucially, demonstrated the shifting importance of these activities when conducted in the chamber. The presence of the bed in the chamber changed what the games and music meant to those playing them. I have also shown that there was a culturally recognised relationship between the book and the bed, which was understood to affect the ways in which books were received. Finally, I have demonstrated that the chamber was understood to be the most appropriate place in which to let one's guard down and display emotions. These different uses and conveyed meanings associated with the bed and chamber support my continuing argument that the chamber had a much greater and wider significance than as simply a space to sleep.

Though the understanding that the chamber was the most appropriate space in which to be one's self was widespread, access to chambers was not. Not only did the chamber allow its owner to

---

[81] A survey of all cultural and social effects on individuals' responses to grief and trauma is beyond the scope of this book. See, for example, W. Stroebe and M. S. Stroebe, *Bereavement and Health: The Psychological and Physical Consequences of Partner Loss* (Cambridge, 1987), pp. 7–55 (esp. pp. 29–35); M. Eisenbruch, 'Cross Cultural Aspects of Bereavement. 11: Ethnic and Cultural Variations in the Development of Bereavement Practices', *Culture, Medicine and Psychiatry* 8 (1984), 315–47; S. Schreiber, 'Migration, Traumatic Bereavement and Transcultural Aspects of Psychological Healing: Loss and Grief of a Refugee Woman from Begameder Country in Ethiopia', *British Journal of Medical Psychology* 68.2 (1995), 135–42; Samir Al-Adawi, Rustam Burjorjee and Ihsan Al-Issa, 'Mu-Ghayeb: A Culture-Specific Response To Bereavement in Oman', *International Journal of Social Psychiatry* 43.2 (1997), 144–51.

cast off restrictions associated with the outside world, but the cultural ideas associated with the chamber restricted the actions of all who did not have access to a chamber of their own. The privileged few could, therefore, 'go to [...] bed myrely' in the knowledge that their merriment was sanctioned, appropriate and, indeed, necessary to maintain the established order.

5

'Plesse and Loffe Thy Wyffe Dewly/ And Basse Hyr Onys or Tewys Myrely'

This book has so far shown that part of what made the chamber meaningful in late medieval England was the fact that it was considered to be the most appropriate space for certain activities. As evidenced by didactic texts such as the precepts upon which this book is structured, it was understood that there was a time and a place for all activities, including the appropriate expression of sexual desire. To date, scholarship on sex in late medieval England rarely focuses on the locus of sexual intercourse, often focusing instead on the way authorities tried to regulate sexual activity.[1] This chapter will explore the notion that the bed and chamber were at the heart of the late medieval English understanding of both licit and illicit sexual encounters, despite the exclusive nature of the chamber.

---

[1] See, for example, P. J. Payer, 'Sex and Confession in the Thirteenth Century', in *Sex in the Middle Ages: A Book of Essays*, ed. J. E. Salisbury (New York, 1991), pp. 126–42; C. Jorgensen Itnyre, 'A Smorgasbord of Sexual Practices', in *Sex in the Middle Ages: A Book of Essays*, ed. J. E. Salisbury (New York, 1991), pp. 145–72; D. Jacquart and C. Thomasset, *Sexuality and Medicine in the Middle Ages* (Princeton, 1988); A. L. Martin, *Alcohol, Sex and Gender in Late Medieval and Early Modern Europe* (London, 2001); R. M. Karras, *Sexuality in Medieval Europe: Doing Unto Others* (New York, 2005); J. A. Brundage, *Sex, Law and Marriage in the Middle Ages* (Aldershot, 1993); P. J. Payer, *Sex and the New Medieval Literature of Confession, 1150–1300* (Toronto, 2009); J. Murray, 'Gendered Souls in Sexed Bodies: The Male Construction of Female Sexuality in Some Medieval Confessors' Manuals', in *Handling Sin: Confession in the Middle Ages*, ed. P. Biller and A. J. Minnis (York, 1998), pp. 79–93; *Gender and Difference in the Middle Ages*, ed. S. Farmer and C. Braun Pasternack (Minneapolis, 2003).

The sexuality of the bed

The pursuit of ideas associated with sex in late medieval England is problematic, not least because the term 'sex', in the sense of sexual intercourse or activity, did not exist until the mid eighteenth century.[2] Instead, terms used ranged from the crude to the euphemistic, both of which could have been misconstrued by reading audiences at the time, and certainly by post-medieval audiences reading medieval texts. The lack of socially appropriate terms with which to name sexual organs and activities is highlighted and exploited in the fabliau *De la damoisele qui ne pooit oïr parler de foutre*, in which a young woman cannot hear someone say 'fuck' without feeling sick and does not have the vocabulary to talk about genitalia or sexual acts.[3] Instead, she overcomes her modesty by providing her own euphemistic names so that, for example, her vagina becomes 'une fontenele' (a fountain) in the middle of her 'praiel' (meadow, used to denote the mons pubis), while her bedfellow refers to his penis as 'mes poulains' (a horse).[4] Elsewhere, euphemisms for sex refer to the perceived location of a sexual act, namely the bed and chamber. These expressions are evidence that the bed and chamber had a strong linguistic and physical association with sexuality in the late medieval English collective imagination. In Middle English literature, to have someone 'in bour' is to have sex with them, as shown in *Lay le Freine*, where Le Freine's mother explains the birth of her neighbour's twins by suggesting that 'tvay men hir han hadde in bour', and in *King Horn*, where Fykenyld reports the sexual relationship between Horn and Rymenhild to the king by locating Horn 'in boure/ Al honder couerture/ By reymyld þi douter'.[5] The term 'chamber' has similar connotations: in *Octavian* 'the Emperoure satt appon a daye,/ In his chamber hym to playe/ With his lady bryghte'.[6] Most explicitly, in *Prohemy of a Mariage Betwixt an Olde Man and a Yonge Wife, and the Counsail*, written around 1430 and often ascribed to Lydgate,

---

[2] K. M. Phillips and B. Reay, *Sex Before Sexuality: A Premodern History* (Cambridge, 2011), p. 14; 'sex, n^1, b', 'sexual intercourse', *OED*.

[3] *De la damoisele qui ne pooit oïr parler de foutre*, in *Recueil général et complet des fabliaux des XIIIe et XIVe siècles*, ed. A. de Montaiglon and G. Raynaud, 6 vols. (Paris, 1878), III.

[4] Ibid., pp. 81–5.

[5] *Lai le Freine*, in *Middle English Verse Romances*, ed. D. B. Sands (Exeter, 1986), l. 71; *King Horn: A Middle-English Romance*, ed. J. Hall (Oxford, 1901), ll. 713–16.

[6] *Octavian*, ed. Hudson, ll. 46–9.

sex is referred to as both 'chambre game' and 'chambre werk'; perhaps unsurprisingly the husband uses 'game', while the wife uses 'werk'.[7]

The bed is also used metonymically in literary texts in lieu of a reference to sex or as the locus of sexual desire. Chaucer makes it clear that he locates sexual desire in bed, when he describes lust as 'perilous fyr, that in the bedstraw bredeth' in 'The Merchant's Tale'.[8] Likewise, in Robert Manning's *Handlyng Synne* of 1303, a lech is described as anyone who '3yf he any ouþer wedde/ Or with any go to bedde'.[9] Similarly, in the sixteenth-century Middle English version of *The Wedding of Sir Gawain and Dame Ragnelle*, Dame Ragnelle's imperious instruction to her bridegroom on her wedding night, 'shewe me your cortesy in bed', is clearly a demand for the physical consummation of her marriage to Gawain.[10] As Megan Leitch argues, within literary texts the space is used 'as the operative language of articulating and pursuing the sensual'.[11] Sexual demands in bed or in the chamber and references to those spaces in articulations of sexual desire have resulted in the erotic being firmly entrenched within the chamber in the late medieval cultural mindset. More specifically, the bed was the culturally recognised space for sex. Hoccleve uses the location of the bed to denote sexual activity: his 'poore olde hore man' in *The Regiment of Princes* (c. 1410) discusses rich people's tendency to marry off their children 'þogh þei be al to yong & tender of age/ No-wher my ripe ynow to go to bedde'.[12] A similar use is found in Wycliffe's fourteenth-century sermon for Christmas Eve, which explains that the immaculate conception of

---

[7] *Prohemy of a Mariage Betwixt an Olde Man and a Yonge Wife, and the Counsail*, in *The Trials and Joys of Marriage*, ed. M. Ellzey and D. Moffatt, rev. E. Salisbury (Kalamazoo, 2002), ll. 339, 432; for a discussion of the authorship of the text, see C. F. E. Spurgeon, *Five Hundred Years of Chaucer Criticism and Allusion, 1357–1900*, 3 vols. (Cambridge, 1925), I, 36; J. Lydgate, *The Minor Poems of John Lydgate*, ed. H. N. MacCracken, 2 vols. (London, 1911), I, xlviii.

[8] Chaucer, 'The Merchant's Tale', l. 1783.

[9] R. Manning, *Handlyng Synne*, in *Robert of Brunne's 'Handlyng Synne'*, ed. F. J. Furnivall (London, 1901–3), ll. 8387–8.

[10] *The Wedding of Sir Gawain and Dame Ragnelle*, in *Sir Gawain: Eleven Romances and Tales*, ed. T. Hahn (Kalamazoo, 1995), l. 630.

[11] M. Leitch, 'Enter the Bedroom', in *Sexual Culture in the Literature of Medieval Britain*, ed. A. Hopkins, R. A. Rouse and C. J. Rushton (Cambridge, 2014), p. 44.

[12] T. Hoccleve, *The Regiment of Princes*, in *Hoccleve's Works: The Regiment of Princes and Fourteen Minor Poems*, ed. F. J. Furnivall (London, 1897), ll. 122, 1641–2; 'my' might be a scribal error: 'ny' would make more sense in this context.

Christ occurred 'bifore [Mary and Joseph] shulden go to bedde'.[13] This understanding is not only conveyed linguistically; it is also evident through events in literary narratives. For instance, in the Middle English *Floris and Blancheflour*, written around 1250, the audience is given to understand that the young eponymous couple consummate their relationship when they are brought 'to a bedde', even though they are described as children throughout.[14] Blancheflour, who had previously been proven to be a virgin by the emir's virginity test, deliberately avoids re-taking the test after having spent some time in bed with Floris, so we can assume that she no longer retains her virginity. We can also see evidence of the understanding that sex should happen in bed in 'The Merchant's Tale': when January and May have sex in the garden after unsuccessful attempts in the chamber, they are described as doing 'thynges whiche that were nat doon abedde', indicating that the bed is the normal locus for sex.[15]

'Bedde' can be used as both a noun and a verb in reference to sex, referring to the sexual partner or the act rather than the bed itself. For instance, in *The Owl and the Nightingale*, which survives in two thirteenth-century manuscripts, the two creatures refer to a woman's lover as 'hire bedde'.[16] The verb 'to beddy' is used by the fourteenth-century priest William de Shoreham in the sense of having sexual intercourse with someone:

And ȝyf þet one weddeþ þe þral	
And weneþ* þe fyre weddy**;	*considers **burning
And ȝyf a spyet* þat soþe** þrof***,	*sees **truth ***thereof
And wondeþ* nauȝt to beddy […][17]	*holds back

The term 'bedde', as noun or verb, carries with it redolent associations with sexuality. In *King Horn*, Rymenhild is in danger of being married to one of Horn's enemies. In two versions of the text, 'bedde' is used

---

[13] J. Wycliffe, 'Þis is Þe Gospel Þat is Rad on Christemasse Evyn', in *Select English Works of John Wycliff*, ed. T. Arnold (Oxford, 1869), I: *Sermons on the Gospels for Sundays and Festivals*, p. 311.

[14] *Floris and Blancheflour*, in *Middle English Verse Romances*, ed. D. B. Sands (Exeter, 1986), ll. 821–46.

[15] Chaucer, 'The Merchant's Tale', l. 2051.

[16] *The Owl and the Nightingale*, in *Old and Middle English c. 890–c. 1400: An Anthology*, ed. E. Treharne, 2nd edn (London, 2004), 371–405, l. 1500.

[17] W. de Shoreham, 'The Poems of William de Shoreham', in *Early English Poetry, Ballads, and Popular Literature of the Middle Ages, Edited From Original Manuscripts and Scarce Publications*, ed. T. Wright (London, 1851), p. 76.

as a verb: 'a king hire shal wedde/ A sonneday to bedde'.[18] In a third version, the king 'hire wile wedde/ And bringe to his bedde'.[19] The bed seems to be interchangeable as a verb or noun in this instance, though the redolent association with sex remains clear, so it is obvious that the bed is firmly semantically linked with sexual activity. Additionally, the practice of referring to the bed in lieu of an explicit sexual description was not restricted to literary texts. In 1505, the churchwardens of Borstall accuse a married couple of promoting illicit sex, as they 'make one Katherine Bronyng their servant lie in the bed where one John their son is wont to have recourse making her pregnant'.[20] Discussing making a person 'lie in the bed' gives the effect of sanitising the implication that the couple were complicit in rape, while at the same time making it clear that Bronyng was, indeed, being subjected to sexual advances.

The knowledge that references to the bed were used as shorthand for sexual activity sheds new light on church court depositions in which a couple's sexual relationship is called into question. Explicit descriptions, such as the 1471 deposition in which John Palmer testified that 'he saw William Stevenes and Juliana Saunder lying on a bed, having sexual intercourse', are exceedingly rare.[21] It is clear from documentary sources that the suggestion that two people were naked in bed together had the same resonances as the phrase 'sleeping together' has today. For instance, the deposition of Alice de Baumburght in 1381 describes how she found 'Robert and Agnes lying alone together in one bed'.[22] The implication is that they were engaged in sexual activity, as Alice reports that she insisted upon their immediate exchange of vows. In a deposition of 1355, Maud Katerforth (or Katersouth) describes how she witnessed Maud de Bradelay refuse to get into bed with John de Walkyngton until he had pledged her his troth.[23] She later deposes that 'she heard him get into bed and saw him lying in bed with her at dawn of the following day, alone and naked together, and get up from

[18] London, British Library, Harley MS 2253, ll. 957–8 and Oxford, Bodleian Library, Laud Misc. MS 108, ll. 992–3; *King Horn; A Middle-English Romance*, ed. J. Hall (Oxford, 1901).

[19] Cambridge, Cambridge University Library, MS Gg. 4. 27. 2; *King Horn*, ed. Sands, ll. 957–8.

[20] Goldberg, *Women in England*, pp. 95–6.

[21] *Love and Marriage*, ed. McSheffrey, p. 87.

[22] Goldberg, *Women in England*, p. 117.

[23] Ibid., p. 156.

the same bed, and she believes that they lay together in bed the whole night with it in mind to have intercourse together'.[24] Similarly, in 1473 Nicolas Maryot describes in a deposition how he saw Edmund Breme and his new wife Petronilla 'lying in a bed in a certain upper chamber [...] both of them nude' to imply that the couple had consummated their marriage.[25] In a deposition of 1432, Isabel Henryson vocalises the direct link between lying naked in bed together and sex, explaining 'that she believes for sure that John often knew Agnes carnally [...] since this same witness often [...] found John and Agnes lying naked together in Agnes' bed'.[26] It is clear from the fact that she 'believes for sure' that the sexual act took place despite not actually witnessing it that 'alone and naked together in [...] bed' was considered enough to denote sexual intercourse, both in word and in deed.

The understanding that the bed was imbued with sexual meaning is further evidenced by the use of beds as spaces for sexual trial by authors of Middle English romance. A knight in a romance text is usually tried either by his ability to complete a quest in the outside world or by his behaviour within the domestic sphere. While beds in continental romances often pose a physical threat to a knight on trial, threatening to shoot flaming arrows, drop swords, hurl rocks, or unleash a lion onto any knight who fails the challenge, beds in Middle English romances rarely pose an overtly physical threat.[27] Instead, the threat associated with the bed is implicit, relying on the audience's knowledge of the bed's inherent sexual meaning. For example, in each of Gawain's bed trials in various English romances, the bed's sexual connotations work to make a trial of seduction more difficult to resist, while Gawain wins by remaining chaste. Given his reputation, overcoming the typical narrative trajectory of his character in order to resist temptation and prove his worth is arguably more difficult than to expect him to fight off a physical attack. The sexual trial is particularly complex and the bed's inherent sexual associations are especially evident in *Sir Gawain*

---

[24] Ibid., p. 157.

[25] *Love and Marriage*, ed. McSheffrey, pp. 44–5.

[26] Goldberg, *Women in England*, p. 114.

[27] For example, in C. de Troyes, *Lancelot, ou le Chevalier de la Charrette*, ed. J. C. Aubailly (Paris, 1991); *Le Chevalier à l'Épée*, in *Two Old French Gauvain Romances*, ed. R. C. Johnston and D. D. R. Owen (New York, 1973); C. de Troyes, *Le Roman de Perceval, ou Le Conte de Graal*, ed. W. Roach (Geneva, 1959); W. von Eschenbach, *Parzival und Titurel*, ed. K. Batsch (Leipzig, 1875). For more on the bed as a dangerous space during sleep, see ch. 2 above, pp. 55–6.

and the Carle of Carlisle, composed around 1400. After a series of tests of loyalty and obedience, the Carle insists that Gawain and his wife kiss each other in his bed, bringing Gawain with great ceremony to his own marriage bed in order to test Gawain's obedience.[28] Gawain passes the test by following the Carle's orders to embrace and perform sex acts upon the Carle's wife up to but not including penetrative sex, stopping at the last moment 'when Gawen wolde have doun the prevey far' (l. 466), because the Carle says 'Whoo ther!' (l. 467). As a reward for passing the test, Gawain is given permission to 'play wytt' (l. 473) the Carle's daughter to satisfy his aroused sexual desires. The daughter 'dorst not agenst his byddynge doun' (l. 478) so lies obediently beside him. Eventually, but not until after they have spent the night together, the Carle gives his daughter to Gawain, who carries her away along with a horse. The two women in the story are barely given a mention: the challenge was not whether Gawain could control himself and follow instructions around women, but whether he could do so in bed.

The treatment of the bed in fourteenth-century romance *The Avowyng of Arthur* highlights how a bed's sexual meaning was ingrained regardless of the proclivity or chastity of its occupants. In an attempt to provoke Bawdwin's jealousy, a knight is ordered by King Arthur to share a bed with Bawdwin's wife.[29] It is clear that the lady and Arthur associate the idea of being in bed with another man with sex, as Arthur repeatedly assures the lady that she will not be dishonoured, saying 'thou schall have no harmynge' (l. 831), 'thou schall harmeles be' (l. 842), and tells the knight to 'neghe noghte thou that Lady' on pain of death (l. 854). Unlike Gawain's trial by the Carle, the knight in bed with the lady is not the subject of this particular trial: instead, the lady's husband is the one being tested. Arthur's surprise when Bawdwin fails to become jealous shows us that the cultural understanding of the bed is such that jealousy is the normal response to seeing one's wife in the same bed as another man, regardless of whether any sexual activity took place:

> The King sayd, 'And I hade thoghte
> Quy that thou wrathis the noghte,
> And fyndus him in bed broghte
> By thi Laydy.' (ll. 905–8)

[28] *Sir Gawain and the Carle of Carlisle,* in *Sir Gawain: Eleven Romances and Tales,* ed. T. Hahn (Kalamazoo, 1995), ll. 330–58.
[29] *The Avowying of Arthur,* ed. Hahn, ll. 846–8.

Arthur's behaviour throughout the scene, repeatedly insisting that the man and woman do not touch in bed, remaining in the chamber to keep guard all night and expressing surprise at Bawdwin's reaction, indicates that he considers it natural that two people in bed together would have sex given the chance, regardless of their feelings towards each other. The characters' reactions to Arthur, as well as the lack of judgement voiced by the narrator, suggests that the audience would be inclined to share Arthur's surprise. It is clear, therefore, that the concept of the bed in the late medieval cultural imagination had inherent sexual meanings, even when sex was far from the bedfellows' minds.

'To be bonour and buxom in bed': beds and marriage

The semantic relationship between beds and chambers and sex and the role they had in a couple's relationship was most pertinent within the context of marriage in late medieval English society. In particular, the idea of a couple in bed was at the centre of the idea of marriage, as it was considered to be the only appropriate space in which to engage in marital sex. However, the marriage bed was understood to be more than simply a space for sex. As we saw in chapter 3, the bed played an important role in communication within the marriage, as it was understood to be the only domestic space in which a married couple were free to speak equally and openly to one another.[30] Additionally, the bed's role as a sacred space in which one could communicate with God, as explored in Chapter 2, meant that it was a particularly fitting locus for the consummation of a Christian marriage. Marriage vows reflect the importance placed on the marriage bed in late medieval England. They do not explicitly refer to sex – though the association shines through – but they do focus on the two objects most intimately associated with sharing within a marriage: the bed and board (or table). In the Salisbury marriage vows, the woman promises 'to be bonour and buxom in bed and at borde' and in the York marriage vows, both the man and the woman use the phrase 'to haue and to holde, at bedde and at borde', so it is clear that the bed was considered to be a vital space in which the theatre of marriage is played out.[31] Indeed, the

---

[30] See ch. 3 above, pp. 77–80.
[31] *The Ancient Liturgy of the Church of England According to the Uses of Sarum Bangor York & Hereford and the Modern Roman Liturgy Arranged in Parallel Columns,*

sharing of 'bed and board' was considered to be at the heart of marriage, even though it was not what made a marriage legally binding. This much is clear from rare instances of judicial separation, known as divorce *a mensa et thoro*: from bed and board.[32] Judicial separation was granted following accusations of adultery, heresy or extreme domestic violence but was not a formal annulment of the marriage.[33] This suggests that the bed was considered to play an important role within what was culturally understood to be a marriage, rather than what was legally required for a marriage to be binding.

The marriage bed was recognised in marriage ceremonies as a meaningful space for the newly-weds. In both the Salisbury and York missals, the priest is instructed to say a blessing 'super thorum in sero' (over the bed at a late hour).[34] Both the bed and the chamber are remembered in the blessing: according to the *Sarum Missal*, after the bride and groom have gone to bed, the priest first enters the chamber and says, 'Bless, O Lord, this chamber and all the dwell therin, that they may be established in thy peace and abide in thy will, and live and grow in thy love, and that the length of their days may be multiplied', before saying a 'blessing over the bed only', followed by a blessing of the couple in the bed.[35] The emphasis on sleeping and rest in these blessings suggests that the marriage bed was not only considered to be the space for marital sex, but also for resting in each other's presence. Meanwhile, the specific blessing over the chamber and the 'blessing over the bed only' demonstrates the cultural awareness that both the chamber and the bed were considered significant

ed. W. Maskell, 2nd edn (London, 1846), p. clv; *The Library of Liturgiology and Ecclesiology for English Readers* IX: *The Sarum Missal in English*, ed. V. Staley (London, 1911), p. 156; *Manuale et Processionale ad Usum Insignis Ecclesiae Eboracensis*, ed. W. G. Henderson (London, 1875), p. 27; *Love, Sex and Marriage in the Middle Ages: A Sourcebook*, ed. C. McCarthy (London, 2004) conflates the York and Sarum Missals, stating that the female-only reference to bed and borde is part of the York marriage vows.

[32] S. M. Butler, 'Lies, Damned Lies, and the Life of Saint Lucy: Three Cases of Judicial Separation from the Late medieval Court of York', in *Trompe(-)l'œil: Imitation and Falsification*, ed. P. Romanski and A. Sy-Wonyu (Rouen, 2002), pp. 1–16 (p. 2); S. M. Butler, *Divorce in Medieval England: From One to Two Persons in Law* (New York, 2013).

[33] Butler, *Divorce in Medieval England*, p. 16.

[34] *Manuale et Processionale*, ed. Henderson, p. 35; *The Sarum Missal*, ed. Staley, p. 156. This practice also reinforces the cultural idea that the time to be in bed is at night, as explored in ch. 1 above.

[35] *The Sarum Missal*, ed. Staley, p. 160.

as a meaningful space and object associated with the marriage. They were not only where a couple would live out their marriage, but were also meaningful in themselves.

The idea that the marriage bed was culturally valuable and worthy of respect is demonstrated in *Lai le Freine*, which survives in the Auchinleck manuscript written around 1330, showing that the cultural meaning of the marriage bed was not only known to the clergy.[36] The protagonist, le Freine, was separated at birth from her mother and twin sister and abandoned in the grounds of a convent with a ring and a 'baudekyne' (a richly brocaded cloth) marking her status.[37] She is brought up in the convent and falls in love with the knight Sir Guroun, who is subsequently pledged to her estranged sister, Le Codre. Despite her own feelings towards the marriage, Le Freine's reaction to the marriage bed illustrates the culturally ingrained idea of the importance of the bed in marriage:

> Than to the bour the damsel sped,
> Whar graithed* was the spousaile bed;   *made ready
> She demed it was ful foully dight*,   *prepared
> And ill beseemed a may so bright;
> So to her coffer quick sche cam,
> And her riche baudekyn out-nam,
> Which from the abbesse sche had got;
> Fairer mantel nas ther not;
> And deftly on the bed it laid;
> Her lord would thus be well apaid. (ll. 359–68)

Even though she is so emotionally opposed to the marriage that 'her herte wel nigh to-broke' (l. 353), Le Freine finds the marriage bed's 'foully dight' condition so incongruous to the event that she gives up her 'baudekyn', one of only two possessions connecting her with her past, which she was bound to keep by the abbess, in order to make the bed suitable for the newly-wed couple. Eventually, Le Freine's mother recognises her by the 'baudekyn' on the bed, the family is reconciled and the protagonist marries Guroun in place of her sister. The marriage bed's role in reuniting the lovers as well as the heroine's family is pertinent, as it reinforces the idea that the bed is at the centre of a marriage and by extension, a family unit.

---

[36] Edinburgh, National Library of Scotland, Advocates MS 19. 2. 1, ff. 261ra–262ra.
[37] *Lai le Freine*, ed. Sands, l. 364.

There are striking parallels between Le Freine and Chaucer's Grisel-da from 'The Clerk's Tale', who is made to prepare the beds for her husband's wedding to a younger woman and does so efficiently and pleasingly, though it 'peyned hire to doon al that she myghte,/ Preyyn-ge the chambereres'.[38] In both cases, the marriage beds are understood by the protagonists to be culturally valuable, so that each heroine takes care to prepare them properly and carefully, at great personal cost. Regardless of how they feel about the marriages, they understand that the marriage beds are worthy of respect. The compulsion to adorn the marriage beds for the special occasion of the consummation of a marriage is reminiscent of the way in which lying-in chambers are prepared, in which in some cases at least as much care is taken in pro-curing the materials to make the chamber aesthetically suitable as in vouchsafing the welfare of the mother and child.[39]

Probably the most important role of the marriage bed was as the locus for the consummation of the marriage. Marriages did not have to be formal contracts made at the church door and did not necessar-ily require witnesses. It was also possible to have chaste marriages of present consent, in which a couple would pledge their troths but never physically consummate the marriage. However, when the marriage vows were vows of future consent (in which a couple would express only an intention to marry), the marriage contracts became binding from the moment at which the marriage was physically consummat-ed.[40] As the only space in which marital sex was appropriate, the mar-riage bed was thus incredibly significant to the legal standing of some marriages. Literary evidence tells us that the beds were linked not only with the consummation of the marriage, but with the marriage vows themselves. Evidence from church court documents suggests that vows were often exchanged in public or in front of witnesses, before the couple consummated their marriage in bed at night.[41] Meanwhile, in romance texts, characters often pledge their troths in bed or in the chamber, before or during sexual activity. For example, in *Sir Degrevant* the protagonists 'trouthus thei plyghtes' in the aptly named Chamber

---

[38] G. Chaucer, 'The Clerk's Tale', in *Riverside Chaucer*, ed. Benson, ll. 976–7.

[39] See ch. 6 below, pp. 192–4.

[40] Goldberg, *Women in England*, p. 10.

[41] See, for instance, the marriages discussed in F. Pedersen, *Marriage Disputes in Medieval England* (London, 2000), esp. pp. 59–84; *Love and Marriage in Late Medieval London*, ed. S. McSheffrey (Kalamazoo, 2005); S. McSheffrey, *Marriage, Sex and Civic Culture in Late Medieval London* (Philadelphia, 2011).

of Love, 'and whan here trouthus was plight,/ Than here hertus were lyghth', as they believed themselves to be married even though Degrevant had not yet got Melidor's 'fadyr wylle'.[42] Similarly, in *Sir Launfal*, the eponymous protagonist pledges his troth to the fairy princess in her 'bed of pris', before they spend the night in 'play' in bed together.[43] In some cases, the characters deliberately seek out a chamber in order to pledge troths. For instance, in Chaucer's 'The Clerk's Tale', Walter forgoes a public wedding ceremony in favour of pledging troths in Griselda's 'chambre'.[44] In *Eglamour of Artois*, Eglamour, having gained entry to Christabelle's chamber, insists on marrying her before they spend the night together in bed:

> "Damysell", he seyde, "so haue I spedde
> With the grace of God I shall you wedde".
> Thereto here trowthes they plight
> […]
> And there he dwelled all nyght.[45]

The propensity for romance characters to pledge troths in the chamber is interesting, as it goes against our existing knowledge of real-world convention. As McSheffrey notes, records of marriages contracted in chambers are rare, and the weddings usually took place ostensibly because either the bride, groom or witness was bedridden.[46] Of course, if the exchange of vows takes place in the chamber and there are no witnesses or no subsequent need to discuss the marriage in a court setting, there would be no record of it. Sometimes, it seems, there may have been an ulterior motive for keeping the wedding away from public view. For example, depositions of 1472 describe how Rose Langtoft and Robert Smyth were married in a chamber in Thomas and Alice Hynkeley's house, where Alice 'was lying sick': 'at the time of the contract, Robert sat on the side of the bed and Rose at the time of the contract stood between his legs'.[47] It was convenient for this couple to marry in the chamber, as the marriage was not considered suitable by Rose's employer and so could not be made in public.[48] However,

---

[42] *Sir Degrevant*, ed. Kooper, ll. 52, 53–4, 50.
[43] *Sir Launfal*, ed. Sands, ll. 283, 349.
[44] Chaucer, 'The Clerk's Tale', l. 324.
[45] *Sir Eglamour of Artois*, ed. Hudson, ll. 781–9.
[46] McSheffrey, *Marriage, Sex, and Civic Culture*, p. 126.
[47] *Love & Marriage*, ed. McSheffrey, pp. 60–1.
[48] Ibid., p. 64.

the chamber as a setting for marriage could become inconvenient, as the intimate location and small number of witnesses meant that false testimonies about marriages could be given, or the exchange of vows could be denied. In *Eglamour of Artois*, a similar predicament befalls the protagonists. As the exchange of vows between Eglamour and Christabelle was not witnessed, Christabelle's subsequent pregnancy is considered to be out of wedlock and she is duly punished. Likewise, in most romances in which troths are pledged in the chamber, the relationship remains a secret until a later date, when a more public wedding is held. It seems that, in the late medieval English imagination, the bed was an obvious place for an exchange of vows, when people were marrying for love. However, social practice dictated that serious marriage vows were exchanged elsewhere. As the majority of our evidence for late medieval marriages comes from disputed cases, it is unsurprising that very few of the recorded weddings were reported as taking place in the chamber. Conversely, given that the audience was almost always on the side of the lovers, the literary trope of characters pledging their troths in bed suggests that the chamber was considered an appropriate place in which to exchange marriage vows. It is likely that when couples exchanged vows in an intimate setting such as the bed they pledged them again in a public place, in order to have witnesses in case of future discrepancies.[49] If we take patterns in romance as possible reflections of social practice, it is arguable that the bed and chamber played an even larger part in marriage than extant documentary evidence suggests.

As suggested by the missals discussed above, it was assumed that the consummation of marriage would take place within the marriage bed. The idea of a couple 'alone and naked in bed together' was enough to denote sexual activity, and so was often used in witness statements to prove that marriages had been consummated. Conversely, the physical consummation of marriage required two people to be in bed together but, intriguingly, they did not have to be the married couple in question. The bed's symbolic role in marriage was considered to be so vital that, in the case of marriage by proxy, in which either the bride or the groom were unable to attend the event, a representative of the absentee would publically share a bed with the other party. An example of this practice is the proxy marriage between Philippa of

---

[49] P. J. P. Goldberg, *Women, Work, and Life Cycle in a Medieval Economy: Women in York and Yorkshire c. 1300–1520* (Oxford, 1990), pp. 236–7.

Lancaster and João I of Portugal. According to Froissart, Philippa and João Rodriguez de Sá, the King's representative, 'were laid courteously in bed, as husband and wife ought to be', in order to symbolise the consummation of the royal marriage.[50] Similarly, Mary Tudor's proxy marriage to Louis XII was considered consummated when Mary's bare leg touched that of the King's proxy Marquis of Rothelin in bed.[51] The concept of consummating a proxy marriage by the use of real (if substitute) people sharing a bed without actually engaging in sexual activity is incredibly revealing about how late medieval people understood the idea of the bed. The trope of two people in bed together was so powerful that it transcended linguistics, so that the bed and its occupants acted out the meaning behind 'alone in bed together', validating an estranged couple's marriage.

The marriage bed was considered to play an important part in late medieval English marriage. More than a symbol of commitment and a site of consummation, it was considered to be the only space in which marital sex was understood to be appropriate. As such the bed and, by extension, the chamber legitimised marital sex, so that it was socially acceptable not only to have sex with one's spouse but also to enjoy it. As indicated by the precepts structuring this book, late medieval English society understood that sex could be approached with gleeful abandon, as long as it was marital sex in bed. In particular, the instruction to 'go to thy bed myrely […] plesse and loffe thy wyffe dewly/ And basse hyr onys or tweys myrely' highlights that the fulfilment of sexual desire was expected to be enjoyed and that all levels of enjoyment were appropriate, as long as it took place in the chamber and within marriage.[52] Other manuscript versions of the poem, which do not have marital sex as their final goal, instruct the addressee to please

---

[50] J. Froissart, *The Antient Chronicles of Jean Froissart, of England, France, Spain, Portugal, Scotland, Brittany and Flanders, and the Adjoining Countries. Translated from the Original French at the Command of King Henry the Eighth*, ed. J. Bourchier and Lord Berners, 3 vols. (London, 1815), III, 375–6; A. H. De Oliveira Marques, *Daily Life in Portugal in the Middle Ages* (Madison, 1971), p. 167.

[51] M. C. Brown, *Mary Tudor, Queen of France* (London, 1911), p. 99; Terence McCarthy argues that a similar event took place between Prince Arthur and the Spanish envoy Roderigo Gonzaléz De Puebla, who was the proxy for Catherine of Aragon. T. McCarthy, 'Old Worlds, New Worlds: King Arthur in England', in *The Social and Literary Contexts of Malory's* Morte DArthur, ed. D. T. Hanks Jr and J. G. Brogdon (Cambridge, 2000), pp. 5–23 (p. 9).

[52] See Introduction, p. 10.

'thy love' or 'thy make'.[53] The 'wyffe' of the Brome precepts reminds the addressee that sex is to be enjoyed with one's spouse. The command to 'basse' the addressee's wife can be read as a gentle reminder to kiss one's spouse, as 'basse' can refer to a kiss.[54] Alternatively, 'basse' can be read as a euphemism for sex, carrying with it a similar mixture of joyful impropriety and carnality as the modern English verb 'to fuck'. Scholarly works on medieval sex have focused on the theological and medical arguments against sexual intercourse for anything other than procreation within marriage, to the point at which one may assume that sex was never permissible or enjoyable in the Middle Ages.[55] On the contrary, the chamber sanctioned sexuality. The double interpretation of 'basse' in the 'Arise Early' precepts sums up the dichotomous cultural meaning of the bed and chamber in relation to marital sex. It was both a pure, sacred space for chaste kisses and the site of joyful, regular fucking.

The understanding that the chamber was the only appropriate space for licit sexual encounters is evident in many literary texts. Some literary couples engaging in licit sexual intercourse do so in bed not because of any plot device, but because the author and the audience locate marital sex within the marriage bed: in *Sir Launfal*, Launfal and the lady 'wente to bedde [...] for play' and in *Sir Tryamour*, Sir Ardus and Margaret conceive their child in 'bedd'.[56] Conversely, couples who have sex outside of the chamber usually suffer negative consequences. A contrast between sex inside and outside of the chamber is set up in Chaucer's 'The Merchant's Tale'. As previously mentioned,

---

[53] McDonald, 'Fragments of *(Have Your) Desire*', p. 255; Dublin, Trinity College, MS 661, p. 62, London, British Library, Lansdowne MS 762, f. 16v, and London, British Library, MS Sloane 775, f. 56v use 'love'/'loue'; Cambridge, Magdalene College, MS Pepys 1047, f. 1 uses 'make'.

[54] *MED*, 'bassen (v.)'

[55] See, for instance, J. A. Brundage, *Law, Sex, and Christian Society in Medieval Europe* (Chicago, 1987), especially the flowchart on p. 162 which suggests that sex is rarely an appropriate option, even within wedlock; the essays in *Handbook of Medieval Sexuality*, ed. V. L. Bullough and J. A. Brundage (New York, 2000), especially P. J. Payer, 'Confession and the Study of Sex in the Middle Ages', pp. 3–32 and J. A. Brundage, 'Sex and Canon Law', pp. 33–50; McSheffrey, *Marriage, Sex, and Civic Culture*, pp. 135–90; Phillips and Reay, *Sex Before Sexuality*, pp. 17–39; R. Mazo Karras, *Unmarriages: Women, Men and Sexual Unions in the Middle Ages* (Philadelphia, 2012); Karras, *Sexuality in Medieval Europe: Doing Unto Others*.

[56] *Sir Launfal*, in *Middle English Verse Romances*, ed. D. B. Sands (Exeter, 1986), ll. 347–9; *Sir Tryamour*, ed. Hudson, l. 41.

when Januarie and May have sex in the garden, they are described as doing 'thynges whiche that were nat doon abedde'.[57] Not only does this phrase reinforce the idea that the normative locus for sex was in bed, but it also suggests that they were deliberately flouting societal convention by only having sex in the garden, or by performing sex acts that were not appropriate in the sanctified space of the marriage bed. The repercussions of having sex outside, even within marriage, are unpleasant for Januarie and May. This extramural sexual activity directly precedes the loss of 'worldly joye' (l. 2055) for Januarie, when 'amydde his lust' (l. 2071) the gods cause him to become blind and May takes the opportunity to engage in a sexual affair with Damyan, a squire in Januarie's court. Januarie's blind and cuckolded state can be read as a direct consequence of having had sex outside in the middle of the day, despite a chamber being available to them. Later on in the narrative, sex 'upon a tree' (l. 2374) puts an end to the relationship between May and Damyan when, once again, the gods intervene. May and Damyan's sexual activities outside of the chamber ensure that they were easily caught, even though the only witness had, until that moment, been blind. Sex out of doors was not appropriate, whether within or outside of wedlock, and so could not continue happily.

There are various cautionary tales of couples who receive divine retribution for engaging in sexual intercourse in churches and places of worship, which cast the church building as the antithesis to a suitable space for sex.[58] For instance, in Robert Mannyng's early fourteenth-century didactic text *Handlyng Synne*, written ostensibly as a guide to managing morality and confession, Mannyng uses as an illustration of 'sacrylage' a story of a man and his wife, who had sex with each other too close to a church and were punished by becoming stuck together so that 'þey myghte no more be broghte a-sondre'.[59] A similar story by Geoffroy de la Tour-Landry was printed by Caxton in 1484, in which a man and woman had sex on an altar in a church, resulting in a case of *penis captivus* because God 'tyed hem fast togedre that night

---

[57] Chaucer, 'The Merchant's Tale', l. 2051.

[58] D. Elliot, *Fallen Bodies: Pollution, Sexuality, and Demonology in the Middle Ages* (Philadelphia, 1999), pp. 61–80; J. D. Rolleston, 'Penis Captivus: An Historical Note', in *Sex in the Middle Ages*, ed. Salisbury, pp. 232–8; D. Elliot, 'Sex in Holy Places: An Exploration of a Medieval Anxiety', *Journal of Women's History* 6.3 (1994), 6–34.

[59] R. Mannyng, *Handlyng Synne*, ed. F. J. Furnivall (London, 1901), p. 281.

and the morw all day'.[60] In both stories, repentance and public assistance is required in order for the couple to be parted, emphasising the evil of their previous actions and how far they have transgressed from acceptable social behaviour. Dyan Elliot points out that the protagonists of earlier versions of this narrative are unmarried, while later versions focus on married couples.[61] Elliot argues that this shift reflects the changes in canonistic attitudes towards expressions of sexuality within marriage, particularly in regards to holidays, in which penitential abstinence was required.[62] She goes on to argue that the 'worst case scenario', as she describes an adulterous couple, was no longer necessary to make the situation undesirable: sex in a consecrated space was transgression enough, regardless of the specific circumstances of the sexual encounter. Though Elliot is certainly right to suggest that sex in a consecrated space would have been met with disapproval and anxiety from the Church, the texts have as much to do with society's increasing desire for private space as it does with morality. The chamber was gaining popularity but was still, by far, a space reserved for the few who could afford it. Within bourgeois houses containing only one chamber, the chamber would belong to the master and mistress of the house, though it was a far from private space. As a result, many married couples would have found it difficult to find a space for sex that was not too overlooked, while unmarried couples had nowhere they could legitimately satisfy their sexual desires. Members of late medieval society were thus in a quandary: the only acceptable space for legitimate sex was in the chamber, but there were not enough chambers to go around. A local church could well have looked like an inviting prospect to a couple seeking the intimacy and shelter that a chamber was understood to provide, without having access to a chamber themselves. The warning against copulating in the church is not merely an attempt to prevent the church from being defiled; it is also a reminder that the only suitable space for sex is in bed.

It is clear that sex outside the chamber walls was understood to result in uncontained, unexpected sexual acts and consequences. For instance, in *Sir Gowther* the duchess, having resolved to do anything it

---

[60] *Book of the Knight of Tour-Landry: Compiled for the Instruction of his Daughters: Translated from the Original French into English in the Reign of Henry VI* (London, 1906), ed. T. Wright, p. 51.

[61] Elliot, 'Sex in Holy Places', p. 13.

[62] Ibid., p. 14.

takes to get pregnant, encounters a demon disguised 'as lyke hur lorde as he myghte be', who 'leyd hur down undur a tre,/ With hur is wyll he wroghtth'.[63] After sexual intercourse and the conception of Gowther, the demon gets up, looking like a 'felturd fende',[64] and informs the duchess of the conception. The result of this encounter is a monstrous child, who had slain nine wet-nurses by the time he was a year old, bit his mother's nipple off and grew into a murderous, immoral wretch. Gowther's behaviour, before he is converted, is treated as a direct result of his mother's tryst with the demon. However, it is not merely the fact that he was conceived by a demon, but the fact that the event was in a place and time unfit for legitimate sex, which causes Gowther to be so monstrous. We are told twice that Gowther is Merlin's brother, as the demon engendered them both.[65] *Sir Gowther*'s audience must therefore have been assumed to be aware of narratives in which Merlin's origin is described, and therefore to know that while Merlin was fathered by a demon, his mother's piety ensured that his otherworldly powers were benevolent, rather than evil.[66] By drawing attention to the relationship between Merlin and Gowther, the writer prompts the audience to think on what was lacking in Gowther's mother's conduct. She cannot be accused of having knowingly committed adultery, because the fiend had taken the appearance of her husband. The duchess's misconduct is in the time and place of her child's conception. This idea is brought home by the stark contrast between the two sexual encounters at the start of the romance: the first 'in hur orchard apon a day […] undur a tre' (ll. 67–71); the second in 'hur chambur […] that was so bygly byld' (ll. 80–81), 'at evon [in] beyd' (l. 91). The iteration that the chamber was 'bygly byld' (l. 81) emphasises its security and suitability for the purpose. Similarly, the writer makes it very clear that the duke and duchess restrict their sexual acts to a socially condoned time. The duchess tells her husband that 'tonyght' (l. 83) they would conceive a child, and they wait all day until evening, when they 'wold no lengur wonde' (l. 93). It is apparent that the proper time and place for legitimate sex was considered to be at the end of the day, in bed.

---

[63] *Sir Gowther*, ed. Laskaya and Salisbury, ll. 70–2.
[64] Ibid., l. 74; 'felturd' = shaggy, literally 'made of felt'.
[65] Ibid., ll. 10, 98.
[66] See, for instance, *Prose Merlin*, ed. J. Conlee (Kalamazoo, 1998), ll. 241–5.

Breaking chambers and bleeding beds: extra-marital sex

Though beds and chambers were at the heart of the late medieval idea of marriage, beds and chambers (and the lack thereof) were not only associated with marital sex. Instead, they were considered consciously in relation to illegitimate sex. Perhaps due to the obvious lack of marriage vows in rape cases, rape was often located outside of the chamber in the late medieval cultural imagination. Adultery, on the other hand, nearly always took place in the bed or chamber.

In Middle English literature, rape is usually treated as a direct consequence of the victim having been sexually available out of doors. In fact, rape outdoors in Middle English romance is rarely articulated as such. However, hardship ensues because the mother had sex outside, rather than because her rapist is considered to be a transgressor. For instance, just as the duchess in *Sir Gowther* is punished because she is violated outside, so too is the king's daughter in *Sir Degaré*. Like the fiend in *Sir Gowther*, the knight rapes the maiden and then tells her immediately that they have conceived a child.[67] Even though the king's daughter put up a fight and was certainly not the instigator of the sexual tryst, it is she who is made to suffer, both at the time and later, when she must keep her pregnancy a secret and then give up her son. At no point is the knight reprimanded, either by another character or by the writer. Indeed, he is rewarded in the end with his victim's hand in marriage. As they eventually make what is apparently a suitable couple, one can assume that had the knight been the maiden's suitor from the start, there would have been no perceived problems with the match. The romance thus appears to condone the knight's actions, as the sexual encounter is the propelling event of the narrative and leads to an apparently happy conclusion. Similarly, the conception of Gyngeleyn in the fourteenth-century *Libeaus Desconus* is the result of Gawain having raped 'a gentyll lady' 'under a forest syde'.[68] The immediate repercussions of this conception are that the child's mother raises him away from society, living in fear of the loss of her reputation and the harmful manifestation of her son's 'bastered' (l. 15) status. Despite the shame and hardship cause by her rape, she later 'thankyd [Gawain] many a syth,/ And kissed hym sykerly' (ll.

---

[67] *Sir Degaré*, ed. Laskaya and Salisbury, ll. 111–17.
[68] Item 20, *Lybeaus Desconus*, in *Codex Ashmole 61: A Compilation of Popular Middle English Verse*, ed. G. Shuffleton (Kalamazoo, 2008), ll. 2208–9.

2211–12). Gawain is described in the highest terms: 'a beter knyght, ne more profetabull,/ With Arthor at the Rownd Tabull,/ Herd I never of rede' (ll. 10–12). It is implied that if the woman has suffered, it is her fault for having been in the forest, rather than any fault on the part of Gawain. A further instance of rape outdoors occurs in Chaucer's 'The Wife of Bath's Tale'. Despite the many 'chambres' and 'boures' in the area, the knight rapes a woman by a river.[69] Perhaps surprisingly, it is the women of the court who persuade King Arthur to have lenience on the attacker, which eventually results in the knight being rewarded with a marriage to a beautiful woman. In each of these episodes, the woman's complete passivity is striking. As they do not share a bed with their sexual partners, they are not empowered by the space to speak on an equal footing with their transgressors. Instead, it is suggested that the outside world is full of potential for rape and sexual attack, and the female characters are to blame for anything which befalls them outside of the chamber walls.

In contrast, adultery is nearly always located in the chamber. The bed's inherent sexual connotations, which meant that two people sharing a bed could be considered to be involved in a sexual liaison, are so powerful that in some cases, the presence of two people in one bed immediately suggested adultery. An important example of this association is found in the mid fifteenth-century manuscript shown in Fig. 15. The historiated initial 'A' of 'Adulterium' in James le Palmer's *Omne Bonum*, an encyclopaedia of universal knowledge, shows a man and woman in bed, with the explanation 'Adulterium est alieni thori violacio': adultery is the violation of the bed of another. According to both the text and the accompanying image, the bed itself becomes violated during acts of adultery. It is apparently enough that two people are in bed together to convey the meaning of adultery, without it being necessary to show the couple in any graphic detail. The bed takes up a large proportion of the belly of the A, while the bed curtains form the two downstrokes, so that the bed and the people within it become part of the concept of 'Adulterium'. In contrast, the adulterous couple are represented only by their heads, which rest on a single small pillow, faces inclined towards each other, and give the impression that their bodies lie diagonally across the bed. Although the third person – the cuckolded husband or wife – is not present, the bed itself acts as the

---

[69] G. Chaucer, 'The Wife of Bath's Tale', in *Riverside Chaucer*, ed. Benson, ll. 869, 885–7.

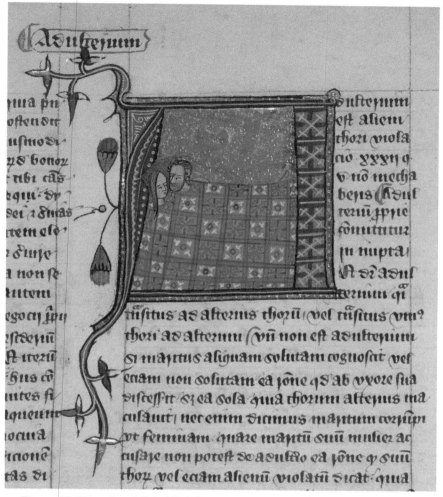

Figure 15: Historiated 'A' of 'Adulterium', c. 1440–60. © The British Library Board. BL Royal 6E. VI, f. 61r.

third party. The intimacy of the shared pillow, combined with the diagonal position, gratuitously taking up space in the bed that could otherwise be filled by another person more legally entitled, enhances the idea of the violation of another's bed.

Adultery as an event understood to take place specifically in the wronged party's bed is a trope found in fabliau, a genre which is most

159

often located in bed. Chaucer demonstrates the understanding that adultery is the violation of another's bed in 'The Miller's Tale', when Nicholas and Alison have sex in the 'bedde/ Ther as the carpenter is wont to lye', even though the audience is aware that Nicholas has a bed and chamber of his own, as it has been painstakingly described by the miller in order to mock the clerk.[70] The author of *Dame Sirith* (*c.* 1275) understands adultery to be particularly bad if it takes place in bed. Marjeri suggests that there are two levels of adultery when she objects to Wilkin's advances, proclaiming 'that ne shal nevere be/ That I shal don selk falseté,/ On bedde ne on flore'.[71] For Marjeri, 'on bedde' is the usual place for adultery, but she will not even condescend to cheat on her husband 'on flore'. Marie de France's fable *Dou vileins qui vit un autre hom od sa fame*, which tells the story of a peasant who sees his wife having sex with another man, shows that adultery was understood more as the trespass of a man's bed by another than as an action done with a man's wife.[72] The marital bed is emphasised in the text: in the initial description, the peasant sees a man 'seur sun lit/ Od sa feme feseit déduit' (on his bed, doing what he will with his wife).[73] When he confronts his wife, the peasant insists that he saw the man 'seur mon lit' (on my bed).[74] The wife does not actually deny that she was having sex with another man, but instead denies that there had been a man in the marital bed, 'proving' her innocence – arguing that the peasant's reflection in a barrel of water does not mean that he is inside the barrel, so he should not believe everything that he sees – by dint of the fact that he could not prove that someone else had been in his bed.

The knowledge that adultery was understood to be the violation of the bed of another sheds new light on the way we understand and interpret episodes in romance. In narratives in which characters are framed for cases of adultery, it is done by planting someone in the chamber. For instance, in *Octavian*, the emperor's mother puts a knave 'into the ladyes beedd' and the lady is immediately found guilty of

---

[70] G. Chaucer, 'The Miller's Tale', in *Riverside Chaucer*, ed. Benson, ll. 3650–1.
[71] *Dame Sirith*, in *The Trials and Joys of Marriage*, ed. E. Salisbury (Kalamazoo, 2002), ll. 100–2.
[72] M. de France, *Poesies de Marie de France, poète Anglo-Normand du VIIIᵉ siècle, ou recueil de lais, fables et autres productions de cette femme célèbre*, ed. B. de Roquefort (Paris, 1820), p. 206.
[73] Ibid., ll. 3–4.
[74] Ibid., l. 9.

adultery, without question, as soon as the knave is discovered.[75] Like-wise, in *Erle of Tolous*, a young man is hidden in the empress' chamber so that he can be 'discovered' and the empress punished for adultery.[76] To a modern reader, it seems incongruous that a romance heroine – often royal or aristocratic and always held in the highest regard for her taste and morality – would be suspected of having an affair with an unnamed, previously unmentioned peasant or knave of dubious social standing. If we bear in mind that adultery was considered to be the violation of another's bed, these scenes in romance, upon which the whole narrative is often hinged, become immediately more compre-hensible. By unwittingly sharing a bed with another man, the women have, indeed, participated in the cultural idea of adultery.

In the late medieval consciousness, the violation of beds was not only understood to mean trespass, but also physical harm. A Notting-ham court case of 1389 illustrates how the violation of another's bed was associated with adultery. John de Bilby files against the chaplain, Roger de Mampton, whom he accuses of having 'entered his chamber', where he was found 'under a curtain of the bed of the aforesaid John'.[77] This trespass into John's chamber and bed was enough to signify adultery, according to the definition provided by James le Palmer. The violation of John's bed, however, does not stop there. Having been warned to stay away from John's wife and houses, Roger subsequently 'broke the wall of the said John' and entered 'his secret places' (i.e. his chambers) 'with the wife of the aforesaid John'.[78] This action re-sulted in the damage of 'two pairs of sheets', which were 'expend-ed and wasted in evil ways'. When questioned by the court, Roger argued that it was 'the custom with parochial clergy to go through their parish with the holy water'. Even laying aside the obvious sexual connotations of the priest repeatedly giving his 'holy water' to John's wife in bed, his actions are described as 'evil' ('in malis').[79] Breaking John's wall, entering his 'secret places' and violating his bed are clear

---

[75] *Octavian*, ed. Hudson, l. 182.

[76] *Erle of Tolous*, in *The Middle English Breton Lays*, ed. A. Laskaya and E. Salisbury (Kalamazoo, 1995), ll. 755–66.

[77] *Records of the Boroughs of Nottingham, Being a Series of Extracts from the Archives of the Corporation of Nottingham* (London, 1882), I: *King Henry II to King Richard II, 1155–1399*, ed. W. H. Stevenson, p. 241.

[78] Ibid., p. 243.

[79] Ibid., pp. 242–3.

indications of adultery and are crimes which are more easily proven and quantified than simply having sex with John's wife.

Physical damage to beds during adulterous sexual encounters also occurs within romance texts. The idea of the violated bed in adulterous relationships manifests itself in the bloodying of beds by the violator (always the male character, though the female characters are equally blamed for committing adultery). For example, male characters in Malory's *Morte DArthur* and other romances tend to bleed while in bed with their paramours. As pointed out by Christina Francis, the four chamber scenes in *Morte DArthur* in which characters shed blood are all within the context of illicit sexual activity.[80] When Tristram has a sexual encounter with Segwarydes' wife, 'in his ragyng' he takes no notice of a fresh wound dealt him by King Mark, and so 'bebled both the ouer shete and the nether & pelowes and hede shete'.[81] The result is that the very centre of the bed is stained with blood, a physical manifestation of its violation, as if the bed itself has been hurt by the illicit sexual encounter. Although the wound was caused by a previous skirmish, the bloodshed in bed is directly caused by the 'ragyng', in which the illicit couple are engaged. Furthermore, Segwarydes' re-action to the stained bed indicates that he (and by extension, Malory and his audience) understands that a violated bed is the signifier for adultery: 'whan he fond her bedde troubled & broken and wente nere and beheld it by candel lyghte thenne he sawe that there had layne a wounded knyght'.[82] Similarly, in an episode taken from *Le Chevalier de la Charrette*, Malory's Lancelot injures his hand on the iron bars outside Guinevere's window upon breaking into her chamber and 'wente vnto bed with the queen & took no force of his hurte hand', bloodying the 'shete & pylowe' (pp. 781–2) in the process. Like Segwarydes, 'whan sir mellyagraunce aspyed that blood thenne he demed in her that she was fals to the kynge', saying 'a wounded knyghte this nyght hath layne by yow' (p. 782). Though Meliagraunce assumes the perpetrator to be one

---

[80] C. Francis, 'Reading Malory's Bloody Bedrooms', in *Arthurian Literature 28: Blood, Sex, Malory: Essays on the* Morte Darthur, ed. D. Clark and K. McClune (Cambridge, 2011), pp. 1–20 (p.1).

[81] T. Malory, *Le Morte Darthur, or The Hoole Book of Kyng Arthur and of his Noble Knyghtes of the Round Table*, ed. S. H. A. Shepherd (New York, 2004), p. 294.

[82] *Le Morte Darthur*, ed. Shepherd, p. 294; see also M. G. Leitch, '(Dis)Figuring Transgressive Desire: Blood, Sex, and Stained Sheets in Malory's *Morte Darthur*', in *Arthurian Literature 28: Blood, Sex, Malory: Essays on the* Morte Darthur, ed. D. Clark and K. McClune (Cambridge, 2011), pp. 21–38 (p. 32).

of the wounded knights lying in the castle, rather than Lancelot, he correctly identifies that an illicit sexual event has taken place. In each of these episodes, the beds are bloodied by the male characters and so are considered to have been despoiled by the perpetrators. The immediate realisation on the part of both Segwarydes and Meliagraunce that bloodied beds signify adultery is intriguing. One would assume that menstruation, rather than adultery, would be a much more obvious explanation for blood found in a bed where a woman has lain. It is very clear, however, that in each episode the blood is not ever considered to be the woman's. Though spilled from the male character, it seems to belong specifically to the violated bed.

The bloodied bed as a signifier for adultery is used to great effect in the Middle English *Sir Tristrem* (c. 1330–40). The dwarf Meriadok, intent on exposing the affair between Tristrem and Ysonde, arranges for them to be bloodlet, explaining to Mark,

Do as Y ye say
And tokening thou schalt se
Ful sone.
Her bed schal blodi bene
Ar he his wille have done.[83]

What is particularly interesting about this plan is that bloodletting was considered necessary. Mark, Tristrem and Ysonde all sleep in one large chamber. One would assume, therefore, that Tristrem and Ysonde would find a less-overlooked space in which to engage in amorous activity, or that they would be caught easily if Mark were to keep watch. Furthermore, Meriadok has taken measures to ensure that any traffic between the beds would be noticed, as he has covered the floor between the beds with flour. As the beds are thirty feet apart, it should be impossible for Mark to jump from one bed to another. It is curious, therefore, that Meriadok insists that a bloodied bed will provide evidence of the adulterous relationship, rather than the footprints between the beds or simply the presence of the two lovers in the same bed. Against all the odds, Mark does indeed manage to long-jump between the beds and, as Meriadok planned, reopens his wounds in the process. Not only was the bloodied bed the proof Mark needed, when he 'her bed hadde sen,/ And al blodi it wes' (ll. 2216–17), but

[83] *Sir Tristrem*, in *Lancelot of the Laik and Sir Tristrem*, ed. A. Lupack (Kalamazoo, 1994), ll. 2185–9.

Meriadok understood that a physical violation of the bed, in the form of bloodstains, was the only way to prove their adulterous relationship. This complex understanding of the damage inflicted upon a bed during an illicit sexual encounter is not explicitly explained within the text, and so we can infer that the symbolism would be obvious to the late medieval audience. Adultery, it seems, was understood to inflict literal damage upon the marriage bed, piercing the heart of the bed until it bled.

A widespread understanding that bloodied beds signify adultery further explains the reaction of Octavian's wrongly accused wife. When Octavian finds the knave who had been secreted into his wife's birthing chamber while she slept, he does not wait to question the boy, but instead immediately draws out a dagger and kills him, so that 'alle was byblede with blode'.[84] The description of the bed, so similar to that of other romance beds in which illicit sexual encounters took place, would be familiar to an audience of romance. If adultery was the violation of another's bed and a bloodied bed is a clear signifier for adultery, on the face of it this scene suggests that adultery has taken place, even though the audience is aware that it has not. His wife's reaction upon waking makes more sense with this knowledge in mind. Elsewhere in the romance, she is a strong character who weathers great hardships, tames lions and defends herself without complaint, and yet upon seeing 'the clothes all byblede':

> Full mekyll was hir care.
> Scho bygan to skryke and crye
> And sythen in swonynge for to ly;
> Hirselfe cho wolde forfare.[85]

Her reaction is understandable, given that her husband had just thrown a severed head at her as she was waking up, but she does not actually scream and swoon at the head, but instead upon seeing the bloodied bedclothes. This reaction indicates an understanding that blood on the bed signifies much more than simply the existence of a decapitated man. The line, 'hirselfe cho wolde forfare' (l. 183) is particularly striking in this episode.[86] Why would she want to destroy herself? Is the bloodied bed such compelling evidence for adultery that

---

[84] *Octavian*, ed. Hudson, l. 159.
[85] Ibid., ll. 179–83.
[86] 'to forfare' is to forfeit.

she is convinced of her own guilt? The state of the bed is so entwined with the sexuality and sexual activity of its occupants that it becomes impossible to separate them out. She becomes entangled within the physical signs of adultery, even though her conscience is clear.

While the bed was considered to have the potential to be violated within the context of adultery, anxiety surrounding the violation of the chamber was often associated with the threat of pre-marital sex. As discussed in Chapter 6, within the late medieval collective psyche, the most female space within the house was the chamber, which was associated with both perceived functions of female genitalia: childbirth and sex. Lying-in and birthing chambers were designed to represent the dark, warm, enclosed womb. Likewise, the entrance into a woman's chamber was symbolic of sexual penetration, so that the chamber door was akin to the vulva. The penetration of a woman's chamber was therefore symbolic of sexual activity. This understanding of an interrelationship between chambers and female sexual organs is evidenced through Chaucer's use of vocabulary. The Wife of Bath euphemistically refers to her 'chambre of Venus', which in her 'Prologue' is certainly a reference to her genitalia but in *The Complaint of Mars*, the chamber of Venus is a chamber within a palace, where Mars and Venus embrace in bed.[87] Despite their obvious differences, each 'chambre of Venus' is the location for sexual activity. Similar to symbols of chastity from previous cultures, such as the *hortus conclusus* in the Song of Songs or the 'bruchele ueat' or fragile vessel in *Hali Meiðhad*, late medieval English society saw a completely sealed chamber to be symptomatic of its occupant's virginal state.[88] This idea can be seen in the architectural constraints associated with anchorites and anchoresses. Their segregation from the world is more than a mental effort and a promise made before God and church officials: they were physically bricked into their anchorholds. The very small hatch, through which the parishioners would deliver food and remove waste, could be compared with the narrower bodily passageways attributed to virgins, as described in medical texts by William of Saliceto, Galen, Henry of Mondeville

---

[87] G. Chaucer, 'The Wife of Bath's Prologue', in *Riverside Chaucer*, ed. Benson, l. 618; G. Chaucer, *The Complaint of Mars*, in *Riverside Chaucer*, ed. Benson, ll. 78–91.

[88] Song of Songs 4.12; *Hali Meiðhad*, in *Medieval English Prose for Women: Selections from the Katherine Group and Ancrene Wisse*, ed. B. Millett and J. Wogan-Browne (Oxford, 1990), pp. 3–43 (p. 11).

and others.[89] The otherwise intact walls of the cells removed, in a very physical way, any opportunity to become less chaste. In a similar way chambers, particularly for female occupants, were seen to physically and symbolically protect the occupants' chastity as long as they remained sealed. A man's entrance into a closed chamber belonging to a woman, or the suspicion thereof, is a common trope in late medieval literature. It is not usually made explicit that the female character's virginity is at stake; rather the focus is on her chamber door. However, the reactions of other characters and the constancy with which the trope occurs indicates that the chamber and parts of the female anatomy are synonymous. In Hue de Rotelande's fifteenth-century text *The Lyfe of Ipomydon*, King Mellyager claims that he is angry at Ipomydon because 'he broke my ladyes boure, þe quene', repeating upon meeting Ipomydon, 'þou dydist dishonour,/ Whan thou brakkist þe quenys boure'.[90] In actual fact, it is not mentioned explicitly that Ipomydon has any sexual relationship with the queen, even though he 'callyd was the quenys lemman' (l. 728). The fact that he had access to the queen's chamber and was able to remove his own maid from the room is perceived to be a violation of the queen's integrity, and thus of the king's property. Access analysis shows that queens are likely to have chambers in the deepest space within a palace, and so would be understood to be harder to reach, with the most severe repercussions if they were transgressed.[91] For instance, Eleanor of Aquitaine's chamber was in the deepest space in Westminster Palace, and had restricted access.[92] Eleanor of Provence's chamber at Clarendon Palace was in the deepest space for all public routes, but with ease of access to the apartments

---

[89] P. J. P. Goldberg, *Medieval England: A Social History 1250–1550* (London, 2004), p. 135; R. Gilchrist, *Gender and Material Culture: The Archaeology of Religious Women* (Abingdon, 1994), p. 178; A. K. Warren, *Anchorites and their Patrons in Medieval England* (Berkley, 1985), p. 29; G. de Saliceto, *Summa Conservationis et Curationis* (Venice, 1489), f. i3ra; *Chirurgie de maitre Henri de Mondeville, chirurgien de Philippe le Bel, Roi de France, composée de 1306 à 1320*, ed. and trans. E. Nicaise (Paris, 1893), p. 75; A. Magnus, *Book of Minerals*, trans. D. Wyckoff (Oxford, 1967), p. 93; D. Jacquart and C. Thomasset, *Sexuality and Medicine in the Middle Ages* (Princeton, 1988), pp. 37–45; E. Lastique and H. R. Lemay, 'A Medieval Physician's Guide to Virginity', in *Sex in the Middle Ages: A Book of Essays*, ed. J. E. Salisbury (London, 1991), pp. 56–79 (pp. 61–3).

[90] H. de Rotelande, *The Lyfe of Ipomydon*, ed. T. Ikegami (Tokyo, 1932), ll. 1441, 1473–4.

[91] Richardson, 'Gender and Space in English Royal Palaces'.

[92] Ibid., p. 137.

of Henry III and Prince Edward.[93] Anne of Bohemia's rooms were the furthest away from all court life and did not provide ease of access to or from any other apartment.[94]

Like *Ipomydon*, in *Undo Your Door*, otherwise known as *The Squire of Low Degree*, the maiden's chamber is a source of much concern. Even before the squire attempts to gain access to the chamber, the guards are told that any attempt to enter the maiden's chamber should be treated as a personal and physical violation, punishable by death:

> Yf he wyl her chamber breke
> […]
> Loke he be taken soone anone,
> And all his meyné* everychone,   *supporters
> And brought with strength to my pryson
> As traytour, thefe, and false felon.
> And yf he make any defence,
> Loke that he never go thence;
> But loke thou hew hym also small
> As flesshe whan it to the potte shall.[95]

To be clear, the Emperor is adamant that if the squire were to attempt to gain access to the maiden's chamber, not only would he and all his men be imprisoned, but any retaliation would result in him being made into squire pâté. It is obvious that the maiden's door is not the focus of her father's concern.

The chamber throughout the poem is symbolic of the emperor's daughter's sexual state. At the start of the poem, 'she was/ Closed well with royall glass' (ll. 93–4) and certainly a virgin, given her behaviour and that of other characters in respect to her. 'Closed' evokes the idea of the *hortus conclusus* while the 'royall glass', as Helene Roberts argues, is symbolic of the Virgin Mary, 'for as light penetrates glass without violating it, so Christ was conceived and born without violating Mary's virginity'.[96] Soon after the maiden becomes aware of the squire underneath her window, she unseals her chamber: 'anone that

---

[93] Ibid., p. 140.

[94] Ibid., pp. 145–6.

[95] *The Squire of Low Degree*, ed. Sands, ll. 511–23.

[96] H. E. Roberts, 'Light II: Divine, Natural, and Neon', in *Encyclopedia of Comparative Iconography: Themes Depicted in Works of Art*, ed. H. E. Roberts (Chicago, 1998), pp. 505–12 (p. 508); M. Meiss, 'Light as Form and Symbol in Some Fifteenth-Century Paintings', *The Art Bulletin* 27.3 (1945), 175–81 (p. 177).

lady, faire and free,/ Undide a pinne of iveré/ And wid the windowes she open set' (ll. 99–102). Upon unsealing the chamber, her virginity is immediately at stake, something which occurs much earlier than the climax of the poem. As Nicola McDonald suggests 'from the moment the princess first unpins the ornately fastened windows in her closet […] the romance simultaneously proposes the method (iteration gone awry) and the matter (practices of sex, gender, and desire that resist normativity) of its own undoing'.[97] Essentially, the maiden has already broken the chamber, so the violation of the chamber has already taken place. The ivory window-pins are reminiscent of the ivory tower, a symbol of virginal purity forming part of the chamber's boundaries.[98] In contrast, the image of the maiden undoing a pin is reminiscent of un-dressing. The emperor's daughter consciously 'undide' the windows, in order to respond to the squire's affection, both breaking the ivory tower and paralleling the removal of clothes. This action both puts her chastity at stake and reaffirms it, as 'the sunne shone in at her closet' (l. 102), reminiscent of the annunciation.[99] The sunbeam reminds the audience that she is a virgin, while at the same time putting us in mind of conception. The idea of light shining into her chamber as a symbol of conception is one that was present in the cultural mindset of late medieval England. For instance, the stage directions for the N-Town representation of the Annunciation include beams of light to signify immaculate conception: 'here the Holy Gost discendit with thre bemys to our Lady, the Sone of the Godhed nest with thre bemys to the Holy Gost, the Fadyr godly with thre bemys to the Sone. And so entre all thre to her bosom'.[100] Such a direction must have required the general populace to understand the significance of beams of light within the context of the annunciation. In *Undo Your Door*, the King's daughter is clearly not Mary, so the audience is aware that any conception that

---

[97] N. McDonald, 'Gender', in *A Handbook of Middle English Studies*, ed. M. Turner (Oxford, 2013), pp. 63–76 (p. 71).

[98] Song of Solomon 7.4.

[99] Compare, for example, with R. Campin's Merode Altarpiece, *c.* 1427–32 in which the window is open and light streams in at the moment of the Annunciation (New York: Metropolitan Museum of Art, accession no. 56.70a–c) <www.metmuseum.org>.

[100] *Play 11, Parliament of Heaven; Salutation and Conception* in *The N-Town Plays*, ed. D. Sugano (Kalamazoo,2007), ll. 292–3; G. McMurray Gibson, *The Theater of Devotion: East Anglian Drama and Society in the Late Middle Ages* (Chicago, 1989), p. 147.

occurs will not be immaculate. The act of opening the window thus leaves the chamber open to penetration. At this point, the boundary between her chamber and the arbour containing the squire becomes unclear. The maiden is 'right in her closet' (l. 150) and there is no mention of the squire coming to join her in her chamber, yet they are able to talk and even kiss without any physical obstruction. Through merely opening the window, breaking the closed chamber, the chamber boundaries have become permeable and unresisting to sexual advances.

The climax of the poem is the squire's unsuccessful attempt to gain entry to the chamber, after repeatedly imploring the maiden to undo her door.[101] Evidently, both characters are aware of the sexual implications of the squire entering the princess's chamber. When the squire returns to 'take leve of that lady free' (l. 499), it is clear that the demand to 'undo thy dore' (l. 539) is more than a request for entry to the chamber. He has no need to return to take leave, as he had already done so around 200 lines earlier, when 'thries he kissed that lady tho/ And toke his leve and forth he gan go' (ll. 281–2). Despite his cries that he is being set upon by attackers, he is not, at this stage, aware that he is about to be attacked. His ruse to gain access betrays his false intentions. Similarly, the princess understands that opening the door to the chamber has sexual associations. Even though she had been wearing a 'mantell of golde' (l. 548) when she first spoke to the squire through the door, she opens her door 'naked as she was borne' (l. 673) rendering void her spoken protestations. She is well aware that she is granting the squire leave to penetrate both her chamber and her body.

The maiden's actions following the discovery of the steward's body, thinking that it is the squire's, are like those of a lover, kissing and embracing the body, which she keeps in her chamber, followed by the actions of a widow, offering masses and mourning. These actions (leaving aside the rather disturbing necrophilia) are similar to what one would expect of a wife or lover. As no 'maidenhede' (l. 575) was actually taken, the princess' perceived loss of virginity is the result of her chamber being broken. The penetration of the chamber is a symbolic sex act in itself, and so the consequences are similar to those of a real sexual encounter.

---

[101] *The Squire of Low Degree*, ed. Sands, ll. 534, 539, 541, 545; N. McDonald, 'Desire Out Of Order and *Undo Your Door*', *Studies in the Age of Chaucer* 34 (2012), 245–75.

A space for sex

This chapter has shown that the bed and chamber were always significant in sexual encounters, whether in their use or absence, and had important associations with sexual desires and practice. It has demonstrated that the marital bed was considered to be the only appropriate space for licit sex and that illicit sex performed in the chamber was considered to be a violation of that sanctified space. This understanding existed in the late medieval consciousness, despite the fact that not everyone had access to an appropriate sexual space, and so poses more questions than it solves: where, then, did people have sex in late medieval England? How could their relationships have been considered valid, if the locus of their marital union was a space considered to be the site of illicit sex? The idea that the chamber was the site of licit sexuality while the violation of the bed and chamber of another was associated with adultery shows the extent to which beds and chambers had a widespread, lasting effect on late medieval society. Without access to a chamber, sex was shrouded by anxiety and restrictions; in a chamber with one's spouse, sex could be approached 'myrely', and with abandon.

6

The Invisible Woman

Let us now turn to the invisible presence in the 'Arise Early' precepts: the addressee's wife. The male addressee moves from place to place, working, conversing with the public and partaking of meals. His wife, however, who has no mention up until the point at which her husband returns to bed, apparently has no role to play outside of the chamber. For all intents and purposes, she is invisible outside of the bed. In fact, we are only aware of the wife's existence in relation to the verb being executed by the male addressee: 'plesse and loffe thy wife dewly'.[1] This invisibility is not presented as strange, but instead as the norm: the man does the everyday tasks required of him as an upstanding man of the community while the woman silently, invisibly, waits in the chamber for her husband to return to bed. This chapter's title, 'The Invisible Woman', acknowledges the many ways in which the late medieval English woman is invisible. Many ordinary – and probably extraordinary – women are left out of history, their influences on the male lead roles rendered invisible. Documentary sources are much more likely to exist for men and, where evidence of individual women is found, it is often in relation to men, such as in proof of marriage depositions. Recent scholarship focusing on late medieval English women goes some way towards closing that gap, but while Women's History is considered a separate focus, women are still presented as other, with the spotlight elsewhere.

Late medieval women's invisibility is also found in the way in which we discuss medieval literature. In romances, the female characters are

---

[1] See Introduction above, p. 10.

deliberately hidden behind almost exclusively masculine titles (notable exceptions including *Le Bone Florence of Rome* and *Emaré*) regardless of their importance within the narrative. This practice was occasionally performed by the scribe, in rubrication or headings, but was continued more broadly by post-medieval editors. It is particularly obvious in the treatment of *Undo Your Door*, which is now more generally known as *The Squire of Low Degree*. As Nicola McDonald argues, there is a marked difference between reading a romance entitled *The Squire of Low Degree* to reading *Undo Your Door*.[2] McDonald points out that conventional romance titles containing the name of the male hero 'work hard to privilege the trajectory of the knight – the pursuit and satisfaction of *his* desires – while simultaneously diminishing the claims of competing story lines, other desires'.[3] In a romance such as *Undo Your Door*, which focuses almost exclusively on the desire and actions of the unnamed princess, the title *The Squire of Low Degree* causes us to read everything the female protagonist does in relation to the squire. Female characters are thus narratorially sidelined from the title of the romance and rarely considered in light of their own merit within their texts. Furthermore, as this chapter will show, within the landscape and architecture depicted in romance, women are contained within chambers. In this way, even the main female characters in romance are invisible, unless we look for them in the chamber.

In this chapter I put women and domesticity at the centre, focusing on the cultural links between women and their beds and chambers in late medieval England. As touched on in other areas of this book, the late medieval chamber, despite being physically closed off from what we might consider to be the wider world, had wider social implications and witnessed events that affected society on both a local and a national level. As such, the aim of this chapter is to explore how the relationship between women and the chamber in late medieval England was not just one of containment, but also one of empowerment. This chapter will begin by looking at the ways in which the bed and chamber are owned by women, physically and linguistically, before exploring notions of empowerment and containment. Concluding this book with a chapter on women is not to slip in some token scholarship devoted to women at the end of an otherwise male-dominated research project, but instead to acknowledge that while both men and women

---

[2] McDonald, 'Desire Out of Order and *Undo Your Door*'.
[3] Ibid., p. 250.

had parts to play in each cultural aspect of beds and chambers, there was a special relationship between women and beds and chambers in late medieval England. Rather than dismissing women's history as domestic, this chapter seeks to move the spotlight to the chamber, where women were located in the late medieval imagination, making visible the invisible. In this chapter I build on evidence already discussed in this book to explore how, while in practice, women may have had little authority at all, the cultural understanding of chambers was such that they were understood to be a female space, an idea which was appropriated by men and women alike, to suit their own end.

Medieval household scholarship and women's history often go together, not only because there is a general consensus among scholars of households such as Shannon McSheffrey and Felicity Riddy that medieval domesticity is 'gendered female', the domestic space being representative of 'the good woman', but also because in the past, both women's history and household history have been marginalised, as if 'real' history took place outside, while women's history ticked along quietly indoors.[4] As Jeremy Goldberg and Maryanne Kowaleski discuss in their introduction to *Medieval Domesticity*, the nineteenth-century bourgeois ideal, which understood men and women to occupy separate spheres, with women controlling the sphere of the home, while men went out to work, perpetuates to the present day and clouds our understanding of both past and present roles.[5] The idea that good women belong in the domestic space is most clearly expressed in scripture in the Book of Proverbs, in the statement that a wise woman builds her house and in the description of the wife of noble character, who manages her household.[6] Christine de Pizan expresses similar ideas in *Le trésor de la cité des dames*, in which she devotes a chapter to advice on how young ladies living on their estates ought to manage their property, including how she should instruct her household.[7] It

---

[4] McSheffrey, 'Place, Space, and Situation', p. 960; Riddy, '"Burgeis" Domesticity', p. 15; Salih, 'At Home; Out of the House', p. 125; Ellis, 'Domesticating the Spanish Inquisition', p. 196.

[5] P. J. P. Goldberg and M. Kowaleski, 'Introduction. Medieval Domesticity: Home, Housing and Household', in *Medieval Domesticity: Home, Housing and Household in Medieval England*, ed. M. Kowaleski and P. J. P. Goldberg (Cambridge, 2008), pp. 1–13 (p. 3).

[6] Proverbs 14.1 and 31.10–31.

[7] C. de Pizan, *Le trésor de la cité des dames de degré en degré et de tous estatz* xxxvi (Paris, 1503), unpaginated.

is worth emphasising that the Biblical view and that of Christine de Pizan is not that men should work and women should stay at home, but rather that women's work is within the home, whereas men's work takes them beyond the boundaries of their houses or estates. While it is generally true that late medieval men were more likely than women to leave the house to work, manorial records indicate that both peasant men and women performed manual tasks in the fields.[8] However, as Barbara Hanawalt argues, records of accidental deaths show that women were more likely to be at home to perform domestic duties at certain times of the day, particularly around meal times.[9] If this is true, then regardless of whether men and women occupied the same working sphere, women were also expected to have control of the domestic sphere. Bourgeois women were likely to have work within the home. As discussed by Eileen Power, Judith Bennett and Jeremy Goldberg, wives of craftsmen would almost certainly work as their husbands' assistants, in the home or in a shop attached to it, while other women would brew and spin for their households, selling any surplus to supplement the family's income.[10] Some late medieval aristocratic English women pursued an active role in the running of the house and estate: Margaret Paston, for instance, describes herself as the 'captenesse' of the household at Haylesdon, which implies both

---

[8] C. Middleton, 'The Sexual Division of Labour in Feudal England', *New Left Review* 113–14 (1979), 147–68; S. Bardsley, 'Women's Work Reconsidered: Gender and Wage Differentiation in Late-medieval England', *Past and Present* 165 (1999), 3–29; J. Hatcher, 'Debate: Women's Work Reconsidered: Gender and Wage Differentiation in Late-medieval England', *Past and Present* 173 (2001), 191–8; S. Bardsley, 'Reply', *Past and Present* 173 (2001), 199–202; P. J. P. Goldberg, 'The Public and the Private: Women in the Pre-Plague Economy', in *Thirteenth Century England III*, ed. P. R. Coss and S. D. Loyd (Woodbridge, 1991), pp. 75–89; Goldberg, 'Space and Gender', pp. 210–11.

[9] B. Hanawalt, *The Ties That Bound: Peasant Families in Medieval England* (Oxford, 1986), pp. 145–7.

[10] E. Power, *Medieval Women*, ed. M. M. Postan (Cambridge, 1975), pp. 53–75; J. M. Bennett, *Ale, Beer, and Brewsters in England: Women's Work in a Changing World, 1300–1600* (Oxford, 1996), pp. 14–36; P. J. P. Goldberg, 'Household and the Organisation of Labour in Late-Medieval Towns: Some English Evidence', in *The Household in Late-Medieval Cities: Italy and Northwestern Europe Compared. Proceedings of the International Conference, Ghent, 21st–22nd January 2000*, ed. M. Carlier and T. Soens (Leuven, 2001), pp. 59–70; Goldberg, *Women, Work, and Life Cycle*, p. 128.

domestic and military governance.[11] Similarly, in 1461 Alice Knyvet defended Bokenham Castle from King Edward IV, claiming 'I will not leave possession of this castle to die therefore [...] I shall defend me, for liever I had in such wise to die than to be slain when my husband cometh home, for he charged me to keep it.'[12] However, such a commanding role was unusual for a married woman and would have been unnecessary, had the respective husbands of Margaret and Alice been present to defend their home: women only usually governed or performed administrative tasks for their households and estates in the temporary or permanent absence of their husbands.[13]

Female control of households only occurred in the place of men, rather than as women in their own right, so domesticity as a whole was not, therefore, female-centred, as the husband or father was head of the house and household. The reason why the domestic setting was considered to be feminine is usually the presence, rather than the governance, of women, even though communal areas within domestic households were often mixed-gender. It has been suggested by Goldberg and others that, among the bourgeoisie and aristocracy, the specifically 'female' space within the house was the chamber.[14] That is not to say that women did not spend time elsewhere, either in other areas of the house or outside the home, but rather that the chamber was understood to give women more freedom and authority than they could enjoy elsewhere.

This book has shown that the chamber was not an entirely female domain: the bed and chamber had both practical and cultural associations with men for various reasons, including national and international politics, which is generally regarded by historians to be a mostly masculine concern.[15] Felicity Riddy argues that male power extended to the chamber, suggesting that 'domestic living – especially urban

---

[11] *Paston Letters and Papers*, ed. Davis I, 298; V. Creelman, 'Margaret Paston's Use of *Captenesse*', *Notes & Queries* 55.3 (2008), 275–7.

[12] *CPR, 1461–7*, p. 67. Cited in Power, *Medieval Women*, pp. 45–6.

[13] R. E. Archer, '"How ladies ... who live on their manors ought to manage their households and estates": Women as Landholders and Administrators in the Later Middle Ages', in *Women in Medieval English Society*, ed. P. J. P. Goldberg (Stroud, 1997), pp. 149–81; Salih, 'At Home', p. 126.

[14] Goldberg, 'The Fashioning of Bourgeois Domesticity', p. 138; R. Lee, 'A Company of Women and Men: Men's Recollections of Childbirth in Medieval England', *Journal of Family History* 27.2 (2002), 92–100; Salih, 'At Home', p. 130.

[15] See Chapter 3.

living – mitigated any simple model of male power and female subordination', and women were still likely to be overruled and exploited within the chamber.[16] In this book I have explored how the chamber had cultural relevance to both men and women, but that the meanings of the bed and chamber affected people in different ways, according to their gender and social status. Although chambers were used by and had great significance to both men and women, it is evident that the late medieval chamber was culturally understood to be a female space.

Linguistic ownership

The bed and chamber were understood to be women's rightful place in the same way that the hall was understood to be the place of men. Within romance texts, the default positions of men and women is 'levedyes in boure, knightes in halle'.[17] These positions in romance reflect the order shown in historical accounts of childbirth where the father of the child typically waited in the hall with his men, while the ladies attended to the mother in the chamber.[18] However, these locations of men and women within romance extended much further than childbirth clichés, situating men and women in their respective, socially recognised spaces. Regardless of the actual spaces inhabited by the owners and audiences of literary texts, there is an implicit understanding between the texts and audience that the woman's true place was in the chamber. Access analysis of palaces and religious institutions supports this understanding, as in separate ladies' quarters and nunneries the chambers and dormitories were situated in the deepest space in the building, while the sleeping spaces of their male counterparts were not.[19] Within the cultural mindset, men lived in the sphere of the outside world and the hall and women existed in the sphere of the chamber. When the male and female worlds meet, as in the episode in *Amis and Amiloun* in which Amis and Belisaunt exchange vows in a garden, secrecy is kept and order restored by resuming normal

---

[16] F. Riddy, 'Looking Closely: Authority and Intimacy in the Late- medieval Urban Home', in *Gendering the Master Narrative: Women and Power in the Middle Ages*, ed. M. C. Erler and M. Kowaleski (New York, 2003), pp. 212–28 (p. 215).

[17] *Havelok the Dane*, ed. Sands, l. 239.

[18] Lee, 'A Company of Women and Men', p. 96.

[19] Richardson, 'Gender and Space in English Royal Palaces', pp. 131–65; R. Gilchrist, *Gender and Archaeology: Contesting the Past* (London, 1999), pp. 138–9; Gilchrist, *Gender and Material Culture*, p. 190.

positions inside the house: 'into hir chaumber sche went ogain' and 'Sir Amis than withouten duelling [...] into halle he went anon'.[20]

Whether the cause or the effect of chambers being considered to be women's spaces, it was not considered fitting for a man to lie late in bed. The sixteenth-century physician Andrew Borde suggests that strong men need only six hours in bed at night and advises against any man lying in bed during the day, suggesting that even if the man is sick, he would be better taking a nap standing against a cupboard or sitting in an upright chair than going to bed.[21] Similarly, Richard Rolle pronounces that 'it is shame if the sunn beme fynd men ydil in thaire bed'.[22] This attitude is reflected in contemporary literature. In *The Wedding of Sir Gawain and Dame Ragnelle*, Gawain stays in bed with his wife the morning after his wedding night and his friends assume that she has killed him![23] Similarly, in *Bevis of Hampton*, when Josian has, in fact, killed her husband on their wedding night, 'the barouns thar-of hadde wonder;/ That th'erl lai so longe a bed,/ Gret wonder thar-of he hadde'.[24] In *Ywain and Gawain*, Gawain's masculinity is put into question when he is told 'that knight es no thing to set by/ That leves al his chivalry/ And ligges bekeand in his bed'.[25] Similarly, in *Sir Gawain and the Green Knight*, Gawain is the only man who stays in bed while the others go out to hunt. The instruction to 'arysse erly', therefore, is expressly for a male audience, leaving the woman to inhabit her domestic sphere during the day. That is not to say that a man was understood to be feminised by lying late in bed. As we have seen in previous chapters, the bed and chamber were considered to be spaces in which external trappings and signifiers of status were stripped off, giving the impression of equality within the chamber. As men had authority within the household because of their sex, the stripping of authority in bed at a time when they should be elsewhere was not so

[20] *Amis and Amiloun*, ed. Foster, ll. 670–5.
[21] A. Borde, *A Dyetary of Helth*, in *The Fyrst Boke of the Introduction of Knowledge made by Andrew Borde, of Physycke Doctor. A Compendyous Regyment or A Dyetary of Helth made in Mountpyllier, compiled by Andrewe Boorde of Physycke Doctor. Barnes in the Defence of the Berde: A Treatyse Made, Answerynge the Treatyse of Doctor Borde upon Berdes*, ed. F. J. Furnivall (London, 1870), pp. 245–6.
[22] Rolle, *The Psalter*, p. 432.
[23] *Gawain and Dame Ragnelle*, ed. Hahn, l. 733.
[24] *Bevis of Hampton*, ed. Herzman, Drake and Salisbury, ll. 3232–4.
[25] *Ywain and Gawain*, ed. Flowers Braswell, ll. 1457–9.

much feminisation as metaphorical castration. Men were thus symbolically rendered powerless in bed during the day.

Without question, characters in late medieval English literature expect female characters to be in the chamber. In *The Erle of Tolous* the earl, upon returning home, 'wendyth [...] to the chaumbur' because 'he longyd hys feyre lady to see'; in *The Avowyng of Arthur* the king 'hiees' to the 'chambur [...] Qwere the lady of the howse/ And maydyns ful beuteowse/ Were'; and in *Bevis of Hampton* the messenger 'fond' his mistress 'in hire bour'.[26] In each case, the woman is sought in the chamber without asking where she might be and with no apparent doubt that they would find her. Women in late medieval English literature are, indeed, located in the chamber. In many texts, they seem to be part of the furniture. For example, in *The Life of St Alexius*, Alex is given a wife from a collection of maidens in 'þe Emperors bour', as if he has a chamber full of women at all times.[27] Similarly, in the fifteenth-century morality play *The Castle of Perseverance*, Mankynd is told that he will find 'serdyn gay gerlys' in his chamber.[28] In one of the Harley lyrics, 'ffurmest in boure were boses ybroht/ Leuedis to honore', as if 'leuedis' were sitting in the 'boure' waiting to be honoured.[29] Furthermore, in *Sir Eglamour of Artois*, Eglamour appeals for the help of the 'chambir wymmen', and in the *Stanzaic Morte Arthur*, Guinevere is 'brought into her bowr/ To ladies and to maidens bright'.[30] The idea that the chamber was the location of many unspecified women is also apparent in linguistic evidence. Within many Middle English literary texts, the location of the chamber is used almost as a stock adjectival phrase in reference to women. For instance, in *Amis and Amiloun*, female characters are called 'levedis and maidens bright in bour', while in *Sir Gawain and the Carle of Carlisle*, Gawain is described as 'meke as mayde

[26] *Erle of Tolous*, ed. Laskaya and Salisbury, ll. 839–40; *The Avowyng of Arthur*, ed. Hahn, ll. 815–19; *Bevis of Hampton*, ed. Herzman, Drake and Salisbury, l. 160.
[27] *The Life of St Alexius*, in *Adam Davy's 5 Dreams about Edward II. The Life of St Alexius. Solomon's Book of Wisdom. St Jeremie's 15 Tokens Before Doomsday. The Lamentacion of Souls*, ed. F. J. Furnivall (London, 1878), l. 51.
[28] *The Castle of Perseverance*, ed. D. N. Klausner (Kalamazoo, 2010), l. 1160.
[29] *Altenglische Dichtungen des MS Harl, 2253*, ed. K. Boedekker (Berlin, 1878), 161. According to the *MED*, 'boses' are a sort of low hair bun, worn on the neck.
[30] *Sir Eglamour of Artois*, ed. Hudson, l. 799; *Stanzaic Morte Arthur*, in *King Arthur's Death: The Middle English Stanzaic Morte Arthur and Alliterative Morte Arthure*, ed. L. D. Benson (Kalamazoo, 1994), ll. 2314–15.

in bour'.[31] It is a common enough trope that Chaucer's *Sir Thopas*, which consciously satirises the romance tradition, refers to 'fful mony a maide briht in boure'.[32] The textual juxtaposition of women and chambers is not peculiar to romance texts: the phrases 'ledies þat beþ bryht in bour' and 'leuedy so bryht in bour' are used in the Harley lyrics; 'leuedis in her bour' is found in the thirteenth-century spiritual poem *The Sayings of St Bernard*, and 'leuedis of boure' is used in the Middle English Biblical narrative *Iacob and Iosep*, to name just a few instances.[33] The repetition of the phrase throughout Middle English literature indicates an almost subconscious link between women and chambers, which reflects the place that women inhabited within the collective imagination. A thorough search through the *Corpus of Middle English Verse and Prose* and through the Middle English romances does not reveal a single instance in which it was expected that men would be found in the chamber, and chambers are not used in stock adjectival phrases in relation to men in the same way as they are to women.

As shown in Figures 16 and 17, the use of possessive pronouns in late medieval literature indicates that within the cultural imagination, the chamber was a woman's own space. For instance, in *Bevis of Hampton*, Bevis' mother is 'in hire bour'; ladies in *Lybeaus Desconus* listen to jests 'in ther bowre'; in *Richard Coeur de Lion* (*c.* 1300), ladies strew 'theire bowres' with flowers, to name just three of many cases of feminine possessive pronouns referring to chambers.[34] The overwhelming number of feminine nouns and pronouns associated with beds and chambers in literary texts reflects the implicit semantic relationship between women and beds and chambers. This linguistic relationship does not imply that it was normal for women, even in aristocratic households, to have their own individual room, but that the chamber

---

[31] *Amis and Amiloun*, ed. Foster, l. 430; *Sir Gawain and the Carle of Carlisle*, in *Sir Gawain: Eleven Romances and Tales*, ed. T. Hahn (Kalamazoo, 1995), l. 4.

[32] G. Chaucer, 'Sir Thopas', in *The Riverside Chaucer*, ed. L. D. Benson, 3rd edn (Oxford, 1987), l. 1932.

[33] London, British Library, Harley MS 2253, ff. 71vb, 80rb; Edinburgh, National Library of Scotland, Advocates MS 19. 2. 1 (Auchinleck), f. 280ra, l. 4; *Iacob and Iosep: A Middle English Poem of the Thirteenth Century*, ed. A. S. Napier (Oxford, 1916), p. 6.

[34] *Bevis of Hampton*, ed. Herzman, Drake and Salisbury, l. 160; *Lybeaus Desconus*, in *Codex Ashmole 61: A Compilation of Popular Middle English Verse*, ed. G. Shuffleton (Kalamazoo, 2008), l. 162; 'Richard Coeur de Lion from the London Thornton Manuscript', ed. C. Figueredo (University of York, unpublished Ph.D. thesis), l. 3780.

was seen to be the place where women belong, and which belongs to them.

Figure 16: Word cloud representing the ten words surrounding variants of 'chambre' in Middle English romance texts.

In Fig. 16, a word cloud taken from the ten words surrounding all instances of 'chamber' in its various spellings in the *Corpus of Middle English Prose and Verse* and all Middle English Romances, yellow indicates nouns and pronouns that are specifically feminine, while purple highlights indicate those that are specifically masculine. It is evident that the feminine nouns and pronouns are greater in number and frequency (the larger the word in the word cloud, the greater the frequency in the corpus). Note that second-person possessive pronouns are indistinguishable by gender, and so are not colour-coded in the word cloud, but, as indicated above, the majority of them are feminine.

Figure 17: Word cloud representing the ten words surrounding variants of

'bedde' in Middle English romance texts.

As in the previous word cloud, it is clear from Fig. 17 that there are more occurrences of feminine nouns and pronouns associated with the word 'bedde' in its various forms than masculine ones. However, a comparison of the two word clouds might suggest that, while beds are clearly linguistically associated with women, chambers are more associated with women than beds. This pattern correlates with evidence elsewhere: in literary works, characters of both sexes have beds but only women are associated with chambers.

Material ownership and control

The sense of female ownership of beds and chambers found in late medieval English literature is reflected in contemporary wills. Women were linguistically associated with beds and chambers in late medieval English literature even though it is clear that very few female members of the books' audience would have had a chamber of their own; so too were women seen to be the owners and decorators of beds and chambers, despite the fact that married women did not technically own anything in their own right. As beds were often understood to actually belong to women, they represented a sense of independence and ownership that could not be associated with many other household objects. Married women did not legally own any household items, but beds and items belonging to the chamber often featured in dowries and dowers. Women were often given beds to bring with them to their marriage and, when their husbands died, were often left beds and items for the chamber either for their dowry at a future marriage or as a dower, to be used during widowhood.[35] For instance, in 1313 Robert Cook left 'Agnes his daughter for her marriage twenty marks, a featherbed, counterpanes, sheets [...] etc.'.[36] In 1352, John de Blakwell left 'Lucy, daughter of Nicholas de Blakwell [...] two marks in aid of marriage, and a bed, to wit, a chalon, two sheets and a canevas'.[37] In

---

[35] Goldberg, *Women, Work, and Life*, p. 185; B. A. Hanawalt, *The Wealth of Wives: Women, Law and Economy in Late Medieval London* (Oxford, 2007), pp. 50–68; There is, in fact, very little linguistic distinction between 'dowry' and 'dower'. For the sake of clarity, I will use 'dowry' to refer to money or goods given before or at the time of marriage and 'dower' to refer to money or goods claimed by a woman after her husband's death.

[36] *Calendar of Wills Proved and Enrolled in the Court of Husting, London*, ed. and trans. R. R. Sharpe, 2 vols. (London, 1889–90), I, *A.D. 1258–A.D. 1688*, p. 243.

[37] Ibid., p. 698.

1386, Richard de Chaddeslee left his daughter Isabella Norable 'one second best bed, the goods of which the said Richard left to Isabella Norable for her marriage'.[38] There is evidence that some husbands recognised the importance of the bed in the dowry, leaving beds and bedding for their wives' subsequent marriage. For instance, in 1418, John Chelmyswyk left all his 'beddynge & naperie' to his wife, 'in the name of her Dowerye & of her parte belonging to here' – essentially giving her back what was already hers – and in 1425, William New-land left his wife 'C marc to her marriage, and a browded bed wiþ þe costures þerto'.[39]

Discussing sixteenth-century continental marriages, Lyndal Roper argues that the bed's central position in a woman's trousseau resulted in the marriage being consummated 'on feminine territory': 'the man had to enter the female space, risking both physically and symbolically the loss of his own virility and identity', arguably going some way to balance the levels of power and vulnerability, which otherwise natural-ly favours the husband, as the loss of the bride's virginity carries with it the threat of death in childbirth, as well as rendering the woman less culturally valuable.[40] While this symbolism is one aspect of the bed's importance in the late medieval English dowry, it seems unlikely that women were consciously bringing beds to their marriages in order to destabilise their husbands' notions of spousal dominance, or that husbands would welcome such a concept. However, what is apparent from the presence of the bed in many dowries is that women were associated with beds and bring them to the marriage, conforming to the idea expressed through the 'Arise Early' precepts that wives are to be found in their beds.

This special relationship between women and beds is further ev-idenced by the fact that beds often formed part of the dowry given to nunneries when women took the veil.[41] For instance, the 1468 will of Elizabeth Sywardby includes instructions to provide a dowry that includes money 'pro lecto competenti' (for a suitable bed) for another

---

[38] *Calendar of the Plea and Memoranda Rolls of the City of London: III: 1381–1412*, ed. A. H. Thomas (London, 1932), p. 128.

[39] *Fifty Earliest English Wills*, ed. Furnivall, pp. 32, 65.

[40] L. Roper, '"Going to Church and Street": Weddings in Reformation Augsburg', *Past and Present* 106 (1985), 62–101 (p. 90).

[41] E. Power, *Medieval English Nunneries c. 1275–1535* (Cambridge, 1922), pp. 16–20.

Elizabeth Sywardby, upon her entrance to the convent at Monkton.[42] Similarly, a 1526 inventory of household goods at the priory of Minster in Sheppey includes information on 'Dame Agnes Browne's Chamber', which contained 'Stuff given her by her frends: a fetherbed, a bolster, ij pillowys, a payre of blankatts, ij corse coverleds, iiij pare of shets good and bade, an olde tester and selar of paynted clothes and ij peces of hangyng to the same'.[43] The various, non-uniform articles of bedding in the nuns' chambers suggests that many of the nuns brought their own, upon entering the nunnery.

After their husbands' deaths, women were often entitled to claim beds from their husbands' estates. In London, beds and bedding were counted as paraphernalia, allowed to the widow immediately upon her husband's death.[44] In addition, in London law, even if the husband died intestate, the wife would be entitled to her 'widow's chamber', which included 'the principal private chamber' of the tenement in which she resided with her husband, as well as the use of other parts of the property.[45] Alice, widow of John de Harwe, claimed the widow's chamber from her husband's executors in 1314.[46] The widow's chamber would have had to be relinquished if the women were to marry again, but was otherwise hers in her own right. In 1305, Juliana Russel left 'her entire chamber of Doningtone' to her daughter, in order that she could continue to live there after her mother's death.[47] The fact that women were understood to be entitled to a 'chamber' shows a strong cultural relationship between women and the chamber. It is also telling that the 'widow's chamber' meant more than just a chamber, but the use of other domestic space and utensils, too. Even when women were using other space, they were associated with the chamber.

---

[42] *Testamenta Eboracensia*, ed. Raine, III, 168; Power, *Medieval English Nunneries*, p. 19.

[43] 'Inventories of (I) St Mary's Hospital of Maison Dieu, Dover; (II.) The Benedictine Priory of St Martin New-work, Dover, For Monks; (III) The Benedictine Priory of SS. Mary and Sexburga, in the Island of Shepey, For Nuns', ed. M. E. C. Walcott *Archaeologia Cantiana* 7 (1868), 272–306 (p. 296); W. Page, *History of the County of Kent* (London, 1926), II, 149–50.

[44] Hanawalt, *The Wealth of Wives*, p. 58; M. Bateson, *Borough Customs*, 2 vols. (London, 1906), II, xcix.

[45] Hanawalt, *The Wealth of Wives*, p. 61; *Wills of Husting*, ed. and trans. Sharpe, I, xxxix.

[46] *Calendar of Letter-books of the City of London: E: 1314–1337*, ed. R. E. Sharpe (London, 1903), p. 33.

[47] *Wills of Husting*, ed. and trans. Sharpe, I, 174.

Whole, physical chambers, or the effects which make up a chamber, were left exclusively to women in wills, indicating a strong relationship between women and beds. In 1328, William de Braye left 'to Alice his wife in lieu of dower a bequest of thirty pounds and her entire chamber, with tailored cloths for the body and beds'.[48] Similarly, in 1340, John de Knopwed stipulated that 'Roseia his wife [was] to have her dower of all his goods, moveable and immovable; also her entire chamber with all the vessels and utensils belonging to his hall, larder, chamber, and kitchen'.[49] What is pertinent in these bequests is that, in both cases, the husbands refer to the chambers in the possessive: they bequeath a certain amount of their own goods, and also 'her' chamber. The husbands give what is legally owed, *viz.* their goods for her dower, but also acknowledge that while they might legally own the chambers, they were culturally understood to belong to their wives all along. A similar understanding is seen in Alice Ancroft's 1391 claim of 'the sum of 500 marks, being her third part of her husband's goods and chattels coming to her as dower and puparty, and for the clothes belonging to her chamber, to wit, linen and wool for the beds and all the clothing for her body'.[50] This claim highlights the dower and the paraphernalia, making it very clear that Alice considered her chamber and beds to be her own personal property. Despite the fact that married women's goods were technically owned and managed by their husbands, married women continued to receive bequests of beds in their own right. For instance, in 1395 Alice West bequeathed to 'Iohane my doughter, my sone-is wyf, a bed paled blak and whit' and to her married daughter Alianore, 'a tawne bed of silk'.[51] Other bequests include crockery and household textiles, which would have been for use by the household, but the bed in each case was in addition to a bed left to the woman's husband. Similarly, in 1354, William de Wakefeld left 'Johanna, wife of William Tydyman' his best bed.[52] In a will from 1501, Alice Clayton left her daughter, Alice Rowe, a bed including 'a pair of gret shetes that hir name is market thereupon with blue threde'.[53] By 'hir name', she probably meant 'Alice', not 'Alice Rowe'. Stitching her

[48] Ibid., I, 349.
[49] Ibid., I, 448.
[50] *Plea and Memoranda Rolls*, ed. Thomas, pp. 177–8.
[51] TNA PROB 11/1/82; *Fifty Earliest English Wills*, ed. Furnivall, pp. 5–6.
[52] *Wills of Husting*, ed. and trans. Sharpe, I, 677.
[53] *Somerset Medieval Wills. 1501–1530. With Some Somerset Wills Preserved at Lambeth*, ed. F. W. Weaver (London, 1903), p. 22.

name into the sheets is significant, as not only does it imply a sense of ownership – names have power, and sheets marked with a woman's name must certainly be understood to be the woman's own – but also carries with it a memorial function. It is interesting that the memorial object is a pair of sheets, rather than any other object, as it places the locus of remembrance in bed.

As this chapter has so far shown it is apparent that, regardless of legal status, late medieval women considered the bed and chamber in which they slept to be their own. A useful comparison could be made with the room and bed in which sleeps a modern child in fortunate enough circumstances to have his or her 'own' room. Although it is unusual for a child to own any real estate, most children have the understanding that the bed and bedroom in which they sleep belongs to them, and that they should have some control over the decoration and contents of the room. However, the link between women and beds and chambers in late medieval England went beyond the bed and chamber that a woman might occupy to encompass all beds and chambers within their immediate vicinity. Goldberg suggests that late medieval bourgeois wives had a significant part to play in purchasing and putting together articles of use within the principal chamber of the house.[54] Evidence from wills shows that some women asserted similar control over their beneficiaries' chambers. Two women whose wills prove them to have had a definite sense of authority over beds and chambers and an implicit understanding of their cultural value are Lady Alice West and Dame Joan Buckland.

Lady Alice West seemed to delight in creating bed-sets for her beneficiaries. For instance, her will of 1395 includes the bequest of:

> a tawne bed of silk, with hool celure and four curtyns of sute, and a keuerlit of selk yponet in that on side tawne, and in that other side blu; and the stoffe of the bed ther-wyth [...] featherbed with caneuas materas, twey blankettes, a payre shites of reynes, with a neuedshite of sute, and iij pilwes.[55]

While it is possible that these descriptions serve only to ensure that each person receives the correct item, the meticulous detail also conveys a sense of pride in the possessions and in the way that the different materials have been put together, as well as a real desire to exert

---

[54] Goldberg, 'Bourgeois Domesticity', pp. 137–8.
[55] TNA PROB 11/1/82; *Fifty Earliest English Wills*, ed. Furnivall, pp. 5–6.

authority over her own property, demonstrating her capability as a housewife.[56] It is evident from her will that Lady Alice appreciated the cultural value of a bed, as she made a point of leaving her servants and acquaintances each 'a bed conuenable for [his or her] estat'.[57] As her beneficiaries range from gentlewomen to servants, one can assume that their 'estat's varied, and their beds followed suit. As Lady Alice does not stipulate what makes a bed 'conuenable for his estat', we can only deduce that she regarded the distinction to be implicit and obvious. In addition, she left a bequest to her eldest son of a bed of rich cultural meaning: 'to Thomas my sone, a bed of tapicers werk, with alle the tapites of sute, red of colour, ypouthered with chapes and scochons, in the corners, of myn Auncestres armes' (p. 5). The inclusion of 'myn Auncestres armes' is interesting, as it indicates that either she chose to have bedding made which contained the arms of her ancestors, rather than those of her husband, or that her ancestors had a bed featuring their arms, which they thought was important enough to leave to her, and which she valued enough to keep and pass on to her eldest son. It is clear that Lady Alice had a fondness for her ancestors, as she requested to be buried 'in Crischerch in the Priorie of the Chanones in Hamptschire, by the Newe forest, where-as myne Auncestres liggeth' (p. 5). The bequest of the bed comes immediately after this request, so it seems likely that the ancestors buried in Christchurch are the same as those whose arms are depicted on the bed. It seems most likely that the bed depicts the Fitzherbert arms. Alice West was the heiress to her brother, Edmund Fitzherbert.[58] As such, there would have been no male heirs to carry on the family name. Leaving a bed with the Fitzherbert arms to her son would ensure that something to commemorate her side of his heritage continues in the West household. Aesthetically, the Fitzherbert arms are the most likely candidate on the red bed. Lady Alice's will indicates that she concerned herself with colours and patterns, as she carefully picked out bedding that would go together.

---

[56] For a discussion on the cultural responsibility of a housewife for maintaining and keeping track of each item of linen, see V. Sekules, 'Spinning Yarns: Clean Linen and Domestic Values in Late medieval French Culture', in *The Material Culture of Sex, Procreation, and Marriage in Premodern Europe*, ed. A. L. McClanan and K. Rosoff Encarnación (New York, 2002), pp. 79–91.

[57] TNA PROB 11/1/82; *Fifty Earliest English Wills*, ed. Furnivall, pp. 5–6.

[58] J. Burke, *A Genealogical and Heraldic History of the Commoners of Great Britain and Ireland, Enjoying Territorial Possessions or High Official Rank; But Uninvested with Heritable Honours*, 5 vols. (London, 1833–8), IV, 729.

The Fitzherbert arms, with their variegated red and gold field, would coordinate well with the red bedding. It is pertinent that the arms were to be found on a bed, rather than any other type of furnishing. Such a practice is not unheard-of: the princess's bed in 'the chaumbur of love' in *Sir Degrevant* has 'at hur testere/ The kyngus owun banere'.[59] However, unlike the shadow of patriarchal dominance present in the fictional maiden's chamber, Lady Alice's bequest of the bed to her son, like Alice Rowe's pair of sheets, ensured that he remembered his maternal lineage through an object with which she had the closest association, and in which she may well have given birth to him.

Possibly the most extreme example of control over beds and chambers beyond the grave is found in the will of Dame Joan Buckland, written in 1450.[60] Dame Joan hand-picked, from various rooms and houses, very specific bedding and soft furnishings to make up entire chambers for her beneficiaries. For example, Robert Carleton received 'the stayned bed with iij. Courtayns in the Chambre aboue Clarell, and all the Costres for the same Chambir', along with 'vj. qwisshens of Tapstre werk wrought with gootys, j. good fetherbed, j. good matrasse, j. good paire of blankettes & j. hillyng of Red & grene, j. good bolster, j. good pyllow, j. paire of Shetes of ij. leuys & dim' (p. 63), presumably from another chamber. John Greve received bedding and curtains to match the bed in his chamber (p. 40). Richard Clarell received 'j. rede Syllour and the Testour, three Curteyns & the hylling and all the Costres that longe to the same Chambir of Rede', along with items which presumably were not from the 'Chambir of Rede': 'ij. qwysshyens of Red clothe of Sylk; Item, the best carpett of the twayne grete & j. the best of the litell Carpettes; Item, the best ffetherbed, & the best Matrasse with the best bolster, j. paire of the best ffustyans; Item, ij. of the best pyllows with the Beerys; Item, j. payre of Shetis of Raynes with iij. leues & closse seme; j. hedshete of the same, with ij. leues & dim.' (p. 39). John Trotter was bequeathed 'j. bed of Blew bokeram with a testour & iij. Courteyns of the same, with all the Costres longyng to the same Chambir', as well as 'j. good ffetherbed with j. large matrasse hilled with white canuase & j. bolster, a paire of the best blankettes, j. hilling of blew worsted, j. lytell Carpett' (p. 40). Altogether, she assembled eight complete or partial bed-sets, as well as leaving any leftover bedding to her friends

---

[59] *Sir Degrevant*, ed. Kooper, ll. 1501–2.
[60] Lincoln, Lincolnshire Archives, REG/20, ff. 55r–56r; Clark, *Lincoln Diocese Documents*, pp. 37–44.

and servants, as the executors saw fit. While she left some other goods, the attention given to the beds and bedding far outweighs any other bequests. As well as being very precise about the exact colours and sizes of the bedding left to her beneficiaries, Dame Joan also sought to gain control over an entire chamber. She stipulated that:

> whosoeuer shall reioyse this Maner of Ochecote after my decesse that ther be leffte in the olde Chaumbir the sellure and the Testure enbrowdred and iij. Curtaynes of the same, and all the Costres of the same sewte, the federbed, & a matrasse, j. bolster, & j. paire of fustyance that lyeth on the same bed, and a hilling of the same sewte, j. grete Carpette (the secunde) and a litell Carpet (next the best), the new mattes that lyen in the same Chaumbir; Item, I wol that the Red wosted qwisshens abyde stille in the same Chaumbir, Also j. copeborde. (p. 41)

Dame Joan's insistence that even the cushions stay where she has put them for whoever next resides in the chamber leaves the reader in no doubt that she believes she has authority over the chamber in her house, as well as the chambers of her beneficiaries. To make this point entirely clear, she adds a line that shows that she expects her wishes to be fulfilled long-term: 'all other necessarijs that ar nayled fast in the said place I wol that thei abyde stille' (p. 41). With this much control over chambers even beyond the grave, it is clear that the strong relationship between women and chambers extended even beyond the lifespan of individual women.

Female power and male anxiety

So far, this chapter has focused on the linguistic and material female ownership of beds and chambers. But what is it about beds and chambers that resonated with late medieval women? As discussed elsewhere, it is clear that most women did not have access to their own chamber and while it is evident from wills that some women owned beds, it does not necessarily follow that they slept alone. However, there was a cultural understanding that women had a degree of power in the chamber, which they did not have elsewhere. This understanding is particularly visible in Middle English literature. An extreme example of a woman's power within the chamber is found in *Ywain and Gawain*, where Lunette has the ability to change the qualities of her chamber. When Ywain finds himself trapped between portcullises after slaying the lord of the castle in combat, Lunette leads him through a door that magically appears in the wall behind him into a chamber 'and did him sit opon hir bed'.[61] She has such power over the chamber that she is able to keep Ywain from being found, as long as he sits on the bed. The chamber itself bends to her will. While knights search the castle for Ywain, the narrator remarks that 'dore ne window was thare none' leading from the space between the portcullises (l. 799) to the chamber, despite Ywain and Lunette having entered through a door. A little later in this episode, Ywain wonders if there might be a hole or window that he could look through. Immediately, 'the maiden than ful shone unshet/ In a place a prevé weket' (ll. 853–4), which emphasises the secrecy surrounding her chamber as well as the fact that she has control over her chamber's boundaries. At the same time, Lunette has made the chamber walls transparent for Ywain:

> Hastily than went thai all
> And soght him in the maydens hall,
> In chambers high (es noght at hide),
> And in solers on ilka side.
> Sir Ywaine saw ful wele al that,
> And still opon the bed he sat. (ll. 805–10)

The men had access to each of the known female-dominated spaces (the maidens' hall and chambers) and yet they did not have the knowledge or access rights to Lunette's chamber. This calls into question the nature of women's secrecy. What were women able to hide in chambers? Lunette's power over the chamber is equally impressive and anxiety-provoking. On the one hand, she is hiding and aiding the protagonist and furthering the narrative. On the other, she is harbouring a fugitive who has just killed her lord and master. This disconcerting wealth of power reflects the cultural attitude towards women in the chamber. The cultural understanding of female power within the chamber goes hand in hand with male anxieties surrounding such power.

As I demonstrated in Chapter 3, the bed was considered to be a sort of levelling ground, in which discussions could take place with more freedom than elsewhere. In particular, the chamber allows women the opportunity to speak with authority. Chaucer explores the idea of the

---

[61] *Ywain and Gawain*, ed. Flowers Braswell, l. 750.

bed as a place for women to express feelings in 'The Wife of Bath's Prologue':

[…] by continueel murmur or grucchyng.
Namely abedde hadden they meschaunce:
Ther wolde I chide and do hem no plesaunce;
I wolde no lenger in the bed abyde,
If that I felt his arm over my syde,
Til he had maad his raunson unto me;
Thanne wolde I suffre hym do his nycetee.[62]

Not only is the bed the site of 'continueel' murmuring, grouching and chiding, but it is a space in which the Wife of Bath's husband has to listen. The bed and its sexual connotations provide the leverage in her discussion: if he does not listen and change his mind based on what she says, she will not allow him to have sex with her. The Wife of Bath seems to be in charge of the chamber. While 'suffre hym do his nycetee' suggests sexual submission on her part, it is a role of submission which has been granted at her leisure, based on her satisfaction with the conversation in hand. That is not to say that every medieval woman had such authority in the chamber, but the caricature of the grumbling housewife suggests a cultural idea of the talkative woman in bed. As Jerry Root argues, 'this is the privileged "space to speke" for women: in bed'.[63]

In romance, female characters often have authority to speak in the chamber, but do so at the expense of being unable to have any authority elsewhere. In *King Horn*, Rymenhild cannot speak to Horn 'at borde […] ne noght in halle', although she willingly summons him to her chamber.[64] In *Le Bone Florence of Rome*, Florence's father goes with her to 'a chaumbur' to ask if she is willing to marry Garcy.[65] She answers, gives her reason and is listened to by her father, who 'lykyd hur wordys wele' (l. 250), but he then has to give her answer to the messengers in 'þe halle' (l. 262); although Florence's voice can be heard in the chamber, in the hall he is the voice of authority. Similarly, at the beginning of *Bevis of Hampton*, the chamber is the only space in which a woman's commands will be obeyed unquestioningly. The king of

---

[62] Chaucer, 'Wife of Bath's Prologue', ll. 406–12.
[63] J. Root, *'Space to Speke': The Confessional Subject in Medieval Literature* (New York, 1997), p. 111.
[64] *King Horn*, ed. Sands, ll. 257–9.
[65] *Le Bone Florence of Rome*, ed. Heffernan, l. 239.

Scotland's daughter has little personal control over her husband out-side of the chamber. When she requires Gii to follow her instructions, she lies 'in hire bedde' and calls him 'out of halle' in order to make her demands.[66] Her instructions to servants are obeyed if they are given within her chamber, even if they take them as far as 'Almaine', which, we are reminded, is 'out of me bour!' (ll. 86–7). In contrast, when she is in 'the halle' (l. 420) and issues instructions to her knights to seize Bevis, 'non of hem nolde him take/ Hii lete him pase' (ll. 455–6).

As I discussed in detail in Chapter 3, *Havelok the Dane* makes it evi-dent that the bed and chamber were considered to be spaces in which women's voices could be heard: Goldeboru remains silent throughout the romance, except for when she is in bed, when her nocturnal advice is good enough to restore Havelok to the thrones of both Denmark and England.[67] A similar understanding of the chamber is found in *Sir De-grevant*, in which 'a chamber […] busked was yare' so that Melidore's maid could talk to Degrevant.[68] It is clear that the maid has authority in this exchange, which reflects some anxiety about women on the part of the writer: she secretly entertains him in the chamber 'as wymen conn mychel slyghth/ And ther wylles ware' (ll. 807–8), explaining to him the political and personal situation of her lord and how Degrevant can overcome his difficulties. Although Degrevant asks the questions, her choice of lexis in 'counsayl' (l. 888) and 'teche' (l. 917) imply that she is in control of the discussion. The maid's advice allows Degrevant to gain entry to Melidore's chamber and so continues the narrative and results in the protagonist succeeding in his conquest. At the same time, the suggestion that women are so easily able to use cunning to cover up events betrays a certain anxiety about what goes on behind cham-ber doors, particularly as the maid's actions result in the deception of her lord and master. Women had the ability to speak and be heard in the chamber, but who was listening?

The idea of women's power and secrecy within the chamber, so prevalent in late medieval literature, stemmed in part from social practice surrounding pregnancy and childbirth. In households of sufficient social standing, certain chambers would be female-only for extended periods of time though it must be pointed out, as Goldberg

---

[66] *Bevis of Hampton*, ed. Herzman, Drake and Salisbury, ll. 176, 178.
[67] See Chapter 3, pp. 78–80.
[68] *Sir Degrevant*, ed. Kooper, ll. 803–4; 'a chamber […] was quickly made ready'. My translation.

argues, that the lack of space would not have allowed this practice to be widespread in bourgeois homes.[69] The last four to six weeks of an aristocratic woman's pregnancy would have been spent in her chamber or another chamber within the house, which was converted into a lying-in chamber.[70] The modifications to the room were not primarily practical: as Angela Florschuetz argues, the lying-in chamber was 'ritually and emphatically feminised', by bringing in rich wall-hangings, bed-clothes and new items of furniture.[71] The gathering of decorations for the lying-in chamber was argued by Linda Pollock to be 'a collective female ritual, nurtured and amplified by sisterly solidarity', although there is evidence that male servants may have been employed in procuring and fetching some of the clothes and furnishings.[72] Certain women would borrow specific furnishings used in the lying-in chamber from each other, as is evident from John Husee's 1530's letter to Lady Lisle:

> I have made delygent sywt unto my Lady of Sussex insomuche that this day she hathe made me grant that your Ladiship shall have of her a Riche pane for a bedd of ermyns borderyd with clothe of gold and a shette of lawnde to cover the same and more i or ij payre of ffyne panyd shettes and a travers and this is all that she hathe promest and this shal be delyverd me xx days hens ffor I thinck the Lady Bewchamp usyth part of it.[73]

Given the lengths to which Husee went to buy appropriate and expensive clothing for Lady Lisle to wear during her lying-in period, the practice of sharing of bedding and furnishings between childbeds was evidently not primarily economical. Instead, the shared fabrics

---

[69] P. J. P. Goldberg, 'Life and Death: The Ages of Man', in *A Social History of England, 1200–1500*, ed. R. Horrox and W. M. Ormrod (Cambridge, 2006), pp. 413–34 (p. 415).

[70] A. Florschuetz, 'Women's Secrets: Childbirth, Pollution, and Purification in Northern Octavian', *Studies in the Age of Chaucer* 30 (2008), 235–68 (p. 241); R. Gilchrist, *Medieval Life: Archaeology and the Life Course* (Woodbridge, 2012), pp. 139–40; L. A. Pollock, 'Childbearing and Female Bonding in Early Modern England', *Social History* 22.3 (1997), 286–306.

[71] Florschuetz, 'Women's Secrets', p. 243.

[72] Pollock, 'Childbearing and Female Bonding', p. 289; C. Mann, 'Clothing Bodies, Dressing Rooms: Fashioning Fecundity in *The Lisle Letters*', *Parergon* 22.1 (2005), 137–57 discusses the communication between Lady Lisle and her husband's servant John Husee, who was given the task of procuring clothing and bedding for Lady Lisle's lying in.

[73] Cited in Mann, 'Clothing Bodies, Dressing Rooms', pp. 152–3.

were rich with symbolic meaning, as they denoted a shared experience between women. Moreover, a birthing chamber containing bedding from well-respected members of local society would carry with it a sense of prestige, ameliorating or cementing the family's status.

The emphatic feminisation of the birthing chamber is multi-faceted. As well as reflecting shared experience through shared fabrics and furnishings, birthing chambers were kept 'warm, dark, and enclosed', recreating the environment of the womb.[74] As discussed in the previous chapter, within late medieval narratives involving sexual encounter or the potential thereof, the chamber either represents the chaste maiden as a whole, as an unbroken vessel with the potential to be penetrated, or specifically female genitalia.[75] It only follows that the lying-in chamber should be dressed to emulate the uterus of a pregnant woman. In addition, the room was designed to centre on the expectant mother.[76] Some aristocratic lying-in chambers were comparable to Christine de Pizan's rather scathing depiction of a merchant's wife's lying-in room, which was behind two other richly adorned chambers and itself 'large and beautiful, all enclosed with tapestries made with her own device', with a large, 'beautifully curtained' bed, surrounded by gold-worked carpets and ornamented hangings.[77] In Christine's description, the pregnant woman was richly dressed and propped up on pearled pillows, 'comme une damoiselle' (literally 'like a lady', although from Christine's sarcasm and loaded phraseology, we might better translate it as a scathing 'like a little princess').[78] The result was that the bed and its occupant were the focal point of an elaborately created tableau. In Christine's description, the lying-in chamber is behind two other chambers, the deepest layer of a female-controlled area, corresponding with

---

[74] P. J. P. Goldberg, *Communal Discord, Child Abduction, and Rape in the Later Middle Ages* (New York, 2007), p. 48; A. Wilson, 'The Ceremony of Childbirth and Its Interpretations', in *Women as Mothers in Pre-Industrial England,* ed. V. Fildes (London, 1990), pp. 68–107 (p. 75); K. Phillips, 'Capturing the Wandering Womb: Childbirth in Medieval Art', *The Haverford Journal* 3.1 (2007), 40–55 (pp. 42–3).

[75] Chapter 5 above, pp. 161–3, 167–9.

[76] G. McMurray Gibson, 'Blessing from Sun and Moon: Churching as Women's Theater', in *Bodies and Disciplines: Intersections of Literature and History in Fifteenth-Century England,* ed. B. A. Hanawalt and D. Wallace (Minneapolis, 1996), pp. 139–59 (p. 149).

[77] 'grande et belle, toute encourtinee de tapisserie faicte a la devise d'elle'; 'bel encourtiné' (my translation); C. de Pisan, *Le Trésor de la Cité Des Dames,* xlii.

[78] Ibid.

Roberta Gilchrist's argument that within a castle, the lady's quarters occupied the innermost space.[79] The use of specific bedding and soft furnishings in the birthing chamber supports the argument that there was a relationship between women and beds, as they command the space in a way which is only visible to women, and for a specifically female purpose. It is also intriguing that the 'device' depicted on the curtains by Christine de Pizan is described as specifically belonging to the expectant mother. This description is reminiscent of Lady Alice West's 'Auncestres armes', which she passed to her son.[80] The heraldic images specifically associated with the woman are arguably most appropriate in the room in which she will give birth: a visual reminder of her continuing bloodline present when at the birth of her child into an (albeit fleetingly) entirely female world. As illustrated in Fig. 18, the company that high-born pregnant women had during the lying-in period and childbirth was usually exclusively female, female friends and servants conducting all tasks within the chamber, collecting food and other supplies from male servants at the door.[81] This miniature depicts a mother shortly after the birth of her child. It is clear from the women's dress that they are not lowly servants, but high-born women in attendance at the birth (perhaps the elusive 'levedis and maidens bright in bour' discussed above).[82] The flowing dresses match perfectly with the décor of the birthing chamber and the scene shows a highly controlled female environment. As discussed by Becky Lee, men were not usually permitted to enter the birthing chamber until the baby was born unless they were called upon to help in an emergency or a priest was summoned to attend to a dying mother or child.[83] John Paston II's letter to Margaret or John Paston III in 1472 makes reference to this segregation:

> I feere that he shall nott speke wyth my lady, for þat she hathe takyn hyre chambre […] I thynke þat thoghe nowthere lyfelde nore ye, brother John, maye come in-to my ladyes chambre, þat my moodre, iff

[79] Gilchrist, *Gender and Archaeology*, p. 124.
[80] TNA PROB 11/1/82; *Fifty Earliest English Wills*, ed. Furnivall, p. 5.
[81] This illustration is discussed in more detail in Chapter 1 above, pp. 18–19; Phillips, 'Capturing the Wandering Womb', p. 40; J. L. Laynesmith, *The Last Medieval Queens: English Queenship 1445–1503* (Oxford, 2005), p. 114; Woolgar, *The Senses*, p. 246.
[82] *Amis and Amiloun*, ed. Foster, l. 430.
[83] Lee, 'A Company', pp. 93–4.

Figure 18: Illustration depicting the birth of St Edmund, *c.* 1434–9. © The British Library Board. BL Harley 2278, f. 13v.

she weer at Norwyche, she myght speke wyth hyre, for þat she is a woman and off worshyppe.[84]

The custom for female exclusivity is reflected in manuscript illustrations representing the birth of a child, whose characters are almost always female unless there is a stated reason for a male presence and which, like Fig. 18 above, often depict the child already wrapped up after having been delivered, as the exact details of childbirth appears to be unclear to the (usually male) limners. While Fig. 18 depicts a

[84] *Paston Letters and Papers*, ed. Davis, I, 453–4.

Figure 19: Illustration depicting the birth of Jacob and Esau, *c.* 1350–75. © The British Library Board. BL Egerton 1894, f. 12v.

calm environment after the birth of a baby, some manuscript illustrations reveal their artists' lack of experience in the birthing chamber through their attempts to depict childbirth itself. Fig. 19 shows part of a series of four images on a page of an illustrated Genesis produced in England in the third quarter of the fourteenth century. Rebekah is delivered of Jacob and Esau by a woman, although what exactly the midwife is doing remains unclear, given her positioning in relation to the mother. The rather bizarre positioning of the midwife, the lack of umbilical cords and the way the children seem to have crawled out from under the sheets suggest that the illustrator had only a vague sense of the mechanics of childbirth. It is clear that the illustrator and the adult male figures in this illustrated Genesis are excluded from the birthing chamber.[85] Kay Staniland argues that the exclusion of men was a practical step to avoid the presence of men during treatments such as herbal baths to aid the onset of labour.[86] I would argue that the reason is more deep-rooted. It would surely be equally possible to ask any male servants to leave during baths and other compromising treatments, without issuing an outright ban. There is documentary evidence that some women had male attendants in their chambers at other times, including during baths: for example, Eleanor de Montfort's baths were organised by Roger of the Chamber.[87] The prohibition of men during lying-in and childbirth included the father of the child who, one would assume, was intimately acquainted with his wife's body, so the exclusion of all men cannot be simply out of a concern for the woman's modesty. Perhaps it was because the ordeal of giving birth was imagined as intrinsically female that an all-female company was required. Florschuetz points out that the act of shutting men out of the chamber 'reminds those shut out that there is indeed something occurring in the forbidden space that is both tempting and important to know'.[88] It is also important to consider that the cultural practice of removing any direct contact with men during the last few weeks of pregnancy until around a month after the birth correlates with the late medieval attitude towards women's bodily functions, in a society in which women's bodies were considered monstrous, particularly when they showed any sign of reproductive capabilities and fecundity.[89] As Julia Kristeva argues, the fear of the female body is 'essentially fear of

---

[85] For a facsimile and description of the whole page, see M. R. James, *Illustrations of the Book of Genesis, Being a Complete Reproduction in Facsimile of the Manuscript of the British Museum, Egerton 1894* (Oxford, 1921).

[86] K. Staniland, 'Royal Entry into the World', in *England in the Fifteenth Century: Proceedings from the 1986 Harlaxton Symposium*, ed. D. Williams (Woodbridge, 1987), pp. 297–313 (p. 302).

[87] Salih, 'At Home; Out of the House', p. 131.

[88] Florschuetz, 'Women's Secrets', p. 243.

[89] For a discussion of the monstrous female body, see *Medieval Monstrosity and the Female Body*, ed. S. A. Miller (New York, 2010), especially Part II; T. V. Pearman, '(Dis)pleasure and (Dis)ability: The Topos of Reproduction in *Dame Sirith* and "The Merchant's Tale"', in T. V. Pearman, *Women and Disability in Medieval Literature* (New York, 2010), pp. 19–44.

her generative power'.[90] As such, a pregnant woman must be hidden in order to retain normal patriarchal society. The apparent insalubriousness of a pregnant woman in late medieval England is evidenced by the ritual of purification following childbirth, though this practice certainly pre-dates the Middle Ages.[91] Until she was churched and purified, she remained in the sole company of women. The chamber was, therefore, both a place of shared knowledge and bonding for women and a site of male anxiety.

The lying-in and birthing chamber, the very method provided to dispel male anxiety of the process of reproduction and the monstrous female body, served to provoke and propagate further male anxieties surrounding the woman's confinement and association with other women. As pointed out by Kate Phillips, the change in meaning of the term 'gossip', which originally meant 'godparent' or someone who was present at the birth of the child, and now refers to malicious tongue-wagging and the spreading of rumours, is reflective of the growing anxiety about the existence of an exclusively female space.[92] The birthing chamber is treated suspiciously in romance, and is often used as the site to frame female characters, as discussed in Chapter 5.[93] As Florschuetz argues, the crisis in *Octavian* is provoked by the 'violent intrusion' into the Empress's birthing chamber of both the knave planted by her mother-in-law and the Emperor, suggesting that the female-only chamber should not have been violated by men.[94] At the same time, the secrecy surrounding the birthing chamber and the lack of distinction between the bloodied childbed and the violated, blood-stained bed associated with adultery, as explored in the previous chapter, render the space as a locus for doubt and mistrust.

Anxiety associated with the exclusion of men from the birthing chamber manifests itself in romances in which children are switched at birth or removed from the chamber without masculine knowledge or consent. For instance, in *Lai Le Freine*, Le Freine's mother spitefully

---

[90] J. Kristeva, *Powers of Horror: An Essay on Abjection*, trans. L. S. Roudiez (New York, 1982), p. 77.

[91] Lee, 'Men's Recollections', pp. 224–41. The practice of segregation and subsequent purification after childbirth is an ancient tradition. For example, instructions for the purification of a woman following childbirth are found in Leviticus 12.

[92] Phillips, 'Capturing the Wandering Womb', p. 42.

[93] Chapter 5 above, pp. 160–1.

[94] Florschuetz, 'Women's Secrets', p. 235.

remarks that her neighbour's twins are the result of having sex with two men and then, to her dismay, she also gives birth to twins. Rather than admit that she slandered her neighbour, she decides that 'me is best take mi chaunce,/ And sle mi childe, and do penaunce'.[95] After consultation with her midwife, who refuses to kill the child, and a maiden, who persuades the lady to let her take the child to a convent, the maiden is able to carry out the removal of the child without the lord's knowledge, due to the fact that the lord is waiting 'in the halle' (l. 45), away from the birthing chamber. The maiden is described as 'a maiden fre/ Who ther y-nortured hade y-be' (ll. 121–2), giving the impression that she has spent her life being 'nortured' – literally speaking, another female bodily function – by the lady, within the confines of the chamber. The ties that connect the mother and the maiden, fostered in the female-only environment, lead the maiden to help deceive the lady's husband. The child is wrapped in 'a riche baudekine' (l. 137), which presumably formed part of the birthing-chamber furnishings, and is left outside a nunnery. It is interesting that, even after the child is removed from the birthing chamber, she is delivered into a female-only environment, thus keeping her away from masculine authority. It is also pertinent that the deception is eventually resolved in a chamber, due to the mother's recognition of the 'baudekine', which Le Freine uses as a mantel on the bed.[96] The 'baudekine' evokes the birthing chamber enough for the lady to recognise her daughter and for the bond between them to be renewed, but not enough to exclude men from the room. Her father is fetched, and he accepts the news with joy and good grace. The audience might be left thinking that all of the confusion and heartache might have been avoided, had the knight had access to the birthing chamber at the beginning.

A similar deception occurs in *The Cheuelere Assigne*. Like the lady in *Lai le Freine*, Queen Beatrice accuses the mother of twins of having sex with two different men, is rebuked by her husband and later conceives 'resonabullye manye' children.[97] Beatrice retires to a birthing chamber, but it is ruled by her mother-in-law, Matabryne, who does not let any other woman come near 'for she thow3te to do þat byrthe to a fowle ende' (l. 40). Although Matabryne has the repetitive verse-tag

---

[95] *Lai le Freine*, ed. Sands, ll. 113–14.
[96] Chapter 5 above, p. 148.
[97] *The Romance of the Chevalere Assigne*, ed. Gibbs, l. 34.

'þat cawsed moche sorowe', running throughout the poem, there is no obvious reason why she should wish to do mischief, except that she is a woman in a position of power within the birthing chamber. Contravening cultural practice, she summons a man to the chamber and instructs him to drown the children, before finding a litter of puppies, killing their mother and putting them in the babies' place, in order to frame her daughter-in-law as a bestialist. Such is her authority within the birthing chamber that she can order a man to take the children and convince her son that his wife has committed bestiality, as she is the only witness to the birth. The deception resulting from a female-only birthing chamber is twofold: Matabryne deceives everyone by sending the children away to be drowned, while the king believes that his wife has deceived him by having sex with a dog. Anxiety surrounding the secrecy of the birthing chamber is evident in this romance. It is obvious to the audience that the complication would not have happened, had the birthing chamber been less segregated. The segregation is emphasised by the fact that the king is described as lying 'in langour' (l. 57) away from the chamber during his wife's labour. The same phrase is used a few lines later to describe his wife's imprisonment. The message is clear: being locked out is as debilitating as being locked in and, without male access to the birthing chamber, who knows what mischief could happen within?

Narratives of deception focused on the lying-in chamber and childbirth are a response to male anxieties about an enclosed space which excludes men. However, it was not only female exclusivity within the chamber which provoked male anxiety. The propensity for women in romance to draw power and protection from her chamber indicates a cultural struggle surrounding women and the chamber: on the one hand, containing women's apparent power within the chamber set a precedent for the chamber being the only acceptable site of female authority; one the other, it betrays an anxiety that women did, indeed, have power within the chamber, even when they shared the space with men. As discussed by scholars such as Schofield and Riddy, many houses, including those belonging to the upper bourgeoisie and aristocracy, did not have very much space in which to sleep.[98] This meant that sleeping quarters were very often shared, and that even married couples did not necessarily get a chamber to themselves. An

---

[98] J. Schofield, *Medieval London Houses* (New Haven, 1995), p. 42; Riddy, '"Burgeis" Domesticity', p. 23.

exaggerated reflection of this can be found in *Sir Tristrem*, where Mark, Ysonde and Tristrem all sleep in the same chamber, but in beds 'thritti fete' apart.[99] Despite these relatively cramped conditions, within romance written at the time, female characters often have their own chamber. This trope is not taken to be reflective of society – after all, the geography and architecture of romance is overtly unlike the audience's sense of the real – but instead allows ideas of women and power to be explored in isolation. It does suggest, however, that in the cultural imagination, women inhabited the chambers in a way which men did not.

It is evident that women were associated with domesticity, as narratives in which women are outside of the domestic space frequently show women to be helpless and unsafe. While it was considered normal for men to travel and camp on the road, women wandering outside were considered to be akin to the harlot in the Book of Proverbs, 'not able to abide still at home'.[100] In the romance tradition, women who sleep outside of their chambers almost always suffer from the abuse of masculine human or otherworldly agents: Sir Orfeo's wife is taken away by the fairies because she slept 'opon the grene'; Lybeaus Desconus is conceived through rape 'by the forest syde' and Sir Degarre's mother is raped when she and her 'damaiseles' stop 'upon a grene'.[101] Each of these instances are treated as if the inevitable outcome of the female character spending time outside. Female characters do not seem capable of fighting back outside of the chamber, but instead have to rely on any passing male characters for help. For instance, in *The Avowyng of Arthur*:

> In the forest he mette a knyghte
> Ledand a bird* bryghte;   *woman
> Ho wepputte wundur sore.
> Ho sayd, 'Sayn Maré mygthe me spede
> And save me my madunhede.
> And giffe the kynghte for his dede
> Bothe soro and care!'[102]

---

[99] *Sir Tristrem*, ed. Lupack, l. 2206.
[100] Proverbs 7.11.
[101] *Sir Orfeo*, ed. Sands, l. 48; *Lybeaus Desconus*, ed. Shuffleton, l. 9; *Sire Degarre*, ed. G. Schleich (Heidelberg, 1929), ll. 56, pp. 73–5.
[102] *The Avowyng of Arthur*, ed. Hahn, ll. 278–84.

The trope of the helpless woman terrified of ravishment was so in-grained in the late medieval cultural imagination that it was appro-priated to strengthen the case for the attempted ravishment of Jane Boys in 1451. As McSheffrey and Pope argue, John Paston I borrows from the chivalric tradition in his report of Jane's alleged kidnap and ravishment:

> she was set upon her hors, she revylid Lancasterother and callid hym knave, and wept and kryid owte upon hym pitowsly to her, and seid as shrewdly to hym as coud come to her mende, and fel doune of her hors unto that she was bound, and callid fals traytour […] and seid that what so ever fel of her she shuld neuer be weddyd to that knave, to deye for it.[103]

In *The Avowyng of Arthur* and Paston's account, the woman is defence-less and weeping, and her main concern is the wrong the man is doing to her and the potential loss of her 'madunhede'. Jane's proclamation that she will never consent to marry the 'traytour' is echoed in Middle English romance texts: Melidore calls Degrevant a 'tratur' and profess-es a desire to see him hanged because he surprises her in the woods.[104] As Goldberg points out, several fifteenth-century kidnap narratives involve the victim being tied to a getaway horse and carried off, so it became a trope in documentary narratives as much as similar episodes in romance.[105] McSheffrey and Pope argue that John Paston's account is fictitious and that Jane consented to the ravishment, an argument supported by Jane's own testimony. Regardless of what actually hap-pened, the amalgamation of romance tropes and legal language to create a credible history of events shows the extent to which cultural ideas surrounding inside and outside space are informed by literary traditions.

The cultural idea that the chamber was a space of protection and power for women is shown in the marked difference between the female protagonist's reaction to violence inside and outside of the chamber in *Le Bone Florence of Rome*. Florence, who is attacked periodically throughout the romance, twice successfully defends herself within chambers but appears helpless when she is outside. The different

---

[103] *Paston Letters and Papers*, ed. Davis, I, 70; S. McSheffrey and J. Pope, 'Ravishment, Legal Narratives, and Chivalric Culture in Fifteenth-Century England', *Journal of British Studies* 48.4 (2009), 818–36.
[104] *Sir Degrevant*, ed. Kooper, l. 733.
[105] Goldberg, *Communal Discord*, pp. 137–8.

responses to violence outside and within a chamber are striking. When in the woods, she responds to her Mylys' attack 'wyth mylde mode' and makes 'many a rewfull crye', whilst remaining passive as she is hung from a tree by her hair and beaten.[106] One would assume that the strength required to hang someone by their hair would make it difficult for Mylys to do so, if Florence were to struggle. Florence's silent suffering during a humiliating and painful beating is a common hagiographical trope, so it is possible that the audience would not expect Florence to attempt to defend herself. However, as the text is a romance rather than a saint's life, the genre requires the protagonist to stay alive until the text is approaching an end, so the audience should not expect martyrdom. Her passivity and lack of an attempt to free herself suggests that she is incapable of fighting back, not necessarily that she chooses not to as a martyr. Therefore, the next time she is attacked, the audience likely assumes that she will be raped: unlike in the forest, in the chamber 'sche had no socowre' (l. 1602). However, in the forest, Sir Tyrry came to her aid; in the chamber, it is the chamber itself that saves her. When Machary attempts to attack Florence in her chamber, she is well-equipped to fight back:

> Before hur bedd lay a stone
> The lady toke hyt up anon
> And toke hyt yn a gethe,[107]
> On the mowthe sche hym hyt,
> That hys for tethe owte he spytt
> Above and also benethe.
> Hys mowthe, hys nose, braste owt on blood,
> Forthe at the chaumbur dore he yode,
> For drede of more wrethe. (ll. 1605–13)

The 'stone' 'before hur bedd' with which she hits Machary is not mentioned elsewhere and does not seem to be there for any particular purpose. If anything, it would make more sense for a stone to have been present in the forest during her previous attack. The stone's presence

---

[106] *Le Bone Florence of Rome*, ed. Heffernan, ll. 1510–19.

[107] The meaning of this line is unclear. The *MED* ('gethe, n.') suggests that the phrase 'to take [something] in a gethe' might mean to do something hastily, but the phrase is only extant in this line. As it immediately follows 'toke hyt up anon', I doubt that the *MED*'s definition is very likely, as the phrase would be redundant. It is possible that 'gethe' comes from 'getheren' and is meant to suggest that she 'gathered' it up to a suitable position to strike or, more likely, that she put it in a gathering of material, with which she then hit her aggressor.

in the chamber is portrayed as fortuitous but not illogical, as if the chamber itself, being the culturally understood natural environment for the female protagonist, provided the means for Florence's defence.[108] His immediate retreat is described as 'at the chaumbur dore', highlighting the acceptable boundary between Florence and anyone else. As a result of this violent encounter, Machary has to spend 'a fowrtenyght' in 'hys chaumber' (ll. 1614–15), emulating feminine behaviour. While the chamber is Florence's fortress, it is Machary's prison. Florence is further protected by a chamber in a mariner's cabin on a ship. Once again, her physical environment conspires to prevent Florence from being raped: she struggles against the mariner and calls upon the Virgin Mary for help and immediately a storm rages, sweeping every potential aggressor overboard. The immediacy with which the events take place, upon her struggling in bed and calling for help, give the impression that she was directly responsible for the storm. She demonstrates a command of her surroundings in bed which she does not have elsewhere. Even when the chamber is not a safe space in *Le Bone Florence of Rome,* the text focuses on the potential for women to commit violence in the chamber when Machary cuts the throat of Florence's bedfellow Beatrice and plants the knife in Florence's hand to frame her for the murder. At the same time, the way in which Florence continues to sleep on, despite the number of knights and ladies pressed around her bed 'wondur sore wepeande' (l. 1655) serves to reinforce her innocence. Conversely, the fact that she is acquitted of the crime, despite all evidence to the contrary, betrays an anxiety that women can get away with alleged murder in bed.

The chamber also serves to empower the female protagonist to attack and defend herself in *Bevis of Hampton.* Just as the ship's cabin acts as Florence's chamber, so too does a cave for Josian. She appears to be entirely at a loss while she is in the wilderness, but as soon as she is placed in the equivalent of a chamber, she gains authority. Even though Josian and Bevis are supposed to be hiding, she sends Bevis out hunting, despite his protestations. When two hungry lions kill her saracen companion, whom Josian calls a 'chamberleyn' as they hide

---

[108] It must be remembered that, as shown in Chapter 1 above, late medieval chambers contained more than simply beds and within the romance genre it is possible for them to contain even more than the audience's chambers would be likely to: if in *The Squire of Low Degree* it can be considered credible that a woman's chamber contains the equipment to embalm and entomb a body, a stone in Florence's chamber is hardly a problem.

in a cave, 'Josian into the cave gan shete/ And the two lyouns at hur feete'.[109] The verb 'shete' is not one normally associated with caves, as it suggests there is a door to shut or lock. Assuming that it were possible to shut a cave, one would think that the more logical solution would be to shut herself in the cave with the lions on the outside, or to shut the lions in a cave and hide elsewhere. Instead, she turns the cave into a chamber, in which she has the utmost control. The difference between masculine and feminine control of the chamber is highlighted upon Bevis' return. He finds Josian sitting in the cave with the lions, entirely unscathed, and declares that he will fight them. Josian offers to hold one while he fights the other, but he declines so that he will have a better story. What follows is an awkward, nearly fatal tussle between Bevis and the lions, which is only resolved when she saves him. According to the narrator, Josian's protection against the lions is due to her being a virgin. Her virginity is the result of her ability to keep control of beds and chambers. Even though Josian is twice married against her will in this romance before marrying Bevis, she is able to remain chaste, first through her magic ring and then through violence. In each case, she has control over the marriage bed. Josian prevents Mile from consummating their marriage by using the bed to her advantage:

Thanne was before his bed itight*,	*prepared
Ase fele* han of this gentil knight,	*many [servants]
A covertine on raile tre, [110]	
For no man scholde on bed ise*.	*see
Josian bethoughte on highing*,	*raising up/ hanging
On a towaile she made knotte riding,	
Aboute his nekke she hit threw	
And on the raile tre she drew;	
Be the nekke she hath him up tight	
And let him so ride al the night.	
Josian lai in hire bed.	
No wonder, though she wer adred. (ll. 3215–26)	

Just as women such as Alice West and Joan Buckland have command over every item of linen in their chambers, Josian can command the

---

[109] *Bevis of Hampton*, ed. Herzman, Drake and Salisbury, ll. 2407, 2388–9.
[110] A 'raile tre' is a rail suspended from the wall or ceiling, from which to hang bed curtains. See, for example, the illustration in London, British Library, Harley MS 3487, f. 121v.

materials in her chamber to the point at which the bed is her weapon. Like Florence, the chamber provides the materials she requires for self-defence: while a man of his status could be expected to have a curtained bed, he appears to only have a 'raile tre', which seems to be an afterthought, 'for no man scholde on bed ise'. The presence of the 'raile tre' meant that she was able to kill her husband with the very bed in which their marriage was intended to be consummated. It is notable that Josian requested that every onlooker leave the chamber and the door be locked, before she would consent to consummate the relationship. Allowing Josian to have the upper hand in the chamber ultimately led to Mile's downfall. Her affinity with the bed is epitomised in the final couplet of the hanging episode. Despite her husband's dead body hanging above her all night, she lies in her bed. It is evident that in bed is where she has the most control.

There is a real sense of anxiety surrounding women's capacity for violence in bed, which does not only exist in the world of romance. For example, in a church court case of 1486, Joan Pollard is reported to have 'kept a knife at the head of her bed with the intention of slitting her husband's throat', and in a witness testimony to domestic violence in a plea for the divorce *a mensa et a thoro* of Thomas and Margery Nesfeld in 1396, Thomas is described as being 'roused by anger' at his wife Margery's suggestion that 'she could kill him in bed at night if she wanted'.[111] In *King Horn*, Rymenhild's preparations to kill herself and her new husband by hiding a knife in her bed are treated as matter-of-fact, as if the obvious solution to the problem of marrying against her wishes would be to kill them both.[112] Josian's murder of Mile is presented as justifiable, given that she did not wish to marry him. This matter-of-fact, sympathetic way of dealing with the planned homicide of the characters' respective husbands contrasts with the legal attitude towards mariticide, deemed to be 'petty treason', which was much more of a heinous crime than the killing of a wife by her husband.[113] Such romances problematise marriage against the woman's consent, justifying the characters' actions, which creates discomfort among the audience, who would simultaneously condemn and condone such

---

[111] See Chapter 2 above, p. 56; S. M. Butler, *The Language of Abuse: Marital Violence in Later Medieval England* (Leiden, 2007), p. 12; Goldberg, *Women in England*, p. 142.

[112] *King Horn*, ed. Sands, ll. 1205–11.

[113] Goldberg, *Women in England*, p. 17; L. E. Mitchell, *Portraits of Medieval Women: Family, Marriage and Politics in England 1225–1350* (New York, 2003), p. 79.

behaviour. Whether or not the audience agrees that the murders are justified, the texts suggest that such a murder is possible, indicating that there was cultural anxiety surrounding such possibilities. Interestingly, in romance and elsewhere, when a man and a woman are intended to share the same bed or chamber, it is never presumed that the man has plotted to kill the woman in bed. This is because husbands were capable of killing their wives when they are awake: the only time a man was vulnerable to his wife was when he was in bed asleep. As such, perhaps the popular instruction to 'arysse erly' is not simply good practice, but a warning: get up before your wife, while you still can.[114]

While there was a distrust of women in the chamber, it was also social practice for women to be in charge of nursing and healing within the home, which would often take place in the chamber. There is very little evidence of women who listed their occupation as a healer, midwife or nurse in late medieval England, notable exceptions being two midwives listed in the poll tax returns at Reading in 1381.[115] However, as Mary Fissell and Goldberg point out, this lack of evidence does not mean that women were not tending the sick on a part-time basis.[116] As Carole Hill argues, the medieval woman's inclination is towards looking after the flesh: 'washing and tending bodies [...] was traditionally their business'.[117] Felicity Riddy further suggests that bourgeois women's concern for the 'regimes of the body' was specifically 'inside the house'.[118] Given the nature of the sick-bed, I suggest that the locus of female bodily concern was in the chamber. It is evident from literature that both men and women were capable of tending to the sick and injured, but that women were particularly associated with the sick-bed. When male characters are responsible for looking after the sick and injured, this usually occurs outside of the chamber. Florence of Rome is rescued and tended to by 'the lorde'

---

[114] See Introduction, p. 10.

[115] *The Poll Taxes of 1377, 1379 and 1381: Part 1*, ed. C. C. Fenwick (London, 1998), p. 41.

[116] M. E. Fissell, 'Introduction: Women, Health, and Healing in Early Modern Europe', *Bulletin of the History of Medicine* 82.1 (2008), 1–17; Goldberg, 'The Ages of Man', p. 415.

[117] C. Hill, *Women and Religion in Late-Medieval Norwich* (Woodbridge, 2010), p. 123.

[118] F. Riddy, 'Temporary Virginity and the Everyday Body: *Le Bone Florence of Rome* and Bourgeois Self-making', in *Pulp Fictions of Medieval England: Essays in Popular Romance*, ed. N. McDonald (Manchester, 2004), pp. 197–216 (p. 201).

and 'hys men' before they lead her to a 'chaumber dere'.[119] Similarly, Amouraunt 'hadde gret care' for Amiloun and looks after him whilst they wander from town to town, but once they reach Amis' home it is Belisaunt who looks after Amiloun in her own chamber.[120]

It is evident from romance that women were understood to have significant power over the sick-bed and that there were male anxieties associated with that presumed power. In some cases, female characters are expected to look after the sick and wounded simply because they are female: women attend sick-beds because it is their duty or inclination to do so, as hostesses or ladies of the house. On the other hand, the trope of powerful women with supernatural abilities who, keeping knights in their chambers, heal but also enthral their patients, betrays an anxiety felt towards women who heal or towards the events that occur behind closed chamber doors. In *Ywain and Gawain*, the 'twa maydens' that tend to Ywain and his lion are not introduced as supernatural beings, but simply 'the lordes doghters'.[121] However, the fact that they 'wele war lered of lechecraft' and managed to cure 'everilka wound' (ll. 2739–40) sustained by both Ywain and the lion so effectually conveys a sense of mystery and suggests that they have an intrinsic adeptness at healing. Further suggestion that they may also have supernatural power over him is found in the narrator's use of time phrases. References to specific lengths of time throughout this romance are usually particularly detailed: the king was with his knights 'aght days and aght nyghtes' (l. 1438); Alundyne allows Ywain a 'twelmoth' to prove himself as a knight, which ends on 'Saint Johns day' (ll. 1570, 1578); Ywain and the lion live in the woods 'a fouretenyght' (l. 2058) and the maidens were allowed 'fourty dayes' respite (l. 2174). These references contrast strongly with the narrator's comment, 'I can noght tel how lang he lay' (l. 2741), referring to the time Ywain spent in his sick-bed. This lack of temporal control suggests a shift in power: for the rest of the romance, the narrator is in control of the pace of the narrative, yet whilst Ywain is being healed, it is the maidens who are in control. The fuzzy sense of time surrounding Ywain's sick-bed can be read as reflective of the writer's and the audience's experience of sickness. It is easy to lose track of time in a darkened sick-room and, when Gawain's very identity as a knight can be questioned if one stays

---

[119] *Le Bone Florence of Rome*, ed. Heffernan, ll. 1543–60.
[120] *Amis and Amiloun*, ed. Foster, ll. 1831, 2179–86.
[121] *Ywain and Gawain*, ed. Flowers Braswell, ll. 2735–7.

in bed until nearly noon, a sustained stay in bed changes the way in which the world is perceived to work.[122] A weak or disabled patient would also be dependent on the person taking care of him or her, so it is likely that healers were understood to have power beyond their ability to heal. Personal experience of the mystery of the sick-bed on the part of the writers and audience of the romances, propagated by literary episodes such as that of Ywain's sick-bed, drew from and fuelled a mistrust of women who have healing and caring roles and a presumption that women are able to have supernatural power over beds and chambers.

A similar lack of temporal control and subsequent mistrust of the female healing character within the chamber is found in *Eglamour of Artois*. It is integral to the narrative that Eglamour be away from Crystabell at the time of his son's birth, in order for their respective exiles to take place. This causes frustration for the audience, who is well aware of Eglamour's time limitations: Crystabell showed signs of pregnancy before Eglamour departed, of which he was aware as he advised her to look after a child, should God send one.[123] However, it seems that Eglamour has forgotten. After injuring himself slaying a dragon, he stays with Dyamuntowre while she 'helys hys heed/ A twelfmonyth in hyr bowre' (ll. 758–9), failing to return in time for the birth of his child. In addition to the sense of scandal created by his location 'in hyr bowre', given that Eglamour's moral conduct and social standing as a man had already been questioned when Arrok the giant called him 'thef' and 'traytour' for stealing his hart, the length of Eglamour's stay suggests disloyalty on his part.[124] Alternatively, an audience could infer that the injuries to the head affected Eglamour's judgement, as the head was understood to contain the mind and therefore the common sense of a person.[125] As such, Dyamuntowre's healing of Eglamour's head is the force that causes the narrative to continue once Eglamour has remembered his responsibilities. On the

---

[122] See p. 177 above.

[123] *Sir Eglamour of Artois*, ed. Hudson, pp. 704–5.

[124] Ibid., l. 304; To call a man a petty thief is to call into question his manliness and social standing. The theft of a hart, given that it was owned by a giant, is comparable to the alleged petty theft of chickens by Robert Smyth, as discussed in D. G. Neal, *The Masculine Self in Late-medieval England* (Chicago, 2008), pp. 13–56 (p. 34).

[125] R. Bacon, *Psychology of Visual Perception*, trans. R. B. Burke, in *A Source Book in Medieval Science*, ed. E. Grant, 2 vols. (Cambridge, 1974), I, 407–10 (p. 408).

other hand, it is equally likely to infer that Dyamuntowre deliberately kept Eglamour in her bed for a year, her status as powerful healing woman causing Eglamour to forget about Crystabell for so long. Whether good or bad, Dyamuntowre is the dominant figure in the relationship, as is clear from her description:

> The Emperour has a dowghtur bryght:
> Sche has unduretane the knyght –
> Hyre name was Dyamuntowre.
> There sche saves hym fro the deed,
> With here handys sche helys hys heed
> A twelfmonyth in hyr bowre. (ll. 754–9)

The choice of lexis here is telling. The verb 'unduretane' has a dual meaning of having taken on the task and having entrapped the knight.[126] Furthermore, the active verb in the phrase 'sche saves hym', the description of Eglamour as nearly 'deed' and the explicit reference to 'here handys' all imply that she has the power physically, socially and medically. Regardless of the characters' intentions, Eglamour's time away is necessary in order for the plot of the romance to develop. The length of time it takes to heal Eglamour allows the audience to ask questions usually left unvoiced about real women's chambers. What exactly went on inside the chamber during that year? What was she doing to him, and he to her? Did it really need to take that long?

A similar sense of discomfort surrounding the sick-bed is found in *Lybeaus Desconus*, in which there appears to be a lack of control of time or direction on the part of the protagonist and the narrator. When Lybeaus is wounded after fighting a giant, Denamowre takes him into a chamber and clothes him in 'paule', from which time he is bewitched by her.[127] The 'paule', with its double meaning of fine cloth and shroud, indicates the fine line between the living and the dead.[128] Women traditionally had the role of shrouding the dead, as is evident in some wills. For example, Alice Bumpsted in 1514 left two pence to each of the 'two women that shall sew my winding sheet' and John Cadeby in 1439 left 'a woman for wrapping the body of the deceased 2d'.[129] The episode in *Lybeaus Desconus* gives voice to the concern that as

---

[126] See *MED*, 'undertāken (v.)'.
[127] *Lybeaus Desconus*, ed. Shuffleton, l. 1506.
[128] *MED*, 'pal (n.)'.
[129] C. Daniell, *Death and Burial in Medieval England 1066–1550* (London, 1997), p. 38; F. Riddy, 'Looking Closely: Authority and Intimacy in the Late Medieval

women are traditionally associated with both healing and preparation of the corpse, the authority that they have is a matter – literally – of life and death. Although Denamowre asks Lybeaus to be 'hyr lord', the language used implies that she has the ultimate control: 'sche made hym to duell thore' (l. 1515). What is unsettling about this part of the narrative is that she is said to 'traye and tene' Lybeaus and give him a death shroud, when what should follow from a woman leading a wounded knight into a chamber is healing and care.[130] Lybeaus is on an errand that had previously been treated with urgency, but he stays under her spell for a lengthy but unspecific length of time, ranging between 'fully thre wekys and more' to 'twelve monthes and more', depending on the manuscript.[131] Not only does Denamowre cause him to forget his errand, and thus delay his trajectory and add to the sense of urgency and suspense, but the narrator cannot be sure of how long he stayed in her castle. In Renaut de Bâgé's twelfth-century Old French text, *Li Biaus Descouneüs*, the closest analogue to the Middle English romance, Lybeaus stays but a day in Denamowre's castle.[132] A later English scribe or minstrel has deliberately chosen to put Lybeaus under the thrall of Denamowre for a greater length of time. This must be reflective of English anxieties surrounding the power women are suspected of having in the chamber.

Eger and Grime highlights the conflicting cultural ideas surrounding women's access to power within the chamber. Loosepaine has power over Eger that is connected to, but not directly related to, temporality. When Eger is defeated in a fight with Greysteel, Loosepaine rescues him

---

Urban Home', in *Gendering the Master Narrative: Women and Power in the Middle Ages*, ed. M. C. Erler and M. Kowaleski (New York, 2003), pp. 212–28 (p. 223); R. Dinn, 'Death and Rebirth in Late Medieval Bury St Edmunds' in *Death in Towns: Urban Responses to the Dying and the Dead, 100–1600*, ed. S. Bassett (Leicester, 1995), pp. 151–69 (p. 154); Stell, *Probate Inventories*, p. 80.

[130] 'betray and harm'. My translation; *Lybeaus Desconus*, ed. Shuffleton, l. 1513.

[131] *Lybeaus Desconus*, ed. Shuffleton, edited from Oxford, Bodleian Library, MS Ashmole 61, suggests around three weeks (l. 1514), as does the text in Naples, Biblioteca Nazionale, MS XIII. B. 29, l. 1501. Lybeaus stays twelve months or more in London, British Library, Cotton MS Caligula A. ii, London, Lambeth Palace, MS 306 and London, British Library, Additional MS 27879 (Percy Folio). The line is partly illegible in London, Lincoln's Inn, MS 150, but the visible 'monyth and more' (l. 712) indicates that it was at least a month. See *Lybeaus Dysconus (Lambeth Palace, MS 306)*, in *Lybeaus Dysconus*, ed. E. Salisbury and J. Weldon (Kalamazoo, 2013), n. 1479.

[132] R. de Beaujeu, *Le Bel Inconnu*, ed. M. Perret and I. Weill (Paris, 2003).

and tends to his wounds in her chamber. She would rather that Eger stayed longer with her, until he 'bee in better plight to goe', although she has healed him so well that it is as if he 'had neuer beene wounded'.[133] Because he 'will not abyde' (l. 326), his wounds are only cured for 'a day or 2' (l. 322). When he reaches his own domestic sphere, 'home within 2 mile' (l. 338), she no longer has control over his wounds, so they bleed anew. Several conclusions can be drawn from this. Firstly, as Eger's wounds reopen upon reaching his own domestic sphere, we can conclude that the woman only has any power within her chamber. Secondly, as he refuses her enticements to stay with her, she no longer has authority over him, so her healing efforts no longer have an effect. Loosepaine, unlike Denamowre and Dyamuntowre, has limits to her power and is unable to entrap the knight. As such, she seems like a much more relatable character. Her treatment of Eger's wounds is unmistakably human: washing and dressing and re-dressing wounds, applying 'spices and salues' (l. 285) and administering a 'grasse greene' drink (l. 291). Her healing powers are essential in keeping Eger alive, but clearly have their limits. Her powers and limitations reflect what appears to be the ideal: women should be allowed some powers in the chamber, particularly when they meet men's needs, but their power must be contained and controlled.

Women of the chamber: empowered or encapsulated?

This chapter has shown that there was a very strong affiliation between women and beds and chambers in late medieval England, which was expressed through literary tropes, social practice and the language of day-to-day speech. There is a definite linguistic link between women and chambers, from adjectival phrases such as 'leuedy so bryht in bour' to the high frequency of feminine nouns and pronouns associated with beds and chambers in the Middle English corpus.[134] It is also evident from ways in which women took ownership of beds and bedding, making decisions about furnishings of their own chambers and those of other people, and the practice of bringing a bed to the marriage as part of the dowry, that late medieval women felt a sense of entitlement in relation to the bed. The majority of women would not have had the luxury of a bed and chamber to call their own. Despite this practicality,

---

[133] *Eger and Grime*, ed. Hales and Furnivall, ll. 302, 319.
[134] London, British Library, Harley MS 2253, f. 80rb.

there was a cultural understanding that women were not only linked to the bed and chamber, but that the chamber allowed them access to some power and authority that is not available to them elsewhere. Such female power can be seen to some extent during lying in and childbirth, in which the chamber was an exclusively female space, and in women's concern with the bodies of members of their households. Male anxieties surrounding the powers allowed to women during these times manifest themselves in stories in which women become powerful when they are in the chamber. These anxieties are played out through narratives of deception surrounding the marriage bed and the birthing chamber or through narratives in which the female protagonist is able to defend herself within the chamber. These stories may have perpetuated male anxieties but would have also spoken to women, encouraging them to feel that they had authority in a space of their very own: the chamber. As very few women had a chamber of their own, it could be said that predominantly male writers of late medieval English literature locate female empowerment in an almost entirely fictional space, removing the threat of any real power outside of romance. However, this chapter has shown that the chamber was a culturally recognised female space and had powerful resonances for late medieval women, despite being a shared space for both genders. Throughout this book, I have shown that the chamber was at the centre of wider ideas and practices associated with religion, politics, sex and culture. Locating women's authority in the chamber did not succeed in eradicating women's power but instead made it easier to find: women within the chamber were not invisible, but instead at the heart of all that was important in late medieval English society.

Conclusion

STARS EXPLODE, WORLDS COLLIDE. THERE'S HARDLY ANYWHERE IN THE UNI-
VERSE WHERE HUMANS CAN LIVE WITHOUT BEING FROZEN OR FRIED, AND YET
YOU BELIEVE THAT A ... A *BED* IS A NORMAL THING. IT IS THE MOST AMAZING
TALENT.

Terry Pratchett, The Hogfather[1]

As vocalised by Terry Pratchett's Death, a bed is only 'a normal thing'
because people believe it to be so. In more theoretical terms, space
'lacks independent existence' without its social and cultural context:
the late medieval bed and chamber were nothing and meant nothing
without the system of assumptions, beliefs and semantic relationships
supporting and surrounding them.[2] Above all this book has shown
that beds and chambers mattered. As demonstrated by the 'Arise
Early' precepts, from the time they got up to the time they went to bed,
and all through life from birth to death, beds and chambers were at the
very heart of how late medieval English people understood the world
around them. My research has shown that the chamber was both consciously and subconsciously considered to be a crucial and meaningful
space, while the bed had powerful value as both space and object.

The paucity of research on the bed in late medieval England is, in
part, due to an assumption that there is not enough material evidence

---

[1] T. Pratchett, *The Hogfather* (London, 1996), p. 408.
[2] Cosgrove, 'Landscape and Landschaft', p. 58. See also Lefebvre, *La production de l'espace*, p. 35; Foucault, *Space, Knowledge and Power*, p. 46; Bachelard, *La poétique de l'espace*.

upon which to base the research.[3] This book has shown that evidence of the physicality of late medieval beds is accessible and worthy of further study and has opened up avenues for research. For instance, the understanding that the chamber was the most appropriate space within the house in which to express emotions could be explored further to contribute to the ongoing discourse on the history of emotions.

Within the constraints of its structure, this book has shed new light on pervasive cultural ideas that informed the way in which late medieval English society functioned. It has shown that socially constructed meanings of this crucial space affected how people understood everyday life, from piety to politics, gender roles to sexual encounters, communication to a sense of self. A similar methodological approach could be usefully applied to other spaces or objects: there is still much about the late medieval reception and interaction with domestic spaces that is not yet fully understood.

This book has illustrated the symbiotic relationship between the bed and chamber in the late medieval English imagination. The chamber, which made its *début* in royal households and whose walls and door separated it from the rest of the house, admitted only a select few.[4] Because of this limited access, the bed contained within the chamber was seen to be the most intimate space in the house. In turn, this intimacy gave meaning to the chamber so that it was considered a space for trust and good judgement – so much so that council chambers and administrative bodies known as 'chambers' no longer needed a physical bed in the room – while the bed's association with sexuality caused the chamber to be understood to carry an intrinsic potential for sex. This sexual potential contributed to the understanding of the chamber in relation to women's bodies and was in part responsible for women being both contained and empowered by the chamber. These cycles of meaning, with each association feeding off the last, meant that the cultural meanings of the bed and chamber went beyond the chamber walls, resonating both with those who had access to chambers and those who did not and affecting social practice inside and outside of the home. This large web of repercussions and associations

---

[3] Pan-European ethnologies and histories of beds do no more than touch on the late medieval and never focus on specifically English medieval beds. See, for example, Dibie, *Ethnologie de la chambre à coucher*; Perrot, *Histoire de chambres*; A. R. Ekirch, *At Day's Close: A History of Nighttime* (London, 2005).

[4] Gilchrist, *Gender and Material Culture*, pp. 125–49; Richardson, 'Gender and Space in English Royal Palaces'.

strung between the bed and chamber meant that there was a vast difference between people's understanding of the space and their actual experience.

One exciting result of this research is the identification of a link between the sense of intimacy surrounding the bed and the secular understanding of faith. Scholars addressing domestic piety tend to focus on the domestic chapel, the practice of reading devotional literature within the home and the provision of materials for the parish church.[5] My research has shown that the bed was also an important locus for domestic piety and that domestic space and everyday objects were being considered by late medieval English society in relation to faith and devotional practice. The bed was not only a place to lie down, but also a space in which to converse with God on a personal level. My research has shown that there was a sophisticated understanding of the bed's significance in relation to God, and a desire to perform actions which reflected it. I have also shown that the intimate setting of the chamber affected modes of play and reading. This book has proven that not only did the chamber affect the ways in which people interacted with each other and behaved individually, but individuals were behaving self-consciously, aware of the chamber's role as an intimate space. City officials' rhetorical application of terms such as 'the King's chamber' or 'the Queen's chamber' in relation to their cities showed an implicit understanding of the potential for relationships and intimate communication inherent in the chamber. The same understanding is visible in the decision made by the beneficiaries of William Paston I to move to a specific chamber in order to discuss his will.[6]

As well as a sense of intimacy, this work has shown that there was an understanding of an appropriate time, place and mode of behaviour for all activities. Crucially, my analysis of the bed and chamber's semiotic relationship with legitimate sex has shown that sex in late medieval England was only considered acceptable within the marriage bed. On the one hand, this approach towards sex moves away from our understanding of late medieval sex as something which was fraught with rules and restrictions – as shaped by scholarly works on

---

[5] See, for example, M. C. Erler, *Women, Reading and Piety in Late medieval England* (Cambridge, 2006); K. L. French, *The Good Women of the Parish: Gender and Religion After the Black Death* (Philadelphia, 2008); K. L. French, *The People of the Parish: Community Life in a Late medieval English Diocese* (Philadelphia, 2001); Webb, 'Domestic Space and Devotion in the Middle Ages', pp. 27–48.

[6] Chapter 3 above, pp. 88–92.

medieval sex that have focused on the theological and medical arguments against sexual intercourse for anything other than procreation
within marriage – and towards an idea that sex could be legitimately enjoyed in late medieval England.[7] On the other hand, given that
chambers belonged to the heads of households, and that most bourgeois and aristocratic houses were occupied by many people above the
age of sexual maturity who did not have access to chambers, this book
has raised important issues surrounding the control and containment
of sexuality within the household. As I have shown, the anxiety surrounding sexual intercourse in any location other than the chamber,
articulated across literary and artistic production, highlights a real
tension between what was considered socially acceptable and what
was actually done.

Finally, this book has proven what scholars of medieval domesticity
have long suspected: that within the late medieval English imagination, women belonged in the chamber. My research has shown that
women were deeply semantically related to the chamber and that,
despite the obvious differences between the imagined chambers of the
romance world and physical chambers in late medieval houses, there
was an understanding that women had more power and more freedom within the chamber than within other domestic spaces. Chapter 6
highlighted a dichotomy between expectations and actual experience
but also showed that the cultural meanings constructed and perpetuated by literary and visual sources had real effects in everyday life.

A return to Hautdesert

The bed and chamber is often at the heart of late medieval literature
and, with the many layers of meaning associated with this space in
mind, many literary works need to be revisited. For a start, let us turn
again to *Sir Gawain and the Green Knight*, with which this book began.
The Green Knight proclaims that Gawain's downfall was that he loved
his life too much, but the motivating factor of the narratorial crisis
was not in Gawain's nature, but in the nature of the chamber, whose

---

[7] See, for instance, Brundage, *Law, Sex, and Christian Society*; Payer, 'Confession
and the Study of Sex in the Middle Ages', pp. 3–32; Brundage, 'Sex and Canon
Law', pp. 33–50; McSheffrey, *Marriage, Sex, and Civic Culture*, pp. 135–90;
Phillips and Reay, *Sex Before Sexuality*, pp. 17–39; Mazo Karras, *Unmarriages*;
Mazo Karras, *Sexuality in Medieval Europe*.

inherent complexity meant that several opposing forces were in play simultaneously. Firstly, the bed's deeply ingrained sense of intimacy causes Gawain to be under the impression that the chamber is his own intimate space. His instructions, to lie in bed at his ease and get up for breakfast when he is ready, suggest that the chamber is his own, in which he can do as he pleases. However, as this book has shown, the chamber in a house belongs to the head of the household, and so is under the control of Bertilak, not Gawain. From the outset, the chamber's claim to intimacy is hanging on the socially constructed idea that the chamber is separate from society, despite evidence that it is heavily scrutinised both by members of society who occupy chambers and those who do not. The public nature of the chamber is articulated in the text: the rich fabrics of the bed, with its 'couertour ful clere, cortyned aboute' (l. 1181) with 'comly cortynes' (l. 1732) and 'gere3 ful ryche of hewe' (l. 1470) are mentioned briefly every time Lady Bertilak enters the chamber. This not only reflects the social practice of publicly showing one's bedding in an attempt to display and perform intimacy; it also suggests that the wider world is right outside the chamber door: each time Lady Bertilak opens the door we are flashed a quick glimpse of the room beyond. The chamber episodes are often described as 'temptation scenes' by literary critics.[8] While Lady Bertilak is presented as lascivious, uttering invitations such as '3e ar welcum to my cors' ('you are welcome to my body', l. 1236) and appearing on the third morning with her throat, breast and back uncovered, we know from other romances that Gawain is perfectly capable of resisting or succumbing to sexual temptation at will. The sexual potential in these episodes is not from Lady Bertilak but from the bed, which is semantically inseparable from sexuality. However, sexual temptation is never really seen as a serious threat in this romance, which might explain why the miniature corresponding to the episodes shows a woman in remarkably modest dress.[9] Instead, the lady's forwardness comes from the fact that as a woman – and particularly as a woman in romance – she has an implicit right to be dominant within the chamber. Gawain's lack of command in these episodes is not because of Lady Bertilak's

[8] Mills, 'An Analysis of the Temptation Scenes', pp. 612–30; Dean, 'The Temptation Scenes in "Sir Gawain and the Green Knight"', pp. 1–12; Brewer, *Sources and Analogues*, p. 7; Putter, *Sir Gawain and the Green Knight and French Arthurian Romance*, pp. 100–48; Cooke, 'The Lady's "Blushing" Ring', pp. 1–8; Cox, 'Genesis and Gender in "Sir Gawain and the Green Knight"', p. 378.

[9] London, British Library, Cotton MS Nero A. x, f. 125/129r.

sexual allure but because she has authority over him in the chamber. Furthermore, the bed was understood to be the most appropriate space for intimate conversation, and the space in which secrets could be told and kept in confidence. As such, it comes as a surprise to the audience that the Green Knight explains that he knows 'þe wowyng of my wyf' (l. 72), claiming, 'I wroȝt hit myseluen' (l. 73). This reflects the difference between the idea of the chamber as an impenetrable, intimate space and the practical experience of chambers in late medieval England, which we know, from sources such as depositions relating to marriage disputes, were permeable to outsiders' ears.[10] Like the idea of the chamber versus its reality, the chamber in *Sir Gawain and the Green Knight* is both controlled and monitored by external forces: Bertilak and Morgan le Fay. What happens in the chamber has wider effects beyond Gawain's trajectory. As with the king's Chamber, decisions made in this chamber affect the wider populace: members of Arthur's court wear girdles without understanding why and the young Gawain does not die, and so is usefully available as the lead in other romances and as a vital member of Arthur's court. The secret to the significance of the three chamber episodes in *Sir Gawain and the Green Knight* lies in them not being secret at all: the space which is considered to be the most removed from society is, in fact, the most public and far-reaching of all.

[10] Chapter 3 above, pp. 77–85, chapter 5 above, pp. 143–4.

BIBLIOGRAPHY

Manuscripts

Cambridge, Gonville and Caius College, MS 175
Cambridge, Magdalene College, Pepys MS 1047
Cambridge University Library, MS Gg. 4. 27. 2
Dublin, Trinity College, MS 661
Edinburgh, National Library of Scotland, Advocates MS 19. 2. 1
Kew, The National Archives, C 54/115, m. 13
Kew, The National Archives, PROB 11/1/82
Kew, The National Archives, PROB 11/3/108
Kew, The National Archives, PROB 11/3/174
Kew, The National Archives, PROB 11/10, q. 25
Leeds, Brotherton Library, Archives of the Dean and Chapter of Ripon, MS 432.1
Lincoln, Lincolnshire Archives, REG/20
London, British Library, Additional MS 27445
London, British Library, Additional MS 27879
London, British Library, Additional MS 34888
London, British Library, Additional MS 34889
London, British Library, Additional MS 43491
London, British Library, Additional MS 61823
London, British Library, Egerton MS 1894
London, British Library, Harley MS 2253
London, British Library, Harley MS 3487
London, British Library, Harley MS 4431
London, British Library, Harley Rolls C. 9
London, British Library, Lansdowne MS 762
London, British Library, Maps Crace Port. 11.47
London, British Library, Royal MS 1 E V

London, British Library, Royal MS 1 E IX
London, British Library, Royal MS 2 A XVI
London, British Library, Sloane MS 775
London, Lambeth Palace, MS 306
London, Lincoln's Inn, MS 150
London, Metropolitan Archives, 9171/1 (Courtney Register)
Naples, Biblioteca Nazionale, MS XIII. B. 29, 1
New Haven, Yale University, Beinecke Library, MS 365
New York, Pierpoint Morgan Library, MS 484
Northampton, Northamptonshire Record Office Westmorland (Apethorpe) 4.
   xx. 4
Oxford, Bodleian Library, Ashmole MS 61
Oxford, Bodleian Library, Laud Misc. MS 108
Paris, Archives Nationales, MS Kk. 42
Vienna, Österreichische Nationalbibliotek, Codex Vindobonensis 1857

Art and objects

Bosch, H., *Death and the Miser*. Washington: National Gallery of Art of the
   United States, *c.* 1485–90.
Campi, R., 'Merode Altarpiece'. New York: The Metropolitan Museum of Art,
   c. 1427–32.
Memling, H., 'The Annunciation'. New York: The Metropolitan Museum of
   Art, *c.* 1465–75.
Paradise Bed. Humshaugh: The Langley Collection, *c.* 1486.
Pricke of Conscience window, All Saints North Street, York, *c.* 1420.
Tristan Quilt. London: Victoria and Albert Museum, *c.* 1360–1400.
Wall paintings. Oxford: 3 Cornmarket Street, *c.* 1540–70.

Printed primary sources

André, B., *The Life of Henry VII*, trans. D. Hobbins (New York, 2011).
Austin, T., ed., *Two Fifteenth-century Cookery-books: Harleian MS 279 (ab 1430), &
   Harl. MS 4016 (ab. 1450), with extracts from Ashmole MS 1439, Laud MS 553,
   & Douce MS 55* (Oxford, 1962).
Bacon, R., *Psychology of Visual Perception*, trans. R. B. Burke, in *A Source Book in
   Medieval Science*, ed. E. Grant (Cambridge, 1974), pp. 407–10.
Benson, L. D., ed., *King Arthur's Death: The Middle English Stanzaic Morte Arthur
   and Alliterative Morte Arthure* (Kalamazoo, 1994).
Black, J., ed., 'Account of the Heresy Trial of Margery Baxter', in *The Broadview
   Anthology of British Literature: Concise Edition, Volume A*, ed. J. Black (Peter-
   borough, ON, 2011).
Boedekker, K., ed., *Altenglische Dichtungen des MS Harl, 2253* (Berlin, 1878).

Borde, A. *A Dyetary of Helth*, in *The Fyrst Boke of the Introduction of Knowledge made by Andrew Borde, of Physycke Doctor. A Compendyous Regyment or A Dyetary of Helth made in Mountpyllier, compiled by Andrewe Boorde of Physycke Doctor. Barnes in the Defence of the Berde: A Treatyse Made, Answerynge the Treatyse of Doctor Borde upon Berdes*, ed. F. J. Furnivall (London, 1870).

Brie, F. W. D., ed., *The Brut, or The Chronicles of England. Edited from MS Raw. B171, Bodleian Library*, 2 vols. (London, 1906–8).

Brown Meech, S., ed., *The Book of Margery Kempe* (New York, 1940).

Calendar of the Close Rolls Preserved in the Public Record Office, Edward I–Edward IV, 37 vols. (London, 1892–1963).

Calendar of the Patent Rolls Preserved in the Public Record Office, Edward I– Henry VI, 49 vols. (London, 1891–1907).

Campbell, K., ed., *The Seven Sages of Rome* (Boston, 1907).

Carpenter, C., ed., *Kingsford's Stonor Letters and Papers 1290–1483* (Cambridge, 1996).

Chabot Perryman, J., ed., *The King of Tars: A Critical Edition* (Heidelberg, 1932).

Chaucer, G., *The Riverside Chaucer*, ed. L. D. Benson, 3rd edn (Oxford, 1987).

—, *The Book of the Duchess*, in *The Riverside Chaucer*, ed. Benson.

—, *The Canterbury Tales*, in *The Riverside Chaucer*, ed. Benson.

—, 'The Clerk's Tale', in *The Riverside Chaucer*, ed. Benson.

—, *The Complaint of Mars*, in *The Riverside Chaucer*, ed. Benson.

—, 'The Merchant's Tale' in *The Riverside Chaucer*, ed. Benson.

—, 'The Miller's Tale', in *The Riverside Chaucer*, ed. Benson.

—, 'The Prioress's Tale', in *The Riverside Chaucer*, ed. Benson.

—, 'The Shipman's Tale', in *The Riverside Chaucer*, ed. Benson.

—, 'Sir Thopas', in *The Riverside Chaucer*, ed. Benson.

—, *Troilus and Criseyde*, in *The Riverside Chaucer*, ed. Benson.

—, 'The Wife of Bath's Prologue', in *The Riverside Chaucer*, ed. Benson.

—, 'The Wife of Bath's Tale', in *The Riverside Chaucer*, ed. Benson.

Child, F. J., ed., *The English and Scottish Popular Ballads*, 5 vols., vol. I (New York, 1884–98).

Clark, A., ed., *Lincoln Diocese Documents, 1450–1554* (Michigan, 1914).

A Collection of Ordinances and Regulations for the Government of the Royal Household, Made in Divers Reigns, from King Edward III to King William and Queen Mary (London, 1790).

Conlee, J. ed., *The Prose Merlin* (Kalamazoo, 1998).

Davidson, C., ed., 'Play 14: The Nativity', in *The York Corpus Christi Plays*, ed. C. Davidson (Kalamazoo, 2011).

Davis, N., ed., *Paston Letters and Papers of the Fifteenth Century*, 2 vols. (Oxford, 2004).

de Beaujeu, R., *Le Bel Inconnu*, ed. M. Perret and I. Weill (Paris, 2003).

de France, M., *Poésies de Marie de France, poète Anglo-Normand du VIIIe siècle, ou recueil de lais, fables et autres productions de cette femme célèbre*, ed. B. de Roquefort (Paris, 1820).

de Montaiglon, A. and Raynaud, G., ed., *De la damoisele qui ne pooit oïr parler de foutre*, in *Recueil général et complet des fabliaux des XIIIe et XIVe siècles*, 6 vols., vol. III (Paris, 1878).

de Oliveira, M. A. H., *Daily Life in Portugal in the Middle Ages* (Madison, 1971).

de Pizan, C., *Le trésor de la cité des dames de degré en degré et de tous estatz* (Paris, 1503).

de Rotelande, H., *The Lyfe of Ipomydon*, ed. T. Ikegami (Tokyo, 1932).

de Saliceto, G., *Summa conservationis et curationis* (Venice, 1489).

de Shoreham, W. 'The Poems of William de Shoreham', in *Early English Poetry, Ballads, and Popular Literature of the Middle Ages, Edited From Original Manuscripts and Scarce Publications*, ed. T. Wright (London, 1851).

de Troyes, C., *Lancelot, ou le chevalier de la charrette*, ed. J. C. de Aubailly (Paris, 1991).

—, *Le roman de Perceval, ou le conte de graal*, ed. W. Roach (Geneva, 1959).

de Viriville, A. V., *Extraits des comptes authentiques du règne de Charles VI, 1380–1422* (Paris, 1859).

Dove, M., ed. and trans., *The* Glossa Ordinaria *on the Song of Songs* (Kalamazoo, 2004).

Doyle, A. I., ed., '"Lectulus noster floridus": An Allegory of the Penitent Soul', in *Literature and Religion in the Later Middle Ages: Philological Studies in Honour of Siegfried Wenzel*, ed. R. Newhauser and J. A. Alford (Binghamton, 1995), pp. 179–90.

Fenn, J., *Original Letters Written during the Reign of Henry VI. Edward IV. And Richard III. By Various Persons of Rank and Consequence; Containing Many Curious Anecdotes, Relative to that Turbulent and Bloody, But Hitherto Dark, Period of our History; Elucidating, not only Public Matters of State, but Likewise the Private Manners of the Age: Digested in Chronological Order; with Notes, Historical and Explanatory; and Authenticated by Engravings of Autographs, Facsimiles, Paper Marks and Seals*, 4 vols., vol. IV (London, 1789).

Figueredo, C., ed., 'Richard Coeur de Lion from the London Thornton Manuscript' (University of York, unpublished Ph.D. thesis).

Fisher, J. H. ed., *An Anthology of Chancery English* (Knoxville, 1984).

Flowers Braswell, M., ed., *Ywain and Gawain*, in *Sir Perceval of Galles and Ywain and Gawain*, ed. M. Flowers Braswell (Kalamazoo, 1995).

Foster, E. E., ed., *Amis and Amiloun*, in *Amis and Amiloun, Robert of Cisyle, and Sir Amadace*, ed. E. E. Foster, 2nd edn (Kalamazoo, 2007).

Fowler, C., ed., *Extracts from the Account Rolls of the Abbey of Durham, from the Original MSS*, 6 vols., vol. III (Durham, 1901).

Fremantle, W. H., Lewis, G. and Martley, W. G., trans., *The Principal Works of St Jerome* (Edinburgh, 1892).

Froissart, J., *The Antient Chronicles of Jean Froissart, of England, France, Spain, Portugal, Scotland, Brittany and Flanders, and the Adjoining Countries. Translated from the Original French at the Command of King Henry the Eighth*, ed. Bourchier, J. and Lord Berners, 3 vols., vol. III (London, 1815).

—, *Œuvres de Froissart*, ed. de K. Lettenhove, 25 vols. (Brussels, 1870–7), vols. IX and XV.

Furnivall, F. J., ed., *Fifty Earliest English Wills in the Court of Probate, London: A. D. 1387–1439; with a Priest's of 1454* (1882).

—, ed., *The Life of St Alexius*, in *Adam Davy's 5 Dreams about Edward II. The Life of St Alexius. Solomon's Book of Wisdom. St Jeremie's 15 Tokens Before Doomsday. The Lamentacion of Souls*, ed. F. J. Furnivall (London, 1878).

Gibbs, H. H., ed., *The Romance of the Cheuelere Assigne* (London, 1868).

Gower, J., *Confessio Amantis*, ed. R. A. Peck (Kalamazoo, 2003).

Grammaticus, G., *Promptorium parvulorum sive clericorum, lexicon Anglo-Latinum princeps*, ed. A. Way, 3 vols., vol. II (London, 1853).

Gregory the Great., *Gregory the Great on the Song of Songs*, trans. M. DelCogliano (Collegeville, 2012).

Hahn, T., ed., *Sir Gawain: Eleven Romances and Tales*, ed. T. Hahn (Kalamazoo, 1995).

—, ed., *The Avowyng of Arthur*, in *Sir Gawain: Eleven Romances and Tales*, ed. Hahn.

—, ed., *King Arthur and King Cornwall*, in *Sir Gawain: Eleven Romances and Tales*, ed. Hahn.

—, ed., *Sir Gawain and the Carle of Carlisle*, in *Sir Gawain: Eleven Romances and Tales*, ed. Hahn.

—, ed., *The Wedding of Sir Gawain and Dame Ragnelle* in *Sir Gawain: Eleven Romances and Tales*, ed. Hahn.

Hales, J. W. and Furnivall, F. J., ed., *Eger and Grime: An Early English Romance. Edited from Bishop Percy's Folio MS, About 1650 AD* (London, 1867).

Hall, J., ed., *King Horn; A Middle-English Romance* (Oxford, 1901).

Harvey, E. R., ed., *The Court of Sapience* (Toronto, 1984).

Hasenfratz, R., ed., *Ancrene Wisse* (Kalamazoo, 2000).

Hayward, M., ed., *The Great Wardrobe Accounts of Henry VII and Henry VIII* (Woodbridge, 2012).

Heffernan, C. F., ed., *Le Bone Florence of Rome* (New York, 1976).

Henderson, W. G., ed., *Manuale et processionale ad usum insignis ecclesiae Eboracensis* (London, 1875).

Herzman, R. B., Drake, G. and Salisbury, E., ed., *Athelston*, in *Four Romances of England*, ed. R. B. Herzman, G. Drake and E. Salisbury (Kalamazoo, 1999).

—, ed. *Bevis of Hampton*, in *Four Romances of England*, ed. R. B. Herzman, G. Drake and E. Salisbury (Kalamazoo, 1999).

Hoccleve, T., *The Regiment of Princes*, in *Hoccleve's Works: The Regiment of Princes and Fourteen Minor Poems*, ed. F. J. Furnivall (London, 1897).

—, *The Regiment of Princes*, ed. C. R. Blyth (Kalamazoo, 1999).

Hudson, H., ed., *Four Middle English Romances: Sir Isumbras, Octavian, Sir Eglamour of Artois, Sir Tryamour*, 2nd edn (Kalamazoo, 2006).

Hugh of St Victor, *Hugh of Saint Victor: Selected Writings*, ed. and trans. A. Squire (London, 1962).

Johnston, R. C. and Owen, D. D. R., ed., *Le Chevalier à l'épée*, in *Two Old French Gauvain Romances*, ed. R. C. Johnston and D. D. R. Owen (New York, 1973).

Kingsford, C. L., ed., *The Stonor Letters and Papers, 1290–1483; Ed. for the Royal Historical Society, from the Original Documents in the Public Record Office*, 2 vols., vol. II (London, 1919).

Klausner, D. N., ed., *The Castle of Perseverance* (Kalamazoo, 2010).

Kooper, E., ed., *Sir Degrevant*, in *Sentimental and Humorous Romances*, ed. E. Kooper (Kalamazoo, 2006).

Langland, W., *The Vision of William Concerning Piers Plowman*, B-text, ed. A. V. C. Schmidt (London, 1995).

Larkin, P., *The Whitsun Weddings* (London, 1964).

Laskaya, A. and Salisbury, E. ed., *Erle of Tolous*, in *The Middle English Breton Lays*, ed. A. Laskaya and E. Salisbury (Kalamazoo, 1995).

—, ed., *Sir Degaré*, in *The Middle English Breton Lays*, ed. Laskaya and Salisbury.

—, ed., *Sir Gowther*, in *The Middle English Breton Lays*, ed. Laskaya and Salisbury.

—, ed., *Sir Launfal*, in *The Middle English Breton Lays*, ed. Laskaya and Salisbury.

le Fevre, R. and Caxton, W., *The History of Jason*, ed. J. Munro (Montana, 2004).

Littlehales, H., ed., *The Medieval Records of a London City Church (St Mary at Hill) A. D. 1420–1559* (London, 1904–5).

Love, N., *The Mirrour of the Blessed Lyf of Jesu Christ*, ed. L. F. Powell (Oxford, 1908).

—, *Nicholas Love's Mirror of the Blessed Life of Jesus Christ: A Critical Edition Based on Cambridge University Library Additional MSS 5478 and 6686*, ed. M. G. Sargent (New York, 1992).

Luders, A. and Raithby, J., ed., *The Statutes of the Realm*, vol. IV: *1377–1504* (London, 1812).

Lupack, A., ed., *Three Middle English Charlemagne Romances* (Kalamazoo, 1990).

Lydgate, J., *Item 31, The Dietary*, in *Codex Ashmole 61: A Compilation of Popular Middle English Verse*, ed. G. Shuffelton (Kalamazoo, 2008).

—, *The Minor Poems of John Lydgate*, ed. H. N. MacCracken, 2 vols., vol. I (London, 1911).

—, *Prohemy of a Mariage Betwixt an Olde Man and a Yonge Wife, and the Counsail*, in *The Trials and Joys of Marriage*, ed. M. Ellzey and D. Moffatt, rev. E. Salisbury (Kalamazoo, 2002).

Macleod Banks, M., ed., *Alphabet of Tales: An English 15th Century Translation of the Alphabetum Narrationum of Etienne de Besançon, from Additional MS Add. 25719 of the British Museum* (London, 1904).

Maidstone, R., *Alliterative Poem on the Deposition of King Richard II; Ricardi May-diston De Concordia Inter Ric. II et Civitatem London*, ed. T. Wright (London, 1838).

Malory, T., *Le Morte Darthur, or The Hoole Book of Kyng Arthur and of his Noble Knyghtes of the Round Table*, ed. S. H. A. Shepherd (New York, 2004).

—, *The Works of Sir Thomas Malory*, ed. E. Vinaver, rev. P. J. C. Field (Oxford, 1990).

Mannyng, R., *Robert of Brunne's 'Handlyng Synne'*, ed. F. J. Furnivall (London, 1901–3).

Maskell, W., ed., *The Ancient Liturgy of the Church of England According to the Uses of Sarum Bangor York & Hereford and the Modern Roman Liturgy Arranged in Parallel Columns*, 2nd edn (London, 1846).

Millett, B. and Wogan-Browne, J., ed., *Hali Meiðhad*, in *Medieval English Prose for Women: Selections from the Katherine Group and* Ancrene Wisse, ed. B. Millett and J. Wogan-Browne (Oxford, 1990), pp. 3–43.

Mirk, J., *Mirk's Festial: A Collection of Homilies by Johannes Mirkus*, ed. T. Erbe (London, 1905).

Morris, R., ed., *Cursor Mundi (The Cursur o the World): A Northumbrian Poem of the XIVth Century in Four Versions* (London, 1893).

Myers, A. R., ed., *English Historical Documents* (Oxford, 1996).

Napier, A. S., ed., *Iacob and Iosep: A Middle English Poem of the Thirteenth Century* (Oxford, 1916).

Nelson, W., ed., *A Fifteenth Century School Book, From a Manuscript in the British Museum (MS. Arundel 249)* (Oxford, 1956).

Percy, T., *Reliques of Ancient English Poetry: Consisting of Old Heroic Ballads, Songs, and Other Pieces of Our Earlier Poets* (London, 1857).

Pratchett, T., *The Hogfather* (London, 1996).

Raine, J., ed., *A Volume of English Miscellanies Illustrating the History and Language of the Northern Counties of England* (London, 1890).

Raine, J., and Clay, J., ed., *Testamenta Eboracensia: A Selection of Wills from the Registry at York* (London, 1869).

Richardson, O., ed., *The Right Plesaunt and Goodly Historie of the Foure Sonnes of Aymon. Englisht from the French by William Caxton, and Printed by Him about 1489* (London, 1884–5).

Rolle, R., *English Prose Works of Richard Rolle: A Selection*, ed. C. Horstmann (London, 1896).

—, *The Psalter, or Psalms of David and Certain Canticles With a Translation and Exposition in English by Richard Rolle of Hampole*, ed. H. Ramsden Bramley (Oxford, 1884).

—, *Richard Rolle: The English Works*, ed. R. Allen (Mahwah, 1988).

Russell, J., *The Boke of Nurture*, in *The Babees Book, Aristotle's A B C, Urbanitatis, Stans Puer ad Mensam, The Lvtille Childrenes Lvtil Boke, The Bokes of Nurture of Hugh Rhodes and John Russell, Wynkyn de Worde's Boke of Keruynge, The Booke of Demeanor, The Boke of Curtasye, Seager's Schoole of Vertue, &c. &c. with Some French and Latin Poems on Like Subjects, and Some Forewords on Education in Early England*, ed. F. J. Furnivall (London, 1868), pp. 117–99.

Salisbury, E., ed., *Dame Sirith*, in *The Trials and Joys of Marriage*, ed. E. Salisbury (Kalamazoo, 2002).

Salisbury, E. and J. Weldon, ed. *Lybeaus Dysconus (Lambeth Palace, MS 306)* (Kalamazoo, 2013).

Sands, D. B., ed., *Middle English Verse Romances*, ed. D. B. Sands (Exeter, 1986).

—, ed., *Floris and Blancheflour*, in *Middle English Verse Romances*, ed. Sands.

—, ed., *Havelok the Dane*, in *Middle English Verse Romances*, ed. Sands.

—, ed., *King Horn*, in *Middle English Verse Romances*, ed. Sands.

—, ed., *Lai le Freine*, in *Middle English Verse Romances*, ed. Sands.

—, ed., *Sir Launfal*, in *Middle English Verse Romances*, ed. Sands.

—, ed., *Sir Orfeo* in *Middle English Verse Romances*, ed. Sands.

—, ed., *The Squire of Low Degree* in *Middle English Verse Romances*, ed. Sands.

Schleich, G., ed., *Sire Degarre* (Heidelberg, 1929).

Sharpe, R. R., ed., *Calendar of Letter-books of the City of London: E: 1314–1337* (London, 1903).

—, ed., *Calendar of Letter-Books Preserved among the Archives of the Corporation of the City of London at the Guildhall*, 11 vols., vol. XI (London, 1912).

—, ed. and trans., *Calendar of Wills Proved and Enrolled in the Court of Husting, London, A.D. 1258–A.D. 1688*: vol. I: *1258–1358* (London, 1889).

Shuffelton, G., ed., *Item 3: How the Wise Man Taught His Son*, in *Codex Ashmole 61: A Compilation of Popular Middle English Verse*, ed. G. Shuffelton (Kalamazoo, 2008).

—, ed., *Item 5, Sir Isumbras*, in *Codex Ashmole 61: A Compilation of Popular Middle English Verse*, ed. G. Shuffelton (Kalamazoo, 2008).

—, ed., *Item 20, Lybeaus Desconus*, in *Codex Ashmole 61: A Compilation of Popular Middle English Verse*, ed. G. Shuffelton (Kalamazoo, 2008).

Smith, T., ed., *English Guilds: The Original Ordinances of more than One Hundred Early English Guilds: Together with The Olde Usages of the Cite of Wynchestre; the Ordinances of Worcester; the Office of the Mayor of Bristol; and the Costomary of the Manor of Tattenhal-Regis* (London, 1870).

Staley, L., ed., *The Book of Margery Kempe* (Kalamazoo, 1996).

Staley, V., ed., *The Library of Liturgiology and Ecclesiology for English Readers* (London, 1911) 9 vols., vol. IX: *The Sarum Missal in English*.

The Statutes: Revised Edition, vol. I: *Henry III–James II. A.D. 1235/6–1685* (London, 1870).

Stell, P. M., ed. and trans., *Probate Inventories of the York Diocese, 1350–1500* (York, 2006).

Stevenson, W. H., ed., *Records of the Boroughs of Nottingham, Being a Series of Extracts from the Archives of the Corporation of Nottingham*, vol. I: *King Henry II. to King Richard II. 1155–1399* (London, 1882).

Stow, J., *Annals of England to 1603* (London, 1603).

Sugano, D., ed., *Play 11, Parliament of Heaven; Salutation and Conception* in *The N-Town Plays*, ed. D. Sugano (Kalamazoo, 2007).

Thomas, A. H., ed., *Calendar of the Plea and Memoranda Rolls of the City of London: III: 1381–1412* (London, 1932).

Thompson, M., ed., *Chronicon Angliae, ab Anno Domini 1328 Usque ad Annum 1388. Auctore Monacho Quodam Sancti Albani* (London, 1874).

Tolkien, J. R. R., and Gordon, E. V., ed., *Sir Gawain and the Green Knight* (Oxford, 1925).

Tomlins, T. E., ed., *The Statutes of the Realm, Printed by Command of his Majesty King George the Third in Pursuance of an Address of the House of Commons of Great Britain, from Original Records and Authentic Manuscripts* (London, 1819).

Toomey, J. P., ed., 'A Household Account of Edward, Duke of York at Hanley Castle, 1409–10', in *Noble Household Management and Spiritual Discipline in Fifteenth-Century Worcestershire*, ed. R. N. Swanson and D. Guyatt (Worcester, 2011).

Treharne, E., ed., *The Owl and the Nightingale*, in *Old and Middle English c. 890– c. 1400: An Anthology*, ed. E. Treharne, 2nd edn (London, 2004).

Tymms, S., ed., *Wills and Inventories from the Registers of the Commissary of Bury St Edmund's and the Archdeacon of Sudbury* (London, 1850).

von Eschenbach, W., *Parzival und Titurel*, ed. K. Batsch (Leipzig, 1875).

Walcott, M. E. C., ed., 'Inventories of (I) St Mary's Hospital of Maison Dieu, Dover; (II.) The Benedictine Priory of St Martin New-work, Dover, For Monks; (III) The Benedictine Priory of SS. Mary and Sexburga, in the Island of Shepey, For Nuns', *Archaeologia Cantiana* 7 (1868), 272–306.

Walsingham, T. *Historia Anglicana*, ed. H. T. Riley (London, 1863–4).

Weaver, F. W., ed., *Somerset Medieval Wills, 1501–1530. With Some Somerset Wills Preserved at Lambeth* (London, 1903).

Weber, H. W., ed., *The Seven Sages*, in *Metrical Romances of the Thirteenth, Fourteenth, and Fifteenth Centuries: Published from Ancient Manuscripts*, ed. H. W. Weber, 3 vols., vol. III (Edinburgh, 1810).

Whitehead, C., Renevey, D., and Mouron, A., ed., *The Doctrine of the Hert: A Critical Edition with Introduction and Commentary* (Exeter, 2010).

Wiggins, A., ed., *Stanzaic Guy of Warwick* (Kalamazoo, 2004).

William of Saint Thierry, *Exposition on the Song of Songs*, trans. Columba Hart (Kalamazoo, 1970).

Withington, L., ed., *Holinshed's Chronicles of England, Scotland and Ireland* (London, 1876).

Wright, T. H., ed., *Book of the Knight of Tour-Landry: Compiled for the Instruction of his Daughters: Translated from the Original French into English in the Reign of Henry VI* (London, 1906).

Wright, W. A., ed., *The Metrical Chronicle of Robert of Gloucester* (London, 1887).

Wycliffe, J., 'Þis is Þe Gospel Þat is Rad on Christemasse Evyn', in *Select English Works of John Wycliff*, vol. I: *Sermons on the Gospels for Sundays and Festivals*, ed. T. Arnold (Oxford, 1869).

Zupitza, J., ed., *The Romance of Guy of Warwick. The First or 14th-Century Version* (London, 1883).

Secondary sources

Adams, J., *Power Play: The Literature and Politics of Chess in the Late Middle Ages* (Philadelphia, 2006).

Al-Adawi, S., Burjorjee, R., and Al-Issa, I., 'Mu-Ghayeb: A Culture-Specific Response to Bereavement in Oman', *International Journal of Social Psychiatry* 43.2 (1997), 144–51.

Ames, K., *Death in the Dining Room and Other Tales of Victorian Culture* (Philadelphia, 1992).

Anglo, S., 'The *British History* in Early Tudor Propaganda, With an Appendix of Manuscript Pedigrees of the Kings of England, Henry VI to Henry VIII', *Bulletin of the John Rylands Library Manchester* 44.1 (1961), 17–48.

Appadurai, A., ed., *The Social Life of Things: Commodities in Cultural Perspective* (Cambridge, 1986).

Archer, R. E., '"How ladies … who live on their manors ought to manage their households and estates": Women as Landholders and Administrators in the Later Middle Ages', in *Women in Medieval English Society*, ed. P. J. P. Goldberg (Stroud, 1997), pp. 149–81.

Armstrong, C. A. J., 'The Piety of Cicely, Duchess of York: A Study in Late-Medieval Culture', in *England, France, and Burgundy in the Fifteenth Century*, ed. C. A. J. Armstrong (London, 1983), pp. 135–56.

Atkinson, C. W., *Mystic and Pilgrim: The Book and the World of Margery Kempe* (Ithaca, 1983).

Bachelard, G., *La poétique de l'espace* (Paris, 1958).

—, *The Poetics of Space: The Classic Look at How We Experience Intimate Places*, trans. M. Jolas (New York, 1964).

Bardsley, S., 'Reply', *Past and Present* 173.1 (2001), 199–202.

—, 'Women's Work Reconsidered: Gender and Wage Differentiation in Late-Medieval England', *Past and Present* 165 (1999), 3–29.

Beattie, C., Maslakovic, A. and Rees Jones, S., ed., *The Medieval Household in Christian Europe, c. 850–c. 1550* (Turnhout, 2003).

Beaudry, M. C. and Hicks, D., ed. *The Oxford Handbook of Material Culture Studies* (Oxford, 2010).

Beckwith, S. 'Problems of Authority in Late-medieval English Mysticism: Language, Agency, and Authority in *The Book of Margery Kempe*', *Exemplaria* 4 (1992), 172–99.

—, *Signifying God: Social Relation and Symbolic Act in the York Corpus Christi Plays* (Chicago, 2001).

Bedos-Rezak, B. M., 'In Search of a Semiotic Paradigm: The Matter of Sealing in Medieval Thought and Praxis (1050–1400)', in *Good Impressions: Image and Authority in Medieval Seals*, ed. N. Adams, J. Cherry and J. Robinson (London, 2008), pp. 1–7.

Bennett, J. M., *Ale, Beer, and Brewsters in England: Women's Work in a Changing World, 1300–1600* (Oxford, 1996).

Berenson, K., 'Tales from the "Coilte"', *V&A Online Journal* 2 (Autumn 2009).

Binski, P., *The Painted Chamber at Westminster* (London, 1986).

Blair, W. J., 'Hall and Chamber: English Domestic Planning 1000–1250', in *Manorial Domestic Planning in England and France*, ed. G. Merion-Jones and M. Jones. Society of Antiquaries of London Occasional Papers 15 (London, 1993), pp. 1–21.

Boffey, J. and Edwards, A. S. G., ed., *A New Index of Middle English Verse* (London, 2005).

Brewer, E., *Sir Gawain and the Green Knight: Sources and Analogues*, 2nd edn (Cambridge, 1992).

Brundage, J. A., *Law, Sex, and Christian Society in Medieval Europe* (Chicago, 1987).

—, 'Sex and Canon Law', in *Handbook of Medieval Sexuality*, ed. V. L. Bullough, V. L. and J. A. Brundage (New York, 2000), pp. 33–50.

—, *Sex, Law and Marriage in the Middle Ages* (Aldershot, 1993).

Burger, G., 'In the Merchant's Bedchamber', in *Thresholds of Medieval Visual Culture: Liminal Spaces*, ed. E. Gertsman and J. Stevenson (Woodbridge, 2012), pp. 239–59.

Burke, J., *A Genealogical and Heraldic History of the Commoners of Great Britain and Ireland, Enjoying Territorial Possessions or High Official Rank; But Uninvested with Heritable Honours*, 5 vols., vol. IV (London, 1838).

Butler, S. M., *Divorce in Medieval England: From One to Two Persons in Law* (New York, 2013).

—, *The Language of Abuse: Marital Violence in Later Medieval England* (Leiden, 2007).

—, 'Lies, Damned Lies, and the Life of Saint Lucy: Three Cases of Judicial Separation from the Late-medieval Court of York', in *Trompe(-)l'œil: Imitation and Falsification*, ed. P. Romanski and A. Sy-Wonyu (Rouen, 2002).

Caille, P. R., 'The Problem of Labour and the Parliament of 1495', in *The Fifteenth Century V: Of Mice and Men: Image, Belief and Regulation in Late-medieval England*, ed. L. Clark (Woodbridge, 2005), pp. 143–56.

Carruthers, M., *The Book of Memory: A Study of Memory in Medieval Culture* (Cambridge, 1990).

Cave, C., *Roof Bosses in Medieval Churches: An Aspect of Gothic Sculpture* (Cambridge, 1948).

Chrimes, S. B., *An Introduction to the Administrative History of Medieval England* (Oxford, 1959).

Cohen, M. and Madeline, F., ed., *Space in the Medieval West: Places, Territories, and Imagined Geographies* (Farnham, 2014).

Coleman, J., *Public Reading and the Reading Public in Late-Medieval England and France* (Cambridge, 1996).

Compton Reeves, A., 'Bishop John Booth of Exeter', in *Traditions and Transformations in Late-Medieval England*, ed. D. Biggs, S. D. Michalove and A. Compton Reeves (Leiden, 2002), pp. 125–44.

Cooke, J., 'The Lady's "Blushing" Ring in *Sir Gawain and the Green Knight*', *The Review of English Studies* n.s. 49 (1998), 1–8.

Copeland, R., 'Why Women Can't Read: Medieval Hermeneutics, Statutory Law, and the Lollard Heresy Trials', in *Representing Women: Law, Literature, and Feminism*, ed. S. S. Heinzelman and Z. Batshaw Wiseman (Durham, NC, 1994), pp. 273–86.

Cosgrove, D., 'Landscape and Landschaft', *GHI Bulletin* 35 (2004), 57–65.

Cox, C. S., 'Genesis and Gender in "Sir Gawain and the Green Knight"', *The Chaucer Review* 35.4 (2001), 378–90.

Creelman, V., 'Margaret Paston's Use of *Captenesse*', *Notes & Queries* 55.3 (2008), 275–7.

Croom Brown, M., *Mary Tudor, Queen of France* (London, 1911).

Crowley, John E., *The Invention of Comfort: Sensibilities and Design in Early Modern Britain and Early America* (Baltimore, 2003).

Cussans, J. E., *A History of Hertfordshire II: Hitchin, Hertford, and Broadwater* (London, 1870–1).

Daniell, C., *Death and Burial in Medieval England 1066–1550* (London, 1997).

Daston, L., *Things That Talk: Object Lessons from Art and Science* (New York, 2008).

Davis, I., 'Calling: Langland, Gower, and Chaucer on Saint Paul', *Studies in the Age of Chaucer* 34 (2012), 53–97.

de Certeau, M., *The Practice of Everyday Life*, trans. S. Rendall (Berkeley, 1984).

—, 'Practices of Space', in *On Signs*, ed. M. Blonsky (Baltimore, 1985).

de Saussure, F., *Course de Linguistique Générale*, ed. C. Bally, A. Sechehaye and A. Riedlinger (Lausanne, 1916).

Dean, C., 'The Temptation Scenes in "Sir Gawain and the Green Knight"', *Leeds Studies in English* n.s. 5 (1971), 1–12.

Delany, S., *The Naked Text: Chaucer's Legend of Good Women* (Berkeley, 1994).

Diamond, A., '*Sir Degrevant*: What Lovers Want', in *Pulp Fictions of Medieval England: Essays in Popular Romance*, ed. N. McDonald (Manchester, 2004), pp. 82–101.

Dibie, P., *Ethnologie de la chambre à coucher* (Paris, 2000).

Dinn, R., 'Death and Rebirth in Late-Medieval Bury St Edmunds', in *Death in Towns: Urban Responses to the Dying and the Dead, 100–1600*, ed. S. Bassett (Leicester, 1995), pp. 151–69.

Dobson, R. B., 'The Crown, the Charter, and the City, 1396–1467', in *The Government of Medieval York: Essays in Commemoration of the 1396 Royal Charter*, ed. S. Rees-Jones (York, 1997), pp. 34–55.

—, *The Peasants' Revolt of 1381* (London, 1983).

Duby, G., *The Age of Cathedrals: Art and Society, 980–1420*, trans. E. Levieux and B. Thompson (Chicago, 1981).

Duby, G., and Ariès, P., ed., *A History of Private Life*, 2 vols., vol. II (Cambridge, 1987–91).

Duffy, E., *Stripping of the Altars: Traditional Religion in England 1400–1580*, 2nd edn (New Haven, 2005).

Dyer, C., *An Age of Transition? Economy and Society in England in the Later Middle Ages* (Oxford, 2005).

Eames, P., 'Furniture in England, France and the Netherlands from the Twelfth to the Fifteenth Century', *Furniture History* 13 (1977), 1–303.

Eden, M. and Carrington, R., *The Philosophy of the Bed* (London, 1961).

Egan, G., 'Material Culture of Care of the Sick: Some Excavated Evidence from English Medieval Hospitals and Other Sites', in *The Medieval Hospital and Medical Practice*, ed. B. S. Bowers (Aldershot, 2007), pp. 65–76.

Eisenbruch, M., 'Cross Cultural Aspects of Bereavement. 11: Ethnic and Cultural Variations in the Development of Bereavement Practices', *Culture, Medicine and Psychiatry* 8 (1984), 315–47.

Ekirch, A. R., *At Day's Close: A History of Nighttime* (London, 2005).

Elliot, D., *Fallen Bodies: Pollution, Sexuality, and Demonology in the Middle Ages* (Philadelphia, 1999).

—, 'Sex in Holy Places: An Exploration of a Medieval Anxiety', *Journal of Women's History* 6.3 (1994), 6–34.

Ellis, D. S., 'Domesticating the Spanish Inquisition', in *Violence Against Women in Medieval Texts*, ed. A. Roberts (Gainesville, 1998), pp. 195–209.

Emery, A., *Discovering Medieval Houses* (Princes Risborough, 2007).

—, *Greater Medieval Houses of England and Wales, 1300–1500*, vol. III: *Southern England* (Cambridge, 2006).

Eming, J., 'The Discussion of Emotions in the Study of Medieval Literature', *Journal of Literary Theory* (2007), 251–73.

Emmerson, R. K. and Lewis, S., 'Census and Bibliography of Manuscripts Containing Apocalypse Illustrations, ca. 800–1500', *Traditio* 41 (1985), 370–409.

Erler, M. C., *Women, Reading and Piety in Late-Medieval England* (Cambridge, 2006).

Fagan, B., *The Little Ice Age: How Climate Made History 1300–1850* (New York, 2000).

Fairclough, G., 'Meaningful Constructions: Spatial and Functional Analysis of Medieval Buildings', *Antiquity* 66 (1992), 348–66.

Farmer, S., and Pasternack, C. B., ed., *Gender and Difference in the Middle Ages* (Minneapolis, 2003).

Faulkner, P. A., 'Castle Planning in the Fourteenth Century', *The Archaeological Journal* 127 (1963), 150–83.

—, 'Domestic Planning from the 12th to 14th Centuries', *The Archaeological Journal*, 115 (1958), 150–83.

Fenwick, C. C., ed., *The Poll Taxes of 1377, 1379 and 1381: Part 1* (London, 1998).

Fissell, M. E., 'Introduction: Women, Health, and Healing in Early Modern Europe', *Bulletin of the History of Medicine* 82.1 (2008), 1–17.

Florschuetz, A., 'Women's Secrets: Childbirth, Pollution, and Purification in Northern Octavian', *Studies in the Age of Chaucer* 30 (2008), 235–68.

Foucault, M., *Space, Knowledge and Power*, in *The Foucault Reader*, ed. P. Rabinow (New York, 1984), pp. 239–56.

Francis, C., 'Reading Malory's Bloody Bedrooms', in *Arthurian Literature 28: Blood, Sex, Malory: Essays on the* Morte Darthur, ed. D. Clark and K. McClune (Cambridge, 2011), pp. 1–20.

Frank, D., 'Karaite Commentaries on the Song of Songs from Tenth-Century Jerusalem', in *With Reverence for the Word: Medieval Scriptural Exegesis in Judaism, Christianity, and Islam*, ed. J. Dammen McAuliffe, B. D. Walfish and J. W. Goering (Oxford, 2010), pp. 51–69.

French, K. L., *The Good Women of the Parish: Gender and Religion After the Black Death* (Philadelphia, 2008).

—, *The People of the Parish: Community Life in a Late-Medieval English Diocese* (Philadelphia, 2001).

Ganim, J., 'Landscape and Late-medieval Literature: A Critical Geography', in *Place, Space and Landscape in Medieval Narrative*, ed. L. Howes (Knoxville, 2007), pp. xv–xxix.

Gardiner, M., 'Buttery and Pantry and their Antecedents: Idea and Architecture in the English Medieval House', in *Medieval Domesticity: Home, Housing and Household in Medieval England*, ed. M. Kowaleski and P. J. P. Goldberg (Cambridge, 2008), pp. 37–65.

Gibbons, R. C., 'The Queen as "Social Mannequin". Consumerism and Expenditure at the Court of Isabeau of Bavaria, 1393–1422', *Journal of Medieval History* 26.4 (2000), 371–95.

Gilchrist, R., *Gender and Archaeology: Contesting the Past* (London, 1999).

—, *Gender and Material Culture: The Archaeology of Religious Women* (London, 1994).

—, 'Medieval Bodies in the Material World: Gender, Stigma and the Body', in *Framing Medieval Bodies*, ed. S. Kay and M. Rubin (Manchester, 1994), pp. 43–61.

—, *Medieval Life: Archaeology and the Life Course* (Woodbridge, 2012).

Giles, K., *An Archaeology of Social Identity: Guildhalls in York, c. 1350–1630* (Oxford, 2000).

Glenn, C., 'Author, Audience, and Autobiography: Rhetorical Technique in the Book of Margery Kempe', *College English* 54.5 (1992), 540–53.

Goldberg, P. J. P., *Communal Discord, Child Abduction, and Rape in the Later Middle Ages* (New York, 2007).

—, 'The Fashioning of Bourgeois Domesticity in the Later Medieval England: A Material Culture Perspective', in *Medieval Domesticity: Home, Housing and Household in Medieval England*, ed. M. Kowaleski and P. J. P. Goldberg (Cambridge, 2008), pp. 124–44.

—, 'Household and the Organisation of Labour in Late-medieval Towns: Some English Evidence', in *The Household in Late-medieval Cities: Italy and Northwestern Europe Compared. Proceedings of the International Conference, Ghent, 21st–22nd January 2000* (Leuven-Apeldoorn, 2001).

—, 'Life and Death: The Ages of Man', in *A Social History of England, 1200–1500*, ed. R. Horrox and W. M. Ormrod (Cambridge, 2006), pp. 413–34.

—, *Medieval England: A Social History 1250–1550* (London, 2004).

—, 'The Public and the Private: Women in the Pre-Plague Economy', in *Thirteenth Century England III*, ed. P. R. Coss and S. D. Loyd (Woodbridge, 1991), pp. 75–89.

—, 'Space and Gender in the Later Medieval House', *Viator* 42.2 (2011), 205–32.

—, *Women in England, c. 1275–1525* (Manchester, 1995).

—, *Women, Work, and Life Cycle in a Medieval Economy: Women in York and Yorkshire c. 1300–1520* (Oxford, 1990).

Goldberg, P. J. P. and Kowaleski, M., 'Introduction. Medieval Domesticity: Home, Housing and Household', in *Medieval Domesticity: Home, Housing and Household in Medieval England*, ed. M. Kowaleski and P. J. P. Goldberg (Cambridge, 2008), pp. 1–13.

Green, H., 'Cultural History and the Material(s) Turn', *Cultural History* 1 (2012), 61–82.

Grenville, J., *Medieval Housing* (Leicester, 1997).

—, 'Urban and Rural Houses and Households in the Late Middle Ages: A Case Study from Yorkshire', in *Medieval Domesticity: Home, Housing and Household in Medieval England*, ed. M. Kowaleski and P. J. P. Goldberg (Cambridge, 2008), pp. 92–123.

Gunn, S. J., 'The Accession of Henry VIII', *Historical Research* 64.155 (1991), 278–88.

Hamburger, J., *Nuns as Artists: The Visual Culture of a Medieval Convent* (Berkeley, 1997).

Hanawalt, B. A., 'Medieval English Women in Rural and Urban Space', *Dumbarton Oaks Papers* 52 (1998), 19–26.

—, *The Ties That Bound: Peasant Families in Medieval England* (Oxford, 1986).

—, *The Wealth of Wives: Women, Law and Economy in Late-Medieval London* (Oxford, 2007).

Hanawalt, B. A. and Kobialka, M., ed., *Medieval Practices of Space* (Minneapolis, 2000).

Hanna, R., *The English Manuscripts of Richard Rolle: A Descriptive Catalogue* (Exeter, 2010).

Harvey, P. D. A. and MacGuiness, A., *A Guide to British Medieval Seals* (London, 1995).

Hatcher, J., 'Debate: Women's Work Reconsidered: Gender and Wage Differentiation in Late-Medieval England', *Past and Present* 173.1 (2001), 191–8.

Heard, K., 'Such Stuff as Dreams Are Made On: Textiles and the Medieval Chantry', in *The Medieval Chantry in England*, ed. J. M. Luxford and J. McNeill, *Journal of the British Archaeological Association* 164 (2011), 163–5.

Henrick, T. S., 'Sport and Social Hierarchy in Medieval England', *Journal of Sport History* 9.2 (1982), 20–37.

Herbert McAvoy, L., '"Ant nes he him seolf reclus i maries wombe?" Julian of Norwich, the Anchorhold and Redemption of the Monstrous Female Body', in *Consuming Narratives: Gender and Monstrous Appetite in the Middle Ages and the Renaissance*, ed. L. Herbert McAvoy and T. Walters (Aberystwyth, 2002), pp. 128–43.

Hicks, D., 'The Material-Cultural Turn: Event and Effect', in *The Oxford Handbook of Material Culture Studies*, ed. M. C. Beaudry and D. Hicks (Oxford, 2010), pp. 25–98.

Hill, C., *Women and Religion in Late-Medieval Norwich* (Woodbridge, 2010).

Hirsch, J. C., 'Author and Scribe in the *Book of Margery Kempe*', *Medium Ævum* 44 (1975), 145–50.

Hodder, I., *Reading the Past: Current Approaches to Interpretation in Archaeology*, 3rd edn (Cambridge, 2003).

Hopkins, A., Rouse, R. A. and Rushton, C. J., ed., *Sexual Culture in the Literature of Medieval Britain* (Cambridge, 2014).

Houston, J. F., *Fetherbedds and Flock Bedds: A History of the Worshipful Company of Upholders of the City of London* (Sandy, 1999).

Hutchinson, R., *Young Henry: The Rise of Henry VIII* (London, 2011).

Itnyre, C. J., 'A Smorgasbord of Sexual Practices', in *Sex in the Middle Ages: A Book of Essays*, ed. J. E. Salisbury (New York, 1991), pp. 145–72.

Jacquart, D. and Thomasset, C., *Sexuality and Medicine in the Middle Ages* (Princeton, 1988).

James, M. R., *Illustrations of the Book of Genesis, Being a Complete Reproduction in Facsimile of the Manuscript of the British Museum, Egerton 1894* (Oxford, 1921).

Johnston, A. F. and Rogerson, M., ed., *Records of Early English Drama: York*, 2 vols., vol. I (Toronto, 1979).

Jones, E., 'Literature and the New Cultural Geography', *Anglia* 126.2 (2008), 221–40.

Karras, R. M., *Sexuality in Medieval Europe: Doing Unto Others* (London, 2005).

—, *Unmarriages: Women, Men and Sexual Unions in the Middle Ages* (Philadelphia, 2012).

Kermode, J., *Medieval Merchants: York, Beverley and Hull in the Later Middle Ages* (Cambridge, 1998).

King, P., 'Emotions in Medieval Thought', in *The Oxford Handbook of the Philosophy of Emotion*, ed. P. Goldie (Oxford, 2009), pp. 167–88.

Klein, P. K., 'Introduction: The Apocalypse in Medieval Art', in *The Apocalypse in the Middle Ages*, ed. R. K. Emmerson and B. McGinn (Ithaca, 1992), pp. 159–99.

Kooper, E., 'The Squire of Low Degree: Introduction', in *Sentimental and Humorous Romances*, ed. E. Kooper (Kalamazoo, 2005).

Kowaleski, M. and Goldberg, P. J. P., ed., *Medieval Domesticity: Home, Housing and Household in Medieval England* (Cambridge, 2008).

Kristeva, J., *Powers of Horror: An Essay on Abjection*, trans. L. S. Roudiez (New York, 1982).

Larson, L. M., *King's Household in England before the Norman Conquest* (Madison, 1904).

Lastique, E. and Rodnite Lemay, H., 'A Medieval Physician's Guide to Virginity', in *Sex in the Middle Ages: A Book of Essays*, ed. J. E. Salisbury (London, 1991), pp. 56–79.

Lawton, D., 'Voice, Authority and Blasphemy in "The Book of Margery Kempe"', in *Margery Kempe: A Book of Essays*, ed. S. J. McEntire (London, 1992), pp. 93–115.

Laynesmith, J. L., *The Last Medieval Queens: English Queenship 1445–1503* (Oxford, 2005).

LeBlanc, L., 'Social Upheaval and the English Doomsday Plays', in *End of Days: Essays on the Apocalypse from Antiquity to Modernity*, ed. K. Kinane and M. A. Ryan (Jefferson, 2009), pp. 87–102.

Lee, R., 'A Company of Women and Men: Men's Recollections of Childbirth in Medieval England', *Journal of Family History* 27.2 (2002), 92–100.

Leeds, E. T., 'A Second Elizabethan Mural Painting in No. 3, Cornmarket Street, Oxford', *Journal of the British Archaeological Association* 37 (1932), 144–50.

Lefebvre, H., *La production de l'espace* (Paris, 1974).

—, *The Production of Space*, trans. D. Nicholson-Smith (Oxford, 1991).

Leitch, M. G., '(Dis)Figuring Transgressive Desire: Blood, Sex, and Stained Sheets in Malory's *Morte Darthur*', in *Arthurian Literature 28: Blood, Sex, Malory: Essays on the* Morte Darthur, ed. D. Clark and K. McClune (Cambridge, 2011), pp. 21–38.

—, 'Enter the Bedroom', in *Sexual Culture in the Literature of Medieval Britain*, ed. A. Hopkins, R. A. Rouse and C. J. Rushton (Cambridge, 2014).

Lewis, S., 'The *Apocalypse* of Margaret of York', in *Margaret of York, Simon Marmion, and* The Visions of Tondal, ed. T. Kren (Princeton, 1992).

—, *Reading Images: Narrative Discourse and Reception in the Thirteenth-Century Illuminated Apocalypse* (Cambridge, 1995).

Liddy, C. D., 'The Rhetoric of the Royal Chamber in Late-Medieval London, York and Coventry', *Urban History* 29.3 (2002), 323–49.

—, *War, Politics and Finance in Late-Medieval English Towns: Bristol, York and the Crown, 1350–1400* (Woodbridge, 2005).

Luxford, J. M., 'The Origins and Development of the English "Stone-Cage" Chantry Chapel', *Journal of the British Archaeological Association* 164 (2011), 39–73.

Lynch, K. L., *Chaucer's Philosophical Vision* (Cambridge, 2000).

Magnus, A., *Book of Minerals*, trans. D. Wyckoff (Oxford, 1967).

Mann, C., 'Clothing Bodies, Dressing Rooms: Fashioning Fecundity in *The Lisle Letters*', *Parergon* 22.1 (2005), 137–57.

Martin, A. L., *Alcohol, Sex and Gender in Late Medieval and Early Modern Europe* (London, 2001).

Mate, M. E., 'Work and Leisure', in *A Social History of England, 1200–1500*, ed. R. Horrox and W. M. Ormrod (Cambridge, 2006), pp. 275–92.

Matheson, L., *The Prose 'Brut': The Development of a Middle English Chronicle* (Tempe, 1998).

Matter, E. A., *The Voice of My Beloved: The Song of Songs in Western Medieval Christianity* (Philadelphia, 1990).

McCarthy, C., ed., *Love, Sex and Marriage in the Middle Ages: A Sourcebook.* (London, 2004).

McCarthy, T., 'Old Worlds, New Worlds: King Arthur in England', in *The Social and Literary Contexts of Malory's* Morte DArthur, ed. T. Hanks and J. G. Brogdon (Cambridge, 2000).

McDonald, N., 'Desire Out of Order and *Undo Your Door*'. *Studies in the Age of Chaucer* 34 (2012), 245–75.

—, 'Fragments of (*Have Your*) *Desire*: Brome Women at Play', in *Medieval Domesticity: Home, Housing and Household in Medieval England*, ed. M. Kowaleski and P. J. P. Goldberg (Cambridge, 2008), pp. 232–58.

—, 'Gender', in *A Handbook of Middle English Studies*, ed. M. Turner (Oxford, 2013), 63–76.

—, 'A Polemical Introduction', in *Pulp Fictions of Medieval England: Essays in Popular Romance*, ed. N. McDonald (Manchester, 2004), pp. 1–21.

McIntosh, M. K., *Controlling Misbehaviour in England, 1370–1600* (Cambridge, 1998).

McMurray Gibson, G., 'Blessing from Sun and Moon: Churching as Women's Theater', in *Bodies and Disciplines: Intersections of Literature and History in Fifteenth-Century England*, ed. B. A. Hanawalt and D. Wallace (Minneapolis, 1996), pp. 139–59.

—, *The Theater of Devotion: East Anglian Drama and Society in the Late Middle Ages* (Chicago, 1989).

McNeill, J., 'A Prehistory of the Chantry', *Journal of the British Archaeological Association* 164 (2011), 1–38.

McSheffrey, S., ed., *Love & Marriage in Late-medieval London* (Kalamazoo, 2005).

—, *Marriage, Sex and Civic Culture in Late-medieval London* (Philadelphia, 2011).

—, 'Place, Space, and Situation: Public and Private in the Making of Marriage in Late-medieval London', *Speculum* 79 (2004), 960–90.

—, McSheffrey, S. and Pope, J., 'Ravishment, Legal Narratives, and Chivalric Culture in Fifteenth-century England', *Journal of British Studies* 48.4 (2009), 818–36.

McSheffrey, S. and Tanner, N., ed., *Heresy Trials in the Diocese of Norwich, 1428–31* (London, 1977).

Meiss, M., 'Light as Form and Symbol in Some Fifteenth-century Paintings', in *The Art Bulletin* 27.3 (1945), 175–81.

Middleton, C., 'The Sexual Division of Labour in Feudal England', *New Left Review* 113–14 (1979), 147–68.

Miller, D., 'Materiality: An Introduction', in *Materiality*, ed. D. Miller (Durham, 2005), pp. 1–50.

Miller, S. A., ed., *Medieval Monstrosity and the Female Body* (New York, 2010).

Mills, D., 'An Analysis of the Temptation Scenes in "Sir Gawain and the Green Knight"', *The Journal of English and Germanic Philology* 67.4 (1968), 612–30.

Mitchell, L. E., *Portraits of Medieval Women: Family, Marriage and Politics in England 1225–1350* (New York, 2003).

Moule, A. C., *Quinsai, with Other Notes on Marco Polo* (Cambridge, 1957).

Mueller, J. M., 'Autobiography of a New "Creatur": Female Spirituality, Selfhood, and Authorship in *The Book of Margery Kempe*', in *Woman in the Middle Ages and the Renaissance: Literary and Historical Perspectives*, ed. M. B. Rose (Syracuse, 1986), pp. 155–72.

Murray, J., 'Gendered Souls in Sexed Bodies: The Male Construction of Female Sexuality in Some Medieval Confessors' Manuals', in *Handling Sin: Confession in the Middle Ages*, ed. P. Biller and A. J. Minnis (York, 1998), pp. 79–93.

Neal, D. G., *The Masculine Self in Late-medieval England* (Chicago, 2008).

New, E. A., *Seals and Sealing Practices* (London, 2010).

Nicaise, E., trans. and ed., *Chirurgie de maitre Henri de Mondeville, chirurgien de Philippe le Bel, Roi de France, composée de 1306 à 1320* (Paris, 1893).

Nolan, C. J., *The Age of Wars of Religion, 1000–1650: An Encyclopedia of Global Warfare and Civilisation* (Westport, 2006).

Oliva, M., 'Nuns at Home: The Domesticity of Sacred Space', in *Medieval Domesticity: Home, Housing and Household in Medieval England*, ed. M. Kowaleski and P. J. P. Goldberg (Cambridge, 2008), pp. 145–61.

Orme, N., *Medieval Children* (New Haven, 2003).

—, 'Schoolmasters, 1307–1509', in *Profession, Vocation and Culture in Later Medieval England: Essays Dedicated to the Memory of A. R. Myers*, ed. C. H. Clough (Liverpool, 1982).

Ormrod, W. M., 'In Bed with Joan of Kent: The King's Mother and the Peasants' Revolt', in *Medieval Women: Texts and Contexts in Late-medieval Britain. Essays for Felicity Riddy*, ed. J. Wogan-Browne, R. Voaden, A. Diamond, A. Hutchinson, C. Meale and L. Johnson (Turnhout, 2000).

—, 'York and the Crown Under the First Three Edwards', in *The Government of Medieval York: Essays in Commemoration of the 1396 Royal Charter*, ed. S. Rees Jones (York, 1997), pp. 14–33.

Pantin, W. A., 'The Golden Cross, Oxford', *Oxoniensia* 20 (1955), 46–89.

Payer, P. J., 'Confession and the Study of Sex in the Middle Ages', in *Handbook of Medieval Sexuality*, ed. V. L. Bullough and J. A. Brundage (New York, 2000), pp. 3–32.

—, 'Sex and Confession in the Thirteenth Century', in *Sex in the Middle Ages: A Book of Essays*, ed. J. E. Salisbury (New York, 1991), pp. 126–42.

—, *Sex and the New Medieval Literature of Confession, 1150–1300* (Toronto, 2009).

Pearman, T. Vandeventer, *Women and Disability in Medieval Literature* (New York, 2010).

Pedersen, F., *Marriage Disputes in Medieval England* (London, 2000).

Perrot, M., *Histoire de chambres* (Paris, 2009).

Phillips, K., 'Capturing the Wandering Womb: Childbirth in Medieval Art', *The Haverford Journal* 3.1 (2007), 40–55.

Phillips, K. M. and Reay, B., *Sex Before Sexuality: A Premodern History* (Cambridge, 2011).

Pickavé, M. and Shapiro, L., ed., *Emotion and Cognitive Life in Medieval and Early Modern Philosophy* (Oxford, 2012).

Pile, J., *A History of Interior Design*, 2nd edn (London, 2005).

Pollock, L. A., 'Childbearing and Female Bonding in Early Modern England', *Social History* 22.3 (1997), 286–306.

Poole, R. M., *The Exchequer in the Twelfth Century* (Oxford, 1912).

Power, E., *Medieval English Nunneries c. 1275–1535* (Cambridge, 1922).

—, *Medieval Women*, ed. M. M. Postan (Cambridge, 1975).

Prestwich, M., *Edward I* (New Haven, 1997).

—, 'Training', in *The Oxford Encyclopaedia of Medieval Warfare and Military Technology*, ed. C. J. Rogers, 3 vols., vol. I (Oxford, 2010), pp. 272–3.

Putter, A., *Sir Gawain and the Green Knight and French Arthurian Romance* (Oxford, 1995).

Quiney, A., 'Hall or Chamber? That is the Question. The Use of Rooms in Post-Conquest Houses', *Architectural History* 42 (1999), 24–46.

Quinn, W. A., '*The Book of the Duchess*: Introduction', in *Chaucer's Dream Visions and Shorter Poems*, ed. W. A. Quinn (New York, 1999).

Redstone, L. J., *Survey of London* 12: *The Parish of All Hallows Barking* (London, 1934).

Reeves, C., *Pleasures and Pastimes in Medieval England* (Stroud, 1995).

Richardson, A., 'Corridors of Power: A Case Study of Access Analysis from Medieval Salisbury, England', *Antiquity* 77. 296 (2003), 373–84.

—, 'Gender and Space in English Royal Palaces *c.* 1160–*c.* 1547: A Study in Access Analysis and Imagery', *Medieval Archaeology* 47 (2003), pp. 131–65.

Riddy, F., '"Burgeis" Domesticity in Late-Medieval England', in *Medieval Domesticity: Home, Housing and Household in Medieval England*, ed. M. Kowaleski and P. J. P. Goldberg (Cambridge, 2008), pp. 14–36.

—, 'Looking Closely: Authority and Intimacy in the Late-medieval Urban Home', in *Gendering the Master Narrative: Women and Power in the Middle Ages*, ed. M. C. Erler and M. Kowaleski (New York, 2003), pp. 212–28.

—, 'Middle English Romance: Family, Marriage, Intimacy', in *The Cambridge Companion to Medieval Romance*, ed. R. L. Krueger (Cambridge, 2000), pp. 235–52.

—, 'Temporary Virginity and the Everyday Body: *Le Bone Florence of Rome* and Bourgeois Self-making', in *Pulp Fictions of Medieval England: Essays in Popular Romance*, ed. N. McDonald (Manchester, 2004), pp. 197–216.

Roberts, H. E., 'Light II: Divine, Natural, and Neon', in *Encyclopedia of Comparative Iconography: Themes Depicted in Works of Art*, ed. H. E. Roberts (Chicago, 1998), pp. 505–12.

Robertson, E., *Early English Devotional Prose and the Female Audience* (Knoxville, 1990).

Roffey, S., *Chantry Chapels and Medieval Strategies for the Afterlife* (Stroud, 2008).

—, *The Medieval Chantry Chapel: An Archaeology* (Woodbridge, 2007).

Rolleston, J. D., 'Penis Captivus: An Historical Note', in *Sex in the Middle Ages: A Book of Essays*, ed. J. E. Salisbury (New York, 1991), pp. 232–8.

Root, J., *'Space to Speke': The Confessional Subject in Medieval Literature* (New York, 1997).

Roper, L., '"Going to Church and Street": Weddings in Reformation Augsburg', *Past and Present* 106 (1985), 62–101.

Salih, S., 'At Home; Out of the House', in *The Cambridge Companion to Medieval Women's Writing*, ed. C. Dinshaw and D. Wallace (Cambridge, 2003), pp. 124–40.

Sarti, R., *Europe at Home: Family and Material Culture, 1500–1800*, trans. A. Cameron (New Haven, 2002).

Schofield, J., *Medieval London Houses* (New Haven, 1995).

Schofield, P., *Seals and their Context in the Middle Ages* (Oxford, 2015).

Schreiber, S., 'Migration, Traumatic Bereavement and Transcultural Aspects of Psychological Healing: Loss and Grief of a Refugee Woman from Begameder Country in Ethiopia', *British Journal of Medical Psychology* 68.2 (1995), 135–42.

Scott, R. F., *Notes from the Records of St John's College* (Cambridge, 1913).

Sekules, V., 'Spinning Yarns: Clean Linen and Domestic Values in Late-Medieval French Culture', in *The Material Culture of Sex, Procreation, and Marriage in Premodern Europe*, ed. A. L. McClanan and K. Rosoff Encarnación (New York, 2002), pp. 79–91.

Sheeran, G., *Medieval Yorkshire Towns: People, Buildings and Spaces* (Edinburgh, 1998).

Sheingorn, P., *The Easter Sepulchre in England* (Kalamazoo, 1987).

Société des Médiévistes de l'Enseignement Supérieur Public, ed., *Constructions de l'espace au Moyen-âge: pratiques et représentations. Actes du XXXVIIe Congrès de la SHMESP, Mulhouse, Juin 2006* (Paris, 2007).

Soja, E., *Postmodern Geographies: The Reassertion of Space in Critical Social Theory* (London, 1989).

—, *Thirdspace: Journeys to Los Angeles and Other Real-and-Imagined Places* (Oxford, 1996).

Spurgeon, C. F. E., *Five Hundred Years of Chaucer Criticism and Allusion, 1357–1900* (Cambridge, 1925).

Staley Johnson, L., 'The Trope of the Scribe and the Question of Literary Authority in the Works of Julian of Norwich and Margery Kempe', *Speculum* 66.4 (1991), 820–38.

Staniland, K., 'Royal Entry into the World', in *England in the Fifteenth Century: Proceedings from the 1986 Harlaxton Symposium*, ed. D. Williams (Woodbridge, 1987), pp. 297–313.

Storey, R. L., 'Gentleman-bureaucrats', in *Profession Vocation, and Culture in Later Medieval England: Essays Dedicated to the Memory of A. R. Myers*, ed. C. H. Clough (Liverpool, 1982), pp. 90–129.

Stroebe, W. and Stroebe, M. S., *Bereavement and Health: The Psychological and Physical Consequences of Partner Loss* (Cambridge, 1987).

Strohm, P., *The Poet's Tale: Chaucer and the Year that Made* The Canterbury Tales (London, 2014).

Szittya, P., 'Domesday Bokes: The Apocalypse in Medieval English Literary Culture', in *The Apocalypse in the Middle Ages*, ed. R. K. Emmerson and B. McGinn (Ithaca, 1992), pp. 374–97.

Taylor, A., 'Into His Secret Chamber: Reading and Privacy in Late-medieval England', in *The Practice and Representation of Reading in England*, ed. J. Raven, H. Small and N. Tadmor (Cambridge, 1996), pp. 41–61.

Tout, T. F., *Chapters in the Administrative History of Mediaeval England: The Wardrobe, the Chamber and the Small Seals* (Manchester, 1933).

Tortora, P. G. and Johnson, I., *The Fairchild Books Dictionary of Textiles*, 8th edn (New York, 2013).

Tuck, J. A., 'The Cambridge Parliament, 1388', *The English Historical Review* 331 (1969), 225–43.

Tudor-Craig, P., 'The Painted Chamber at Westminster', *The Archaeological Journal* 114 (1957), 92–105.

Vance Smith, D., *Arts of Possession: The Middle English Household Imaginary* (Minneapolis, 2003).

Voaden, R., 'All Girls Together: Community, Gender and Vision at Helfta', in *Medieval Women and Their Communities*, ed. D. Watt (Toronto, 1997), pp. 72–91.

Ward, J. C., *Women in England in the Middle Ages* (London, 2006).

Warf, B. and Aries, S., ed., *The Spatial Turn: Interdisciplinary Perspectives* (Abingdon, 2009).

Warren, A. K., *Anchorites and their Patrons in Medieval England* (Berkeley, 1985).

Webb, D., 'Domestic Space and Devotion in the Middle Ages', in *Defining the Holy: Sacred Space in Medieval and Early Modern Europe*, ed. A. Spicer and S. Hamilton (Aldershot, 2005), pp. 27–48.

Wheeler, B., 'Grief in Avalon: Sir Palomydes' Psychic Pain', in *Grief and Gender: 700–1700*, ed. J. C. Vaught with D. Bruckner (New York, 2003), pp. 65–77.

Wilson, A., 'The Ceremony of Childbirth and Its Interpretations', in *Women as Mothers in Pre-Industrial England*, ed. V. Fildes (London, 1990), pp. 68–107.

Windeatt, B., 'Literary Structures in Chaucer' in *The Cambridge Companion to Chaucer*, ed. P. Boitani and J. Mann (Cambridge, 2003), pp. 214–32.

Withers, C., 'Place and the "Spatial Turn" in Geography and History', *Journal of the History of Ideas* 70.4 (2009), 637–58.

Wolfthal, D., *In and Out of the Marital Bed: Seeing Sex in Renaissance Europe* (New Haven, 2010).

Woolgar, C. M., *The Great Household in Late-medieval England* (New Haven, 1999).

—, *The Senses in Late-Medieval England* (London, 2006).

Worsley, L., *If Walls Could Talk: An Intimate History of the Home* (London, 2012).

Wright, L., *Warm and Snug: The History of the Bed* (London, 1962).

Youngs, D. and Harris, S., 'Demonizing the Night in Medieval Europe: A Temporal Monstrosity?', in *The Monstrous Middle Ages,* ed. B. Bildhauer and R. Mills (Toronto, 2003), pp. 134–54.

Digital resources

British History Online (2010) <http://www.british-history.ac.uk/report.aspx?compid=118120>.

Cambridge Dictionaries Online (2013) <www.dictionary.cambridge.org>.

Catalogue of Illuminated Manuscripts (London, 2014) <http://www.bl.uk/catalogues/illuminatedmanuscripts>.

Catholic Bible: Douay-Rheims Bible and Challoner Notes. <www.drbo.org>.

Given-Wilson, C., Brand, P., Curry, A., Horrox, R., Martin, G., Ormrod, W. M. and Phillips, S., ed., *The Parliament Rolls of Medieval England* (Leicester, 2005) <http://www.sd-editions.com/PROME>.

Leung, H. < www.tagxedo.com>.

Manuscripts Online: Written Culture 1000–1500 <www.manuscriptsonline. org>.

McDonald, N., ed., *The Database of Middle English Romance* (York, 2012) <www. middleenglishromance.org.uk>.

McSparren, F., ed., *The Middle English Dictionary*, in *The Middle English Compendium* (Michigan, 2006) <http://quod.lib.umich.edu/m/med/>.

Mooney, L. R., Mosser, D. W. and Solopova, E., ed., *The Digital Index of Middle English Verse.* 2012 <www.dimev.net>.

Oxford English Dictionary Online, 2nd edn, Oxford, 2012. <www.oed.com>.

Rimmer, M., *The Angel Roofs of East Anglia* (2012) <www.angelroofs.com>.

INDEX